AF559882

CHILD LABOUR IN INFORMAL SECTOR

CHILD LABOUR IN INFORMAL SECTOR

By

Dr. Bishnu Mohan Dash

M.S.W., M.Phil., Ph.D.

Assistant Professor in Social Work

Bhim Rao Ambedkar College

(University of Delhi)

(INDIA)

DISCOVERY PUBLISHING HOUSE PVT. LTD.

NEW DELHI-110 002

Published by:
Tilak Wasan

DISCOVERY PUBLISHING HOUSE PVT. LTD.
4383/4B, Ansari Road, Darya Ganj
New Delhi-110 002 (India)
Phone : +91-11-23279245, 43596064-65
Fax : +91-11-23253475
E-mail : discoverypublishinghouse@gmail.com
sales@discoverypublishinggroup.com
web : www.discoverypublishinggroup.com

***First Edition:* 2015**

ISBN: 978-93-5056-728-9

Child Labour in Informal Sector

Printed at:
Infinity Imaging Systems
Delhi

Preface

In the present work, an attempt has been made to scientifically present the various aspects pertaining to working and living conditions of child labourers and factors contributing to the incidence of child labour engaged in small scale commercial establishments. The problem of child labour is no longer a matter of merely regional and national concern, but it has become an issue of serious debate at various international forums as it is linked to the violation of children's rights. The issue of child labour has already been placed firmly in the dialectical universe of human rights. In recent years, the issue has increasingly drawn the attention of policy-makers, governments, non-governmental organizations and international agencies. India has the dubious distinction of being a nation with the largest number of child labourers in the world. A large number of children in India are engaged in labour that is hindering their education, development and livelihood, and many of them are involved in the worst forms of child labour that cause serious physical-psychological damage, and even threaten their lives. The fact that, not the mere workbut it is the labour that the children are coerced to do, has manifold repercussions for them, their families and for the society as a whole. The Government of India has been making efforts to curb the menace of child labour but the problem continues to pose a challenge before the nation.

The present study on child labour aimsat examining the factors contributing to the incidence of child labour; living and working conditions of the children engaged in small scale commercial establishments in Delhi, as well as critically examine the various provisions of all legislations prohibiting and regulating child labour.

In order to accomplish the objectives of the study, combination of both qualitative and quantitative research methods have been adopted. The design of the study is descriptive. The Non-Probability sampling method was used to draw the required sample of child labourers. It was done by using Quota sampling techniques. The sample size consisted of 120 child labourers working in shops, subzimandis (vegetable markets), motor garages and dhabas/tea stalls (30 from each stratum). Besides these respondents, the qualitative data was collected using narrative analysis as a method of data collection. Ten cases were identified from all the four strata for the narrative analysis. A sample of parents and employers was selected by Using Non-probability method of Purposive sampling. Total sample size was 40 parents (selecting 10 from each stratum) and 40 employers (selecting 10 from each stratum). Besides that, the lawyers, social activists and social workers selecting 5 from each category were interviewed for the purpose of for formulating the recommendations for reducing the incidence of child labour. The data was collected using self administered interview schedule with the child labourers and interview guide with the parents and employers. The secondary sources were tapped and information procured from them was analyzed. This was primarily pertaining to the constitutional provisions, various legislations, census data, ILO reports, and relevant reports of Ministry of Labour, Government of India, Reports of Government of Delhi, Books, Journals, Periodicals and Reports of Non-governmental organizations.

The findings of the study reflected that, along with a series of enactments of child labour legislations, a number of welfare programmes, policies have been implemented. Along with this, a series of committees and commissions have been appointed by Government of India, either specifically on the question of child labour or on labour conditions in general to enquire into the causes or consequences of the problem and to suggest measures to reduce the incidence of child labour and to ameliorate the conditions of child labourers. Though the laws exist to regulate and prohibit employment of children in hazardous occupations, there is neither blanket prohibition on the use of child labour nor is there any universal minimum age that has been set for child labourers. The inadequate legislation as well as insufficient enforcement is responsible for the continuation and perpetuation of the phenomenon of child labour.

The study reveals that the most important factor which led the children (respondents) to work was to supplement family income. Besides that, family pressure, poverty, lack of interest in studies and school drop out, migration of parents, self desire, death of parent/s were found as other important determinants (as reported by child labourers). In addition to these, illiteracy of parents, occupation of parents in petty jobs, employers' preference for hiring children were reported to be primary reasons for children's engagement in jobs.

The study reveals that the working conditions of child labourers were very appalling. Majority of such children were found to be engaged in unskilled jobs doing full time work with petty wages. The children were put through longer hours of work by their employers, in some cases even more than 12 hours. The living conditions of the child labourers were very deplorable, with most of them staying in slum clusters in unhygienic atmosphere without proper sanitation facilities.The study manifests the denial of denial of rights of those children engaged in small scale commercial establishments in terms of survival and development, education, leisure and play, opportunity for developing physical and mental talents, and protection from abuse and neglect which eventually impair their growth and development.

Child labour is a complex socio-economic demographic problem which can be reduced and eliminated by multiplicity of actions, both by the Government and the civil society sector. The study has emphasized on the promotion of income generation activities, provision of social safety nets, educational opportunities for all, awareness generation, strict implementation of the legislations, involvement of local governance institutions, implementation of fair trade labeling initiatives, provision of proper housing/avenues for recreation/purposeful utilization of leisure time.There is an urgent need for attitudinal change, political mobilization and aggressive campaign against the scourge of child labour. The coordinated efforts of Government, Non-governmental organizations, employers and social workers through active public support are likely to help in ameliorating or controlling the problem. Social workers should provide guidance and counseling to the child labourers in confronting their problems and tackling them. Counseling is also needed for the families of the child labourers as well as those who are on the verge of sending their children to the labour market. Counseling and guidance are also needed for those children who are poor in studies and are truants so that they are prevented from dropping out of the school and entering into the labour market.Social work intervention is necessary at the family level, especially where the fathers are drug addicts or are unemployed.Social workers should work with children to bring about a change from an essentially welfare-based, charitable approach to a more children-centered, rights based approach.They social should take systematic efforts to ensure that work places and communities remain child labour free. This can be facilitated by awareness raising activities by using participatory approach involving employers, parents, and adult workers in the work places, community leaders, service providers and enforcement agencies.

Dr. Bishnu Mohan Dash

Acknowledgements

Let me first say that it was one of my long cherished dreams to conduct a study on the child labourers engaged in the small scale commercial establishments in the city of Delhi.While doing so I was lucky to have the guidance and support of many.

I express my heartfelt gratitude to Prof. Sushma Batra and Dr. Neera Agnimitra for their valuable guidance and support. I feel highly indebted for their time, effort and inputs provided to me during the course of research. I also thank Prof. Sanjai Bhatt, Department of Social Work, University of Delhi for his kind cooperation and providing relevant literature for my research work. I also thank Prof. Giriswar Misra, Professor in Psychology and Dean, University of Delhi (Now Vice Chancellor, International Hindi University, Wardha) for providing valuable inputs during the research work. I also express my sincere thanks to the faculty members at the Department of Social Work, University of Delhi particularly Dr. Manoj Kumar Jha and Dr. Seema Sharma for their support and cooperation.

I would like to thank all the respondents for being part of this research. I am also very thankful to the staff of various libraries and information centers, particularly V.V. Giri National Labour Institute, Noida; ICSSR Library, Ratan Tata Library, Department of Social Work Library who had granted permission and rendered prompt information about the books, journals and articles I needed for my research study.

I am grateful to my parents and elder brothers who have always encouraged me in this academic endeavour. I also thank all my friends and colleagues who stood by me during these trying years. My heartfelt thanks are due to Dr. S.S. Chawla, Dr. Ravindra Singh, Dr. Sanjoy Roy, Mr. Kumar Satyam and my student Lokender Prasad for their support and assistance. I also thank Dr. G.K. Arora, for his encouragement and motivation which I received from him throughout this period.

I also wish to thank the University Grants Commission for giving me the financial support to pursue this research exercise as well as travel grant support for presenting a paper in the international conference held in Toronto, Canada. I also thank University of Delhi for providing me financial assistance to present a paper related to my research in the 21st Asia Pacific Social Work Conference, held at Waseda University, Tokyo, Japan (July, 2011).

Lastly, I would like to appreciate my kids (Bhavini and Lokesh) and wife Dr. Mitu Dash who had supported me during the period of my study.

Dr. Bishnu Mohan Dash

Contents

List of Acronyms

ILO	International Labour Organization
UN	United Nations
NCPCR	National Council for Protection of Child Rights
NGO	Non Governmental Organization
VVGNLI	V.V.Giri National Labour Institute
ICCW	Indian Council of Child Welfare
UNICEF	United Nations International Children's Emergency Fund
ORG	Operational Research Group
GOI	Government of India
NIPCCD	National Institute of Public Cooperation and Child Development
NIRD	National Institute of Rural Development
NCLP	National Child Labour Project
NRCCL	National Resource Centre on Child Labour

1

Introduction

INTRODUCTION TO THE RESEARCH PROBLEM

The problem of child labour has moved from a matter of regional and national concern to one of international debate and in recent years, the issue of child labour has increasingly drawn the attention of policy-makers, governments, non-governmental organizations, and international agencies. Despite general acceptance that child labour is harmful and having international accords aimed at its eradication, progress on lowering the incidence of child labour has been slow. Child labour in general, and child caring in particular, has been placed ûrmly in the dialectical universe of human rights (Aldridge and Becker, 1995). The issue of child labour has been gaining considerable international attention particularly as it is linked to the rights of the child. The United Nations Convention on the Rights of the Child (CRC), adopted by the General Assembly in 1989, calls for the right of the child to be protected from economic exploitation and any work that is likely to be hazardous, interfere with the child's education or harmful to the child's health or physical, mental, spiritual, moral or social development. Since the beginning of the 1990s, child labour has become the focus of increasing attention, in developing as well as in developed countries. As a result, practical action against child labour in the form of policies, programmes and projects has been building up on an unprecedented scale. The struggle against child labour has thus gained momentum and a wide variety of actors have joined in, including governments, NGOs, trade unions, employers' organizations, and international organizations, to name just a few(Colombini, 2008).

The problem of child labour continues to pose a challenge before the nation. Child labour represents a fundamental abuse of child rights and a violation of various child related laws. India has the dubious distinction of being the nation with the largest number of child labourers in the world. A large number of children in India are engaged in labour that is hindering their education, development and livelihoods, even many of them are involved in the worst forms of child labour that cause serious physical or psychological damage, and even threaten their lives. Children's engagement in occupations negatively affects their physical, mental and emotional well being. This situation represents an intolerable violation of the rights of children, it perpetuates poverty and it compromises economic growth and equitable development. It harms not only the present generation but also the posterity.

The International year of the child was celebrated in 1979 and since then working children and their problems have been receiving the attention of researchers, voluntary organizations, activists and the media. Described as a vexed problem, child labour, in general, has gained 'currency' in recent times as result of 'bringing injustice into the open' and 'articulation' of child abuse by academicians, activists and journalists (Lieten et.al. 2004).

MEANING AND CONCEPT OF CHILD LABOUR

The term 'child labour' means different things in different societies. Defining child labour has always been a contestable term. Not a single definition of child labour is exhaustive and acceptable to all concerned including governments, social scientists, non-governmental organizations etc. A universally accepted definition of child labour is not available because it is a social construct, not a natural phenomenon, and social constructs are cultural ideas that differ between actors, histories, contexts and purposes (Ennew et al, 2007).

The terms: 'child', 'work', and 'labour' are not timeless, uniform concepts; their definitions are subject to change and variation. Wherever and whenever these terms are used inconsistently, confusion and contradiction are likely to arise. Different societies demarcate the threshold of childhood differently, according to age, legal status and custom. 'Work' does not necessarily equate with 'labour' although they are more often used interchangeably. The work children do to help the family in non-hazardous occupation and processes is different from the work done by a child in a production process on a waged (part-time/full-time) employment. In India in the home –based industries, in the informal sector, in the areas of brassware, carpet, lack-making, fire works even if children are apparently seen to be working to help family work, but they can't be categorized as working children, rather they are child labourers.

Definitions of child labour vary across time, nations and industries. They range from normative ones based on specifications of minimum age for employment; to education-oriented definitions which define any child out of school as child labourer or as a potential child labourer; to right-oriented definition which consider any work that deprives children of their fundamental childhood rights as constituting child labour (UN, 1998). At times, the definitions change contextually and depending on the situation and environment. The terms 'employed child' and 'working child' were used in the past to denote employment of child. Now, the term 'child labour' is standardized and replaced the above terms.

The Encyclopedia of the Social Science (1963) describes the term child labour as "when the business of wage earning or of participation in itself or family support, conflicts directly or indirectly with business of growth and education, the result is child labour". In simple terms, child labour can be defined as the work undertaken by a child, below a certain age, for gainful purpose within or outside the family.

Article 1 of the United Nations "Convention on the Rights of Child, 1989" (CRC) defines child as "every human being below the age of 18 years unless, under the law applicable to the child, majority is attained earlier". The convention calls for protection of the child from economic exploitation and from performing any work that is likely to be hazardous or to interfere with the child's education or to be harmful to the child's health or physical, mental, spiritual, moral and social development.

Flowing from the above, a distinction has to be drawn between child work and child labour. The term 'Child Work' and 'Child labour' though used synonymously, have different meanings. The term 'Child labour' is used synonymously with other terms like 'employed child' or "working child'. In this sense, it is coextensive with any work done by a child for gain. It signifies employment of children in gainful occupations with a view to add to the household maintenance activities. In the definition of 'child labour' according to 1971 and 1981 census of India, "the stress has been on the concept of main activity i.e. on the economically productive pursuits in which the worker engages himself or herself for most part of the time. As for seasonal work such as agriculture and ancillary pursuits, the main activity of a person was defined with reference to his or her work during the year preceding the enumeration. Further, if a person participated in economically productive work, not as a main activity or for most part of the year, he/she is not treated as worker but as marginal worker. (Mishra and Mishra, 2004).

'Child Work' refers to occasional light work done by children, which in most of the societies is considered to be an integral part of the child's socialization process. While helping parents at home and in family farms, children learn to take responsibility and acquire certain skills and prepare themselves for the tasks of future adulthood.

'Child Labour' implies something different in which young people are being exploited, or over worked or deprived of their rights to health, education and childhood. It impairs their health, their overall physical, mental and social growth.

Fyfe (1989) attempts to provide a distinction by differenting between 'child work' and 'child labour'. The former being seen as permissible and latter as exploitatative.

Children attending to some form of work as part of familiarization and socialization without its effect on his/her education and recreation, which can be termed as child work, is different from that of child labour. A relatively workable and functional definition is provided by ILO (1996) according to which "child labour includes children prematurely leading adult lives, working long hours for low wages under conditions damaging to their health and to their physical and mental development, sometimes separated from their families, frequently deprived of meaningful education and training opportunities that could open up for them a better future".

Homer Folks (1946) of the United States Child Labour Commission defined child labour as "any work by children that interfere with their physical development and their opportunities for desirable minimum level of education or the needed recreation".

The Constitution of India calls for free and compulsory education for all children until they complete the age of 14 years. It also prohibits employment of children below the age of 14 years in factories and certain hazardous employments. Census of India (1991) consider the full time child labour as children below 14 years, whose main activity is economic and who have spent more than half the year(183days or more) in economic activity.

Several Non-Governmental Organizations (NGOs) differ with the definition given by the census and other Government agencies and they believe that every child in the school age group and who is out of school is child labour. The Operations Research Groups (ORG, 1993), Baroda defines child labour as " a child falling within 5 to 15 age group and who is at remunerative work, may be paid or unpaid and busy in any hour of the day, within or outside the family".

According to Encyclopedia of Social Work (1997) "a generally valid definition of child labour is presently not available either in the national or international context. Any definition turns upon the precise meaning we attach to the two components of the terms 'child labour' i.e., 'child' in terms of his chronological age, and 'labour' in terms of its nature, quantum and income generation capacity. It defines child labour as that segment of the child population which participates in work either paid or unpaid.

According to V.V. Giri, the term child labour is commonly interpreted in two different ways; first, as an economic practice and secondly, as a social evil. In the economic sense, it signifies employment of children in gainful occupations with a view to adding to the income of the family. In the social context, it takes into account the damages to which children are exposed, which means the denial of opportunities for development (Tripathy, 1996).

The Indian Factories Act of 1948, which is an elaborate and highly specific act relating to child labour, makes use of three different concepts to classify the workers, i.e., a 'child', a 'young person' or an 'adolescent' and an 'adult'. It has been made explicit in this act that a person below the age of 15 years is to be regarded as a child.

The word 'child labour' also been defined variously in the multiple studies undertaken on the broad theme of child labour. In the study of working of children in Bombay, Singh (1991) and others have held a view that 'child labour' means a working child who is between 6 and 15 years of age, is not attending school during the day, is working under an employer or learning some trade as an apprentice. In the study conducted by Indian council of child welfare (ICCW) in Delhi opines, 'every child below 14 years, who contributed to the family income or treated as a full time/part time worker is a child labourer.

According to the Sen Committee (1981), Child labour, however, can broadly be defined as that segment of child population in work either paid or unpaid. The diversity of opinion among researchers in defining child labour is due to differences in social perceptions.

Age is an important criterion for distinguishing child labour from adult labourers. In the context of child labour, a working definition of a child may be a person below the age limit of 15 years set by minimum age convention (1973). In a wider context, the United Nations Convention of the Rights of the Child (1989) set the age limit of a child at 18 years. In India, many labour acts have fixed the minimum age of employment. But the definition of a child in terms of age differs from act to act. The Factories Act prohibits employment of children below the age of 14 years in factories. The limit in Mines Act is 15 years, whereas it is 12 years in Plantation Labour Act. The Child Labour (Prohibition and Regulation) Act, 1986, defines 'child' as a person who has not completed his fourteenth year of age.

Now days, child labour is a widespread phenomenon. It is not only confined to work on family farms or in traditional family jobs and occupations, but it has also extended to other fields. They work in agriculture and allied activities, unorganized small-scale sectors and even in organized industries. The notion of child labour is intended to cover children under the age of 14 engaged in work or employment with the aim of earning a livelihood for themselves or for their family or themselves directly or indirectly at the cost of their physical, mental or social development." Thus the term child labour not only applies to the children working in industries but also to the children working in all form of non industrial occupations which are injurious to their physical, mental, moral and social development.

In the Indian Context, there has been a tendency to formulate the definition of child labour rather loosely. Even in the latest Labour Commission Report (2001), all working children are taken as one hardly differentiated category. It also includes all the children who are out- of- school. Burra (1999) advocates that; a child labourer is "basically a child who is deprived of the right to education and childhood. What makes her definition important is that it makes it unambiguously clear that all out of school children is working in one form or another. The 'nowhere' children are stated to be potential child labourers and are assumed to be staying at home, away from school so that they can take over some of the household duties of the parents and allow the latter to go out of and work.

FORMS OF CHILD LABOUR

Children are working in all the three sectors of the Indian economy, i.e. the agrarian, industrial and service sector. There are several forms of child labour - migrant, invisible, bonded and wage-based, self employed and so on. UNICEF has classified child labourers into three categories:

1. *Within the family*: Children helping in the domestic chores or family occupations like agricultural - pastoral work, handicrafts, khadi and cottage industries etc.
2. *Within the family but outside the home*: Children do local agricultural work, assist in shops, and help in construction, harvesting crops, laundry/recycling of waste, and so on.
3. *Outside the family*: Children are employed in bounded work doing errands for the rich landlord and various works in the cottage industries.

A. Within the family (unpaid)

1. Domestic/Household tasks: e.g. cooking, cleaning, child-care, water cleaning utensils, washing clothes, poultry etc.
2. Agriculture/pastoral tasks: e.g. ploughing, weeding, harvesting, herding, livestocks etc.
3. Handicrafts/cottage Industries: e.g. weaving, basketry, leather work, wood work, house hold industries in the urban informal sector.

B. With the family but outside the home

1. Agricultural/Pastoral work
   (a) Migrant agricultural labour
   (b) Local agricultural labour (full time/seasonal)
2. Domestic Service
3. Construction work, e.g., building, roads etc.
4. Informal economy e.g. laundry, recycling rubbish
   (a) Employed by others
   (b) Self-employed

C. Outside the family

1. Employed by others
   (a) Tied/bonded/slave

(b) Apprentices
(c) Skilled trades e.g. carpets, embroidery, brass and copper work.
(d) Industries/unskilled occupations/mines
(e) Domestics e.g. maids- of- all- work.
(f) Commercial e.g. shops, restaurants
(g) Begging
(h) Prostitution and pornography

LOCATION SPECIFIC OCCUPATIONS

Informal sector of the rural and urban economies of the developing countries is an important source of employment for a major chunk of labour forces particularly the children and women. Though the sectoral distribution of child labourers differs from country to country, yet child labour is predominantly confined to agricultural sector followed by services and industry.

One of the unique features of the child labour system in India is the location specific nature of the employment. Even though child labourers are spread all through the length and breadth of the country, some specific kind of occupations are observed in some areas only. For example, carpet industry is more common in Jammu and Kashmir, West Bengal and Uttar Pradesh. Working in the construction sites is found in every patch of the country. Glass industry is predominately found in Uttar Pradesh. Like that concentration of large power loom industry can be seen in both Tamilnadu and Maharashtra state because of availability of enough raw materials and cheap labour. Children working in fishing industry are common all along the coastal areas of the country. Garage work and street children are found in many parts of the country.

CHILD LABOUR-HUMAN RIGHTS PERSPECTIVE

The existence of child labour is a concrete manifestation of denial of rights of children. The child labourers are denied of their rights to survival and development, education, leisure and play, opportunity for developing their physical and mental talents, and protection from abuse and neglect which eventually impairs the personality and creativity of children and growth of full well being.

Table 1.1: Location Specific Occupations of Child Labour in India

Glass and Bangles	Firozabad (U.P.)
Handloom	Tamilnadu and Maharashtra
Power Loom	Maharashtra
Carpet Weaving	J&K, Uttar Pradesh and Rajasthan
Gem Cutting and Polishing	Jaipur (Rajasthan)
Diamond Cutting and Polishing	Surat (Gujarat)
Match and Fireworks	Sivakasi (Tamilnadu)
Garages and Petrol Pumps	Throughout India
Cashew Processing and Manufacture of coir products	Kerala
Helpers in Hotels, Restaurants, Canteen, Tea-Stalls, Shops	Throughout India
Rag Picking	Predominantly in Mega cities of the country.
Construction	Throughout India.
Fishing	Kerala, Tamilnadu, Gujarat.
Pottery units	Khurja, (U.P.)
Hawkers, vendors and newspaper sellers	Through out India
Coolies	Through out India.
Lock Industry	Aligarh (U.P.)
State Industry	M.P.

Source: Dak, 2003

The prevalence of child labour has given rise to a number of socio economic problems. It is beyond doubt that children are forced by circumstances to do labour in a tender age when they should have been studying in schools. The mere fact that it is not the work but labour that children are coerced to do which has manifold repercussions for them, the family and for the society as a whole.

The rationale for combating child labour derives from two distinct perspectives. Historically, the dominant perspective has been the development perspective, which lays emphasis on the adverse consequences of child labour for economic development and the labour market, as well as for the development of children as "human capital" contributing to future economic development. One of the most significant and dominant perspective for abolition of child labour comes from human rights perspective (Tabatabai, 2003).The child-centred, rights-based approach received international recognition with the adoption in 1989 of the United Nations Convention on the Rights of the Child (CRC), which has been ratified virtually by all countries. The Convention on the Rights of the Child (CRC), presents a compendium of diverse rights described in nearly forty articles. Article 32 of the CRC recognizes the right of the child (under 18) "to be protected from economic exploitation and from performing any work that is likely to be hazardous or to interfere with the child's education, or to be harmful to the child's health or physical, mental, spiritual, moral or social development" The Convention is intended to promote a holistic view of children, and therefore its other articles have to be taken into consideration as well. One of the CRC's most fundamental provisions (Article 3) requires that "in all actions concerning children ... the best interests of the child shall be a primary consideration". This principle is at the very heart of the child-centered perspective. At least another dozen or so rights articulated by the CRC are relevant to child labour concerns. They include, for example, the right to not be discriminated against (Article 2), the right of children to have their voice and opinion heard in all official actions concerning them (Article 12), the right to freedom of association (Article 15), the right to freedom from violence and abuse (Article 19), the right to an adequate standard of living (Article 27), the right to free and relevant schooling that effectively develops a child's potential (Articles 28 and 29), and the right to rest and play (Article 31), among others.

The Convention on the Rights of the Child is the outcome of the efforts of the international community to arrive at a standard to be followed by all countries in matters relating to children. The Convention lays emphasis on the fundamental freedom and liberties of the individual, protection against discrimination, violence, abuse, neglect and exploitation as well as on the positive measures such as upbringing within the family and under parental care, access of health care, social security, education, and to rest and leisure.

Childhood is required to be a period of 'evolving capacities - of the development of child's personality, talents and mental and physical abilities to their fullest potential", primarily through education. During this period, a child has a right "to a standard of living adequate for the child's physical, mental, spiritual, moral and social development".

The Convention establishes the right of the child to be an actor in his or her own development, to express opinions and to have then taken into account in the making of decisions relating to his or her life. Basic to the development of the child are: the right to express views in all matters affecting her or him and of their being given due weight, freedom of expression including right to information and ideas, freedom of thought, conscience and religion, as well as freedoms of association and peaceful assembly. The child has a right to privacy, and to special protection and assistance provided by the state, where the child is deprived of family environment.

As regards employment, the child, in view of his physical and mental immaturity, has a special right to be protected from "economic exploitation and from performing any work that is likely to be hazardous or to interfere with the child's education, or to be harmful to the child's health or physical, mental, spiritual, moral or social development.

These concerns also underlie the ILO's 1973 Minimum Age Convention (No. 138, henceforth C138) that defines a range of minimum ages – depending on the country's level of development and the type of employment and work – below which no child should work. In 1999, these international instruments were complemented with the adoption by the ILO of the Convention on the Worst Forms of Child Labour (C182). The C182 obligates member States to "take immediate and effective measures" to eliminate the worst forms of child labour. C138 and C182 are the principal international labour standards defining the ILO's mandate on child labour. Such a perspective and approach are also reflected clearly in ILO's

Convention no.182 against the worst forms of child labour adopted in June, 1999. It defines the worst forms as including all forms of or practices similar to slavery, the sale and trafficking of children, debt bondage, use or procurement of children for prostitution or pornographic purposes, forced or compulsory recruitment of children for use in armed conflict, using child in illicit activities, such as the production and trafficking of drugs, and the work that is likely to harm the health, safety and morals of children (UNICEF, 2001). The 'child-centered perspectives are especially influenced by modern ideas of human rights and human development. It understands children to be resilient as well as vulnerable, to be capable as well as inexperienced, to be characterized by knowledge as well as ignorance, to have a variety of intelligences as well as learning needs, and to be active rather than passive agents in their development. It also appreciates that children learn best through personal engagement in life activities, and that crucial self-esteem comes in part from a sense of efficacy in the world. The major contribution of the 'child-centred perspective' has been to refocus primary attention on children and their welfare. It has in effect made national policy and other child labour action more accountable to children. Assertive introjection of the 'child-centred perspective' in to international debate already has turned the 'best interests' provision of the CRC into a central criterion that all parties in the discussion must address in order to maintain their credibility(Myers, 2001). A positive development for abolition of child labour has been shaped and accelerated by the principles and ideals of human rights more particularly with the adoption and ratification of Convention on the Rights of the Child, 1989. According to the Convention, the child labour can be seen in its broadest and most damaging sense as a human rights violation on many different levels. As such, it can be addressed only through a complementary range of measurers from laws and mechanisms to create and enforce minimum working age regulations to the multiple protections enumerated in article 32 of the Convention of the Rights of the Child. And in concert with article 32, virtually every other article of the convention focuses on issues that are in one way or other related to the effects of work on children, including education, protection, exploitation, health, nutrition, rest and relaxation, play, social security, economic well being and the responsibilities of the parents. A human rights approach to child labour therefore permits and indeed requires responses that are as multifaceted as the affronts children endure and the conditions that give rise to them. It also permits and requires wide partnerships and alliances to make the responses a reality.

PROBLEMS OF CHILD LABOUR

Child labourers are not only deprived of proper food, shelter and other necessities, but also deprived of basic rights. They endure miserable and difficult lives. They earn little and struggle to make enough to feed themselves and their families. According to Tiwari (1997), child's developments can be endangered by work as under:

(a) *Physical development*: Including overall health coordination, strength, vision and hearing;

(b) *Cognitive development*: Including literacy, numeracy and the acquisition of knowledge necessary for normal life;

(c) *Emotional development*: Including adequate self esteem, family attachment, and feeling of love and acceptance;

(d) *Social and moral development*: including a sense of group identity, the ability to cooperate with others and the capacity to distinguish right from wrong;

The specific deprivations accruing to the child labour include:

- Deprivation in health care
- Deprivation from psychological support
- Deprivation from recreational opportunities
- Educational Deprivation
- Exclusion from future employment
- Deprivation from social security

Deprivation in Health Care

The health of the child labour is always endangered. Their health status becomes more vulnerable due to high incidence of malnutrition and undernourishment. The child labourers suffer from various infectitious diseases including tuberculosis, anemia, asthma, skin diseases, ear and eye problem etc. There are ample incidences of sexually transmitted diseases among child labourers. Most of the working children are also addicted to drugs. Working children are deprived of basic necessities like immunization protection from job hazards, proper ventilation, toilet facilities protection from sun and rain and proper lightning. The study done by Mitra (1993) on health conditions of child labourers in a small scale leather industry in Calcutta revealed that three specific health problems prevalent among employed children namely backache, ankle pain, and tingling pain in hands. In bidi industry child labourers are exposed to tobacco fumes through out the day which leads to asthma, tuberculosis, continuous cold, backaches, body ache, gas trouble, piles and rheumatic complaints (Naidu & Kapadia, 1985). In the bangle industry and glass industry children work close to the pumices where the temperature ranges from 40 to 45 degree centigrade. Owing to extreme heat and chemical fumes the incidence of tuberculosis is widespread which reduces their life span. They became unable to do work after the age of 35 years (Burra, 1986). In brassware industry due to inhaling of metal dust child labourers suffer from several respiratory diseases. In diamond cutting industries of Surat, diamond polishing industries of Jaipur and in zari embroidery work of Lucknow, children work in ill-ventilated, badly lit rooms where their eyesight get affected (Rao, 1980). In the lock industries of Aligarh and metal industries of Moradabad; Varanasi and Delhi, children work on hand presses, buffing machine, electroplating and spray painting units. Here the chemical fumes affect their respiratory systems and white-hot flames damage their eyesight. The children reported giddiness and tiredness, which influence their working capacity (Pati, 1985). Shah (1985) observed that child labourers come into close contact with several kinds of infections. They also suffer from anemia, fatigue and inadequate sleep makes them more susceptible to infectious diseases. The child labourers are also victims of constant threat of traffic accidents. (Joshi, 2006, Nongia, 1987). Contact dermatitis is a health hazard seen in children working in processes where chemicals are used. Ankylosis, Spondalitis and permanent spinal deformities have been attributed to abnormal posture, which the working children have to adopt while working. Most of the child labourers are highly vulnerable to all kinds of child abuses especially physical abuse, sexual abuse & police abuse etc. (Sekar, 2007).

Deprivation from Psychological Support

A large number of child labourers face the unhappy reality of increasing separation from their natural families. Many of them have the feeling of insecurity, inferiority and low self esteem and fatigue. A large number of child labourers also suffer from various kinds of neurotic disorders particularly anxiety, depression etc. Children who are in risky job fields have no opportunity to build their natural psychosocial health. Long working hours breed their feeling of frustration and inadequacy. Their involvement in risky work resists eventually in building their emotional cognitive skills and they become withdrawn, introvert and uncommunicative. A significant portion of the child labourers are suffering from psychological immaturity and are affected by abnormal psychological growth. They are also deprived of the special care that would be required for their psychological effects (Nasiruddin et.al. 2009). Reddy and Ramesh (2002) in their study reported that the child labourers are deprived of love, affection and sympathy which results in development of the feeling of inferiority and insecurity further leading to the development of fear and anxiety. The development of children and adolescents growing up in adverse circumstances lag behind peers from more advantaged homes (Misra and Mohanty, 2000) and experience a unique set of psychological barriers to change and development (Sinha,1990, Arumani, 2010).They are also deprived of the special care that would be required for their psychological effects (Nasiruddin et.al., 2009).

Deprivation from Recreational Opportunities

The child labourers are unable to participate in leisure and recreational activities, and, therefore, lose the psychological benefits otherwise needed for them. So, most of them child labourers develop a habit of smoking, and liquor drinking. Some of them also become drugs addicts or spend time in gambling and other such criminal activities. Mishra and Mishra, 2004 in their study reported that the child labourers get very less spare time. But whatever spare time they get, they try to utilize it in the best possible manner. Jeyaranjan (2001) in his study reported many children also pooled their money to hire a vehicle and go for excursions during the weekly holidays. But unfortunately, because of their access to cash, many of them had started drinking at a very early age. Since most of the child labour households had a television at home with a cable connection, many children spent their late evenings before these television sets.

Educational Deprivation

Child labourers are deprived of the educational and vocational facilities otherwise available to the non-working children. Child participation in labour force clearly reduces the potential for schooling and educational development. Children from poor families obviously do not have much access to education as those from wealthier families. Even where educational facilities are available to children, such children can not take sufficient advantages of them because of lack of interest of their parents. The chances of benefitting from education diminish more when they work. Most of the child labourers cannot go to school or are bound to leave the school before time (Shandilya, 2006). So, the childhood is lost because of economic concerns. The education provided in government run schools are irrevalent to contemporary needs and changing economic situations. The formal education that is provided to child labour does not match the needs of the local labour market. Therefore, the child labourers further lose interest and remain deprived of educational opportunities.

Exclusion from Future Employment

A large number of children end up working as domestic workers on low wages and facing unhealthy living conditions. The unrelenting poverty forces the parents to push their children in all forms of hazardous occupations. Child labour is a source of income for poor families. Some times children are abandoned by their parents or sold to factory owners. The last two decades have seen tremendous growth of export based industries and mass production factories utilizing low technologies. They try to maintain competitive positions through low wages and low labour standards. The child labourers exactly suit their requirements because of lack of education. Given the low educational achievement, the possibility for acquiring remunerative jobs becomes still more remote. Children thus find themselves locked in unskilled, low paying, unpleasant and unsafe work situations and permanently disadvantaged in the labour market (ILO, 1983). In India, a majority of children work in industries, such as cracker making, diamond polishing, glass, brass-ware, carpet weaving, bangle making, lock making and mica cutting to name a few. Ultimately the poor health status coupled with lack of education and training, they are deprived of future employment.

Deprivation from Social Security

The child labourers are not covered by various social security measures, which operate largely through formal sector employment. Reasons for their exclusion from these systems include the practical difficulties of collecting contributions from them and their employers, their unwillingness or inability to pay contributions (especially when the benefits on offer do not match what they consider to be their most important needs, in particular for health care) and their distruct of the management of the formal schemes. Child labour headed families are especially difficult to reach through formal social protection systems and welfare, particularly because of lack of proper official identities.

CAUSES OF CHILD LABOUR

There is neither one cause of child labour nor any single model that adequately explains the complex phenomenon of child labour. Scholars subscribe to various models in explaining the determinants and analyzing the causes of or forces behind the incidence of child labour of varying degrees across time and space. One accepted model of the 20th century explaining the causes of existence of child labour is Becker's micro theory of fertility. The model was explained with the help of Hicksian indifference curves, showing that the higher level of the curve on the indifference map, the higher is the fertility and higher might be the incidence of child labour(Becker,1960). Dinesh, 1988 strongly supported the Becker's model with quantitative information, according to which child labour is the consequence of large number of siblings in a family fundamentally caused by high fertility of mothers. Mother's fertility is stated to be high, if it is influenced by parent's motive to have children mainly to satisfy (a) the psychic utility; and (b) economic utility.

Economic utility which refers to prospective benefit and/ or tangible returns expected from children may be sub-categorized as

1. income benefits;
2. work benefit; and
3. security benefit in the old age of parents.

This micro fertility theory of child labour can not be accepted as fully valid. Because, it is found that some nuclear or small families too send their children to labour market which shows that the undergoing causes of child labour supply is not necessarily the higher level of fertility of mother. It is the result of macro situation and not of a micro situation in a family.

Another popular theory of child labour is the extreme poverty with high or low fertility (Duraiswamy, 1997). Under such a theory it is argued that the phenomenon of child labour practices is very much determined by the degree of parent's poverty and the survival strategies of parents (Lieten, 2000 cited in Manimekalai, 2001). In a study of child labourers in Kashmir, Sharma et.al, 1993 noted that 97 per cent of children joined carpet weaving industry due to poverty. Thus, poverty has been identified as one of the main determinants of the child labour supply-for, in a non-poor high wage society parents do not send their children to work (Basu & Van, 1998). It is a generally acceptable proposition that poverty is the main reason for which the children are forced to work. Their income is necessary for the survival of their family members and also of themselves (Jain and chand, (1979). Chronic poverty is the largest factors factor responsible for the prevalence and perpetuation of child labour. Due to poverty 'parental authority' is misused. In this context, Marx said: "It was not the misuse of parental authority that created the capitalist exploitation....of children's labour but on the contrary, it was the capitalist mode of production which by sweeping away the economic basis of parental authority, made its exercise degenerated into a mischievous misuse of power". There are many who view the problem in this way and link it with exploitative capitalist mode of production and working of capitalist system. It has been opined: "Child labour more truly mirrors the character of the society and polity including the nature of transition, than any other set of indicators." (Juyal, 1988). Thus, the exploitative capitalist order perpetuates the problem.

A parallel view holds that poverty as the reason for supply of child labour is partly true. ILO (1996) is also of the opinion that poverty combined with traditions, compel the children to follow the footsteps of their parents. But poverty, it is admitted is not the only reason for the existence of child labour (ILO, 1992).

The 'traditional view' of the history of child labour reigned almost unchallenged for a long time. In this view, the process of industrialization led to unprecedented use and exploitation of child labour, producing working conditions for children comparable to those of slavery. Children were ultimately rescued from their fate by campaigners on their behalf, and above all the passage of effective child labour laws (Hammond and Hammond, 1919; Hutchins and Harrison, 1926).

Sociologists consider school drop outs as the important reason for existence of child labour. But as regards, the reason of school drop outs, there is a difference opinion between those who argue poverty as the paramount reason and those who attribute the school. According to the National Council for educational research and training (NCERT) the inability of the school system to retain children who have enrolled in the primary level education-"the push out" has been the single greatest reason responsible for the existence of child labour(Weiner,1991). Thus, poverty can not always be argued to the paramount reason of school drop outs and supply of child labour. It is poverty simply a classical defence offered by sociologists till date (Basu and Van, 1998).

Ahmed (1999) has concluded after a quantitative cross country empirical study that child labour is basically associated with inequality in society but not with poverty. Both inequality and poverty in the society have been currently found to be the consequence of capability deprivation-deprivation from quality of being able to do something. And, hence, the latter is a more responsible variable for the existence and continuum supply of child labour (Foster and Sen, 1998).

Choudhary (1997) theorizes that the phenomenon of child labour- both the incidence of child labour and its occupational pattern undergoes a major transformation in the process of structural changes of the economy caused basically by the complex process of economic growth.

The discourse on of child labour can briefly be analyzed in the classical and contemporary political economy perspectives. Karl Marx in Capital (Volume 1, chapter 15, Section-3) outlined a formal model of the cause of child labour. He first noted how, with the rise of new technology, in a particular mechanism, there arose scope for employing those" whose bodily development is incomplete, but whose limbs are all the suppler. The labour of women and children was therefore, the first thing sought by capitalists who used machinery". Marx also noted the far reaching consequences of child labour with reference to the nature of capitalism.

The urban areas in India are characterized by a strong concentration of urban population, the emergence of slums and the urban poor. While migrating to urban centres, the migrants bring with them a number of children. In order to survive and raise their level of earnings/income they seek employment for the children in a variety of activities of the economy. The child labour, which faces restrictions to entry in the formal sector activities, is comparatively more easily absorbed in the informal sector activities which are out side the purview of the legal restrictions (Gaur, 2005). Tripathy's study also revealed that child labour originates from the flow of labourers or labour mobility towards districts or states or outside where industry and employment are expanding. Though migrant streams are varied in dimensions, the principal current of modern migration all over the world is towards urban areas. Shukla and Shukla (1993) pointed out that, there were certain factors which enabled children to seek employment in the informal sector in comparison to the formal sector. These related to: absence of any statutory minimum age requirement, easy entry, less competition among job seekers, absence of any minimum requirement of education or training, easy nature of work, provision of food, shelter and clothing in the city by the employer and absence of any minimum wage requirement as well as easy entry and easy exit. He had also mentioned that four types of children are found engaged in the informal sector. Those children belonging to poor families undertake jobs to supplement their parent's income, children who have none to support them, children who are sent to urban areas by their parents in rural areas for earning a living and children who run away from their families. Sekar (2004) had conducted a study on child labour in urban informal sector in Noida and it reiterates the fact that the perpetuation of child labour is inextricably linked to the slow pace of poverty reduction. Intersection of poverty with other forms of disadvantages such as caste, gender, ability among others complicate its effects on the incidence of child labour. The study revealed that 97 per cent of the households with rag picking children are migrants and almost all the households migrated after 1980, when the city was being constructed. Poverty and unemployment have been reported as the most common reasons for migration. The study also revealed that the living conditions of the rag pickers were extremely poor with hardly any basic amenities. Most of them lived in dilapidated structures made of cheap building material with temporary ceilings which were highly vulnerable to the vagaries of weather.

In most of the cases, employers prefer children to adults, as children are more active, agile, and quick and feel less tired than adults in certain tasks. They are also more amenable to discipline and control. They can be coaxed, admonished, pulled up and punished for defaults without jeopardizing relations or generating hostile and revengeful reactions. They provide very flexible workforce that can be employed or laid off without difficulty under their non contractual recruitment arrangements. Socially, their status as workers is not recognized and their work is seen as temporary and marginal (Nongia, 1987). The reasons stated in the Report of the Committee on Child Labour (1980) for employer's preference for children in work are: "less age and status conscious, lesser affliction by feeling of guilt and shame, no hesitation to do non-status, even demeaning jobs, activeness, agility and quickness and lesser feeling of tiredness, greater discipline and control, less expensive to maintain, superior adaptive qualities, lack of organization; moral consideration of employers to help and to provide succor to destitute or for saken children and acquisition of fitness through initiation in the early age. The National Commission on Labour (1969) has also pointed out that "quite often it is the feeling of sympathy rather than the desire to exploit which weighs with employers in employing child workers." Dak (2002) pointed out that Most of the employers have vested interests in employing child labour. Child labour is cheap children work at lower wages for long hours without grumbling. Children are easy to be exploited, honest and hardworking and at the same time docile and meek workforce. Managing children is easier than managing adults. Children are found to be better suited for certain types of jobs. The greed for profit and stiff competition for markets in the developed countries encourage employers to use child labour for economic advantage. It is argued that if children who earn meager sums were taken out of employment, there would be no downward swing in the socio economic status of the family. The only downswing would be the profit margin of the employers.

Conceiving the advantages of employment of children, the parents feel that the job disciplines the child, terminates his dependency, protects him against the infection of delinquent culture, and provides some moments of privacy to parents and so on. The parents are so much overwhelmed by the visibility of these gains that they would forego the exploitation of the child (Nangia, 1987).

The National Commission on Labour (1969) has also pointed out that "quite often it is the feeling of sympathy rather than the desire to exploit which weighs with employers in employing child workers."

The roots of the problem lie in the exploitative systems prevailing not only at the national level but also at the international level. At the national level the lopsided development process in the background of socio-economic structure results in marginalization of the poor, who are left with no option but use child labour as a survival strategy. And at the international level the need for foreign exchange, on the one hand, and stiff competition for markets in the developed world, on the other, encourage the producers of export industries in the third world to use cheap and vulnerable child labour. Also, powerful multi national corporations use child labour directly or indirectly, to minimize cost of production and to maximize profits (Indira et al, 1991). The foreign exchange earning aspect has been very well brought out in the article by Mahendra Lama on Tea industry, Neera Burra on lock industry in Aligarh, Manju Gupta on carpet industry. All these industries are export-industries where cheap child labour is used for minimization of production cost and maximization of profits (Singh and Mohanthy, 1993). Child labour is intimately linked to the pace and pattern of economic growth, the structure of the economy, the prevalence of poverty, the inadequacies in social infrastructure and protection, the functioning of the labour market, population growth and dynamics, cultural factors and attitudes, etc. The existence of child labour is a manifestation of inadequate and improper socio-economic development and the problem cannot be effectively addressed in isolation from the broader context of the development process (Tabatabai, 2003).

The reasons of child labour are divided into three main groups as stated by Anker (1996) as follows.

(A) Awareness and innocence

(a) More docile and less troublesome
(b) Greater willingness to do repetitive, monotonous work.
(c) More trustworthy and innocent, so less likely to steal.
(d) Less absenteeism
(e) Don not form trade union.

(B) Tradition

(a) Tradition of hiring child labour by employers.
(b) Traditional occupations have children working along with their parents
(c) Social role of employer to provide jobs to families in the community
(d) Employers need labourers. Children are available and ask for jobs, so they hire child labourers.

(C) Physical Characteristics

(a) Better health (as young)
(b) Nimble fingers (traditional scholars used to call it supple fingers)

Vidyasagar and Kumarbabu (2002) had presented three distinct stages in the evolution of the institution of child labour with regard to India. These are:

A. As far as the traditional Indian context was concerned, formal education had been the prerogative of certain communities in the upper layers of the society in the historical past. As per the hierarchy-based division of labour and inheritance of occupations, the children of peasants, artisans and other service communities were made apprentices in their family occupations, be it crafts or agriculture. It was considered part of the socialization process for the children. So, the problem of child labour was persisted.

B. It is after the industrial revolution in Europe and its gradual impact on the colonies that factory-type units started springing up during the British period. Factories required cheap and plentiful labour. Employment of children as labourers began because they were cheap, docile and uncomplaining. The factory owners could hence minimize costs and maximize profits. Along with modern factory type production, employment of children also emerged in petty commodity production that went to cater to the growing urban demand. Thus along with modern factories, manufacturing also developed in informal sector which could be termed as traditional informal sector (through agriculture remains to be one of the biggest traditional informal sector till date). In this phase, employment of children began, both in organized factory sector as well in the traditional informal manufacturing sector.

C. From the seventies, as an impact of a strong labour movement which has been fighting for the rights of the workers and the resultant national legislation for regulation of labour standards, there has been a process of decentralization of production from the organized sectors to informal sector, where the labour standards remain low and regulation is the least. This process has got intensified in the "new economic regime" where the liberation of the economy and linkage to the global markets are the key principles. In the present era, big factories are breaking into small units and the operations are spatially divided. Given the income and poverty levels of the people, ground for employment of children in large scale has been generated and is next only to agriculture sector.

ESTIMATES OF CHILD LABOUR–GLOBAL AND NATIONAL LEVEL

As per the latest estimates of ILO in 2004, out of an estimated 317 million children in the age group of 5 to 17 years who are globally engaged in some form of economic activity, 218 million fall within the strict definition of child labour. Out of these, 126 million children engaged in hazardous occupations. In other words, more than 2/3rd of the child labourers are still engaged in hazardous form of child labour.

Table 1.2: Global Estimate of Child Labour

Age Group (Years)	Economically Active	Child Labour Occupations	In Hazardous
5-17	317 million	218 million	126 million
5-14	190.7 million	165.8 million	74.4 million

Source: ILO, 2004

Out of the estimated 190.7 million economically active children in the age group of 5-14 years in the world, the Asia-Pacific region harbors the largest number of child labourers. In Sub-Saharan Africa and in Latin America, these figures are 49.3 million and 5.7 million respectively.

Table 1.3: Region Wise Distribution of Children in the Age Group of 5-14 Years by Their Economic activity

Region	Magnitude
Asia and Pacific	122.3
Sub-Saharan Africa	49.3
Latin America and Carribean	5.7
Other region	13.4

Estimates of child labour for different countries depend on the consideration of age that has been set for inclusion in the category. This consideration of age is different in different nations. As a result more or less children get included or excluded in the estimates. As mentioned earlier in India children below 14 years gainfully engaged physically or mentally in any occupation either in agriculture or in industry, are called child labour. The minimum age considered for child labour is 12 years in Egypt, 14 years in Philippines and Hong Kong and 13 years in Malaysia. In Peru, this age is 14 years in agriculture sector, 15 years for industry, and 16 years for ocean fishing and 18 years for working in ports. ILO in its minimum age (industrial) conference (1919) has determined 12 to 13 years for light works and 18 years for hard and dangerous works.

India continues to host the largest number of child labourer in the world today. According to 2011 Census, 12.6 million children in the age group of 5 to 14 are employed in our country. This accounts for 11% of the workforce of India. If we examine the trend from 1971 onwards, the phenomenon of child labour has shown an increasing trend. As can be seen in the period from 1981 to 1991 the child labour figure was seen as declining. Economic liberalisation commenced in 1991 which may be the reason for the increase of child labourers in India. The following table gives a comparative picture of the child labour estimates in our country over the different census period.

Table 1.4: Child labour in India over different censuses

Year	Number of Child Labour
1971	10,753,985
1981	13,640,870
1991	11,285,349
2001	12,591,667
2011	12,626,505

SITUATION OF CHILD LABOUR IN THE ERA OF GLOBALIZATION

After the introduction of globalization era in India, private investment began to flow through foreign direct investments. Multinational corporations are free to establish factories and can sell their products anywhere in the globalized world. The shrinkage of public sector and expansion of private sector economic activities has increased child labour (Das, 2011). Economic activities seem to move from formal sector to informal sector. The flourishing of informal sector has intensified child labour in the developing countries particularly in India. The informalisation of many production activities in the wake of privatization is also associated with outsourcing of job to home based working units employing family labour. Children of the poor families are therefore prone to be engaged in such work. Child Labour (Prohibition and Regulation) Act does not apply to this home based work for children. Many of the processing jobs have been shifted to family based units. This out sourcing have substantially reduced production costs and increased the profits of the enterprises. These enterprises use child labour for production and processing of their products by employing child labour.

According to Census, 2001 there were about 12.7 million economically active children in the age group of 5-14 years. The number was 11.3 million during 1991 census, thus showing an increase in the number of child labourers. The Census data shows that there is a substantial increase in marginal workers in every category of worker irrespective of sex and residence. Despite the number of main workers declining from 9.08 million in 1991 to 5.78 million in 2001 and 4.9 million in 2011 census, the total number of children in the workforce increased. A large part of the increase in marginal workers, which increased from 2.2 million in 1991 to 6.89 million in 2001 showed decreasing trend in 2011 i.e. 5.85 million. The trends between 1991 and 2001 of declining main child workers along with increasing marginal workers may indicate the changing nature of work done by the children. This is also to be seen in the context of decelerating employment growth in general in the economy during the last decade. There is a broad decline in the incidence of child labour in the southern and western Indian states and UTs between 1991 and 2001. However; there has been an increasing trend in eastern and north Indian states and UTs.

Table 1.5: State/UT Showing % Increase in the Incidence of Child Labour during 2001 as Compared to 1991

Punjab 24.08	Uttar Pradesh 41.71	Mizoram 60.65	Chandigarh 102.09
Tripura 32.03	Arunachal Pradesh 49.11	Bihar 61.82	Haryana 131.10
Meghalaya 55.75	Andaman & Nicobar 54.94	Rajasthan 60.38	Nagaland 178.43
Himachal Pradesh 90.96	Delhi 53.19	Manipur 74.84	Sikkim 193.98

Source: NCPCR, 2007

The census data, 2001 shows that only around 20% of the child workers are engaged on farms in agriculture, animal husbandry and fishing and the figure is 27% in 2011 census. There is a sharp decline in this proportion compared to 1991 where around 42% of child labour force was engaged on farms in agriculture, animal husbandry and fishing. Thus, there is a movement of child labour force from farm to non-farm activities. Nearly 48% of the child labour force in the age group of 5-14 in 2001 census is involved in manufacturing both household based and non-household based occupations. Remaining child labour force is involved in service sector operations including construction, trade and domestic service-mostly in the informal sectors of the economy. This partly explains the increase in child labour force in north and East Indian states where the household industries and service sector is growing (NCPCR, 2007). There are some indications that child labour in export production, such as the carpet industry, has increased since liberalization, as reported by Joseph Gathia of the Centre of Concern for Child Labour (Vivekananda, 1996 cited in Hensman, 2001). The 2011 census reported that 40% of the child labour work force are involved in manufacturing both household and non-household occupations which is declined if compared to the 2011 census. This may be due to the increasing role played by the government, media, and civil society organizations.

CHILD LABOUR: DELHI CONTEXT

The child labourers are spread throughout the National Capital Territory of Delhi. There are nearly 4 lakh child workers in Delhi, who comprise about 18% of the child population of the National Capital Territory of Delhi. Out of them about 30,000 work in the 5,000 registered and 25,000 unregistered tea shop and dhabas, about 20,000 work in scooter and car repair shops, and approximately 30,000 children are working as shop assistants and about 40,000 work as labourers (agriculture, construction and coolies etc.) and nearly 1, 00, 000 work as the domestic servants (full time/ part time) (Panicker and Nongia, 2002). As per the census of india, the child labourers in Delhi shows increasing trend.

Table 1.6: **Workers aged 5-14 years between 1971 -2001 Censuses in Delhi**

Year	Number of Child Labour
1971	17120
1981	25717
1991	27351
2001	41899

Major Areas of Concentrating of Child Labour in Delhi

(a) Interstate Bus Terminus and its surrounding areas.

The ISBT and its surrounding areas is one of the major areas of concentration of child labour. The children in this area are employed as vendors, porters, shoes-shining boys, shop assistants, sellers of ready made garments, service boys in tea stalls etc.

(b) Trans Yamuna Area

The Trans Yamuna area is an area of major concentration of child labour. The children in this area are engaged in construction work, rag picking, garage work and work as domestic servants and as service boys in tea stalls and dhabas and apprentices in the tailoring shops etc.

(c) The Railway Station Area

Child labourers are found at all the three railway stations in Delhi, New Delhi Railway Station, Old Delhi Railway Station and Nizammudin Railway Station. Children in these areas are mostly working in tea shops, dhabas, as vendors, shoe-polishers, porters and rag pickers.

(d) Jama Masjid and Surrounding Areas

Many children surrounding Jama Masjid like Chandi Chowk are engaged as helpers in the shops, small workshops, as rag pickers etc. nearly an equal number of children are engaged in the manufacturing processes, like electro-plating, book binding, metal carving etc.

(e) Daryaganj and Surrounding Areas

The areas surrounding Dayraganj like Asaf Ali Road and Ramlila ground, a large number of children are employed in various activities like rickshaw pulling, working in garages, and selling newspaper etc.

(f) Connaught Place

A large number of children are found working in Connaught Place which is known in Delhi as one of the busiest commercial place. A number of children are found working here as vendors, selling glasses, flowers, garlands and also engaged as shoe-shining boys.

(g) Karol Bagh

Karol Bagh, which is one of the busy markets in Delhi, provides employment to a large number of children. They are mostly self-employed as vendors, selling eatables, cold drinking water, cosmetics, handkerchief etc. Some are found working in shops, tea stalls, dhabas, and garages etc.

Besides that, a large number of children in Delhi are found working in zari industry, leather industry, lock industry, and jewellery sector etc. A majority of the children working in zari industry are found in Seelampur, Ghonda, Nurelai, Gautam Puri, Chowanbengar, Kureji, Kalian Bagh (Trilokpuri), Sangam Vihar, Khanpur extension, Kotla Mubarakpur, Sarai Kale Khan, Mehruli, Nizammudin Basti, Uttam Nagar and Janakpuri. In leather industry, a large number of children work in Sadar Bazar (Hanuman Gali), Paharganj. In lock industry, child labourers are found in Sakur Ki Dandi (Near Ramlila Ground), LNJP Colony, etc. In jewellery sector, child labourers are found in Darayaganj, Karolbagh and other localities. A large number of rag pickers are found in Chilagown (Near Mayur Vihar), Yamuna Pusta (both sides of ITO bridge), Seelampur, Badarpur, Mitapur, Jaitpur, and C-Block of Jahangir Puri. There are also organized rag picking in Kalyan Baas, Mitapur etc. Child labourers are found working in Subzi Market in Azadpur Mandi, as well as in Okhla Mandi. A large number of child labourers are working at motor garages in Indira Market, Trilokpuri. In Dhaba/tea stalls, children are found working in North Delhi, Kashmere Gate, Jama Masjid and ITO areas.

2

Review of Literature

INTRODUCTION TO REVIEW OF LITERATURE

Review of Literature constitutes one of the most important aspects of research. A review of literature is a critical summary and an assessment of the current state of knowledge or current state of the art in a particular field. It is the process of reading, analyzing, evaluating, and summarizing scholarly materials about a specific topic. It entails the basic ground work before conducting any research.

The review helps in grasping the concerned issue and knowing the requirements for further investigation. It also enables the researcher to build a logical framework and to conceptualize varied dimensions of the issue under study. A review of relevant documents provides a critical insight into the theoretical and conceptual dimensions of the present study. Additionally, a review also provides an insight about the methodological concerns thus, setting ground to identify the limitations and applications of the available studies. In doing so, it allows the researcher to find the unexpected areas and dimensions of his/her field besides helping in bridging the gap between the present and past researches. It actually guides the researcher through out the research process. Finally, review of literature is an important source of secondary data. Studies conducted at different levels are of immense help for the researcher at every step of the study, beginning from the conceptualization to the conclusion.

A comprehensive and intensive literature review was undertaken by the researcher both prior to and over the entire course of the doctoral study. It entailed a review of empirical studies, reports, books and articles. A summation of the review is provided in the following section. Besides, an overview of the literature review is also presented. This has enabled the researcher to identify the gaps that exist in research work on the theme identified by him and in defining the scope of the present study.

Various studies on the broad theme of child labour have been conducted at different levels including the national, regional or industry wise levels. These came up in different periods of time as many educational institutions, government and non-governmental institutions started assuming research projects/studies on child labour. Child labour being a multidimensional issue, various scholars, planners and researchers has analyzed it from different perspectives. Many of these studies have been reviewed by the researcher. As far as the purview of this study is concerned, the focus has been on the studies undertaken after 1986 in India. This is due to the fact that the Child Labour Prohibition Act was passed in India in 1986 which is a significant legislation for preventing the occurrence of child labour in the country. For review purposes, the studies have been depicted and analyzed chronologically and not thematically, because the scholar observed that most of the studies have covered multiple dimensions and issues pertaining to child labour. On account of this, it was felt that a chronological depiction would be more appropriate as it would highlight the trends pertaining to the significant aspects of child labour in different periods of time.

STUDIES CONDUCTED DURING THE LATE 1980's

NIPCCD (1986) had conducted a study on rag picking children. The study mainly discussed the socio-economic background of the children. It covered 1000 male rag pickers in Delhi. The study revealed that every three out of four children lived in katcha houses with minimum civic facilities. The study also revealed that rag pickers migrated from various states of Haryana, Rajasthan, Tamilnadu, Uttar Pradesh and West Bengal and about 41 per cent of the rag pickers had dropped out before completing their primary education. The sample rag pickers contributed to the extent of 31.24 per cent of the total monthly income of the families.

Madhu et.al (1989) made a survey on the children working in restaurants, garages and domestic sector of the Bombay city on a selected sample of 508 children, 50 parents and employers for the purpose of the study done on random basis. The chief objectives of the study were: to find out the socio-economic conditions, factors responsible for the child labour and the working conditions of the children. The investigators used the field sources as well as documentary sources within their methodology. The study recommended that care should be taken particularly by the head of the family for health, education and welfare conditions of the children. The study also highlighted that protection from exploitation as also from under pay and over work must be ensured for the child labourers.

Singh (1990) conducted a study on carpet industries of Varanasi of Uttar Pradesh. The analysis was based on the sample study of 309 child labourers.These working children aged 11-15 years were mainly from lower economic background and were mostly illiterate. They belonged generally to backward and scheduled castes. In spite of working for more than 11 hours per day, they earned an average of Rs 145 p.m. The study found that abolition of child labour was not favoured either by parents or employers because of economic reasons. Even some of these children were happy in working because it gave them economic independence to certain extent. Singh highlighted that the practice of child labour was predominately found among weaker sections of the society and that the working conditions were grossly detrimental to the growth and development of the child workers.

The studies conducted during the late 1980's revealed that the focus of these studies has been on traditional occupations like beedi industry and carpet industry. The studies were based on large samples and relied on quantitative information. The studies have mainly discussed the incidence of child labour, the related problems particularly the harsh working conditions, possible causes and remedies.

STUDIES CONDUCTED DURING 1990'S

Karunanithi (1990) had conducted a study on the child labourers working in the beedi factory of Melapalayam of Tamil Nadu. The study was based on 112 respondents selected from every alternative households on a systematic sample based method .The study revealed that the child workers were forced by their parents to make 500 beedies and earn Rs. 5 a day. These children were put to work for nearly 10 to 12 hours, from dawn to desk.

Srivasthsava and Bhanumathi (1990) took up their research study on the child labour working in domestic, agriculture and hotel sectors of the Madras city. A sample of 300 child labourers in the age group of 7-14 years was taken for the survey and to study the choice of recreational activities, reasons for school dropouts, income and other aspects. The study found that for a majority of the child labourers the preferred choice of recreation was watching movies and listening to radio. The study also found that the child labourers were given left over food by their employers. The study also revealed that the child labourers suffered from fatigue, lack of rest break and weekly holidays.

Singh (1992) selected 200 children, aged 8 to 14 years working in hotels, truck garages, and doing household chores of Ahmadabad city. It aimed at studying the causes of child labour; size of the families and earnings of child labour.The study disclosed that most of the child labourers belonged to large families and worked due to socio economic compulsions. Children working in hotels and garages were earning very low wages between Rs 1 to 12 per day. The study recommended opening special schools, with non formal education at ten centers in the city.

Shukla and Shukla (1993) pointed out that, there were certain factors which enabled children to seek employment in the informal sector in comparison to the formal sector due to certain reasons viz- absence of any statutory minimum age requirement, easy entry, less competition among job seekers, absence of any minimum requirement of education or training, easy nature of work, provision of food, shelter and clothing in the city by the employer and absence of any minimum wage requirement as well as easy exit. He had also mentioned that four types of children were found engaged in the informal sector: children belonging to poor families who undertook jobs to supplement their parent's income; children who had none to support them; children who were sent to urban areas by their parents in rural areas for earning a living; and children who ran away from their families.

Kumar (1993) had conducted a study on child labour and education. His study had covered fourteen major states of India and had relied on secondary information. The study revealed that high fertility rate resulted in heavy population structure and abundant availability of children. Low level of literacy, in general and failure of educational institutions and institutional infrastructures to attract children to schools for education and higher drop out rate added to this\ problem. He had also pointed out that due to poverty, sometimes there was high economic value attributed to children in our traditional society and this left no other space for the poor parents but to send their children to the labour market.

IAMR (Institute of Applied Man Power Research) study on 'Child Labour in Informal Sector' in 1993 covered 644 child labourers of 492 households. The study reported that out of school children were the main reservoir for the supply of child labour. Most of the children were encouraged by their parents to be engaged as either self employed, wage paid or unpaid family workers. The study also reported that nearly 25% child labourers worked for more than seven hours in a day and most of the child labourers were semi-skilled. The various schemes initiated by government for controlling and banning the child labour practices did not have any impact in that area. The study viewed that child labour was not an economic problem alone; it had social and cultural dimensions too.

Kulshreshtha in 'Indian Child Labour' (1994) considered the child labour problem of India as an enigmatic problem. He attributed the causes of child labour, inter alia, to low wages of the adults, unemployment of the adult workers, lack of social security schemes for poor families, bigger family size, rural-urban migration, high rate of illiteracy, traditions and absence of compulsory education. He appraised the roles of voluntary organisations in creating awareness about the evils of child labour and securing social justice for them.

The study of Burra (1995) 'Born to Work' focused on the working children in some specific industries of glass making, brass ware, gem polishing and lock making. The study had focused on the socio economic conditions of the child labourers and the hazardous processes involved in their work. The study brought to light the fact that a large number of children, as young as five or six years worked through the night under great health and safety hazards, resulting in the stunting of the growth of these children, both psychological and physical. Even the state policies aimed at protecting children were poorly conceived and badly enforced.

Tripathi (1996) studied child labour in Agra city and found that maximum of them were residents of the same region and belonged to large nuclear families with meager family income. These children worked under pathetic working and employment conditions. Most of these children were of the age group of 10-14 years, living in poor socio-economic conditions, earning low wages and worked for long hours with no rest in between. No facilities and benefits like provident fund, medical compensation were provided to the child labourers.

"Working Children in Urban India" by Patil (1997) is a comprehensive survey which attempted to analyse the problem of child labour at the macro level and also highlighted the reasons which compelled children to become wage labourers. The study revealed that among the selected 600 child workers in Bangalore, 79.67% were boys and 65.33% of the child labourers were in the age group of 15 and 17 years and around 10 per cent were below the age of 10 years. The percentage of girls within each group varied and about 41.27% were in the age of below 10 years and 22.67 per cent in the age group of 10-12 years. This study found that girls started working at an early age than do boys. It also brought out the harsh realities of child employment with regard to their wages and monthly earnings/income and revealed that the meager wages the children earned was the means of survival for their families. Finally it outlined some policy measures to tackle the problem of child labour in the short term and its elimination in the long term.

Tripathy's study (1997) revealed that migrant child labourers were mainly from the drought prone poverty stricken scheduled caste and scheduled tribe families. The contributions of child labour to the family income were substantial as they contributed at par with adult members. Work environment of the migrant child labour was poor and they were usually victimized by health hazards of tuberculosis, eye, and hand injuries. The study also revealed that the migrant child labourers toiled hard and usually walked a distance not less than 16 km per day. About 50 per cent of the migrant child labourers families were having a family size of 5 to 8 members. About 80 per cent of child labourers migrated to Surat were in the age group of 11-14 years. An in-depth study of the living conditions of migrant child labourers revealed that the absence of employment in rural areas, failure of crops, poverty and indebtedness were some of the vital factors of migrant child labourers of Ganjam district in Orissa. Tripathy's study also revealed that migrant child labour originated from the flow of labourers or labour mobility towards districts or states or outside where industry and employment were expanding. Though migrant steams were varied in dimensions, but the principal current of modern migration all over the world was towards urban areas.

Gaur (1999) had conducted a study on 'Child Labour in College Canteens in Jaipur city. The study revealed that about 80 per cent of child labourers were living in kachi bastis with their parents. The bastis were located 10 to 15 kms from their work place and they commuted from their villages daily. The study also found that the child labourers were between the age group of 6 to 13 years and about 80 per cent of the child labourers were illiterate. It also revealed that employment of child labour in college canteens was believed to have an economic basis that fitted into a demand supply frame work. Child labourers were source of income for their poor families and were easily available at the lowest wage rates. They were also easily controlled by employers through various methods such as physical torture, wage deduction and abusive language. The study also found that the children in college canteens did various types of work, such as supply of goods (tea, coffee, snack, cigarettes, cold drinks etc.) not only in canteen but also in the entire college campus.

The review of the studies conducted during the designated period 1900's had also emphasized more on traditional occupations viz. gem polishing, lock making, carpet industry. Besides that, some of the studies were also conducted in the domain of the domestic, agriculture and hotel sectors. These studies highlighted the working conditions, terms of employment, causes of child labour as well as the physical and psychological problems faced by the children.

STUDIES CONDUCTED DURING THE YEAR 2000 AND BEYOND

Srivastava and Raj (2000) had conducted a study on child labour employed in the carpet industry of Mirzapur, Uttar Pradesh. The study revealed that about 62% of the children were illiterate and only 35 per cent reported to have completed primary education. The study reported that more than 90 per cent of the child labourers were earning a monthly income of less than Rs. 600/-. The study also indicated that the modal age of entry into the carpet industry was 10 years. While entry was reported even at the age 6-8 years, the entry acquired momentum by the time children were eight years old. The study also showed that poverty was most important reason for non-enrolment of students, as well as drop out of the students. Their parents were not conscious of and interested in the education of their children. This study found that the organization of the carpet industry was fairly informal and most of the carpets were produced at the house hold level. A break-up of the workers in the carpet industry revealed that adults comprised only 42.29 per cent against the children who constituted 57.71 per cent. The study also reported that about 42.26 per cent of the children were between 6-14 years. It also bought out the fact that female children constituted nearly 30 per cent of all children working and belonging to households with child labour in the carpet industry. It also found that the children from child labour households were generally from the poorer economic backgrounds, and most of them were drawn from either backward classes or scheduled caste communities.

Mathur and Bhargava (2000) conducted a study based on the problems of child labour, particularly in the gem-polishing industry, in Jaipur and other areas of Rajasthan. The study revealed that the main cause for the existence of the problem of child labour was the concerned people's ignorance. Most of the parents whose young children worked in these industries were simply unaware of the welfare measures that were being implemented for their benefit and that of their children. Secondly, most of the parents also did not consider anything wrong in making their children work from an early age. They were more concerned about the children's ability to be able to earn wages by becoming skilled, nor about their education. So, schooling of the child was not considered important for these parents. They also felt that if a child is gainfully occupied, it would keep him or her out of mischief.

Desai and Raj (2001) had conducted a study on child labour in the diamond industry of Surat. The study found that the working hours of the child labourers was flexible and varied from one unit to another and their wages were calculated on a piece rate basis. An average worker polished around 7-8 diamonds a day and earned about Rs. 1000 per month. The wage structure was almost similar for adults and children after a training period. All workers including children were initially given on-the-job training for a period. Children were not given the job of polishing diamonds right from the time they were inducted. During the initial one or two months, they were given jobs like cleaning the units, running errands etc. The study showed that child workers in the age group of 13-14 years constituted almost 96 per cent of the total child labour in the sample. The study also found that about 94 per cent of the child labours were found to be migrants mainly from the Bhumihar community of Bihar, Rajasthan, Madhya Pradesh, Orissa and Uttar Pradesh. It also revealed that over 80 per cent of child labourers were reported to have joined the work in the age group of 11 to 12 years and an insignificant proportion below the age of 10. The working conditions in the diamond industry were not different from other informal sector activities. Benefits like permanent status, provident fund, gratuity, earned leave, sick leave, and casual leave were not given to workers even though they were entitled to them.

Mathur and Singh (2001) had conducted a study on child labour in the gem-polishing industry of Jaipur. The study found that the industry was deemed suitable for child labour as it required no knowledge-based skills at least in some processes. Several reasons were cited in the study for the continued presence of children in the industry including the inability of the child labour legislation to pull the children out from work. The increasing number of workshops was also a major reason for the increasing number of employment of children in these industries. The parents also felt that, the earlier a child learns the skill, the better it is since, by the time he is 15 or 16 year old, he would be able to earn Rs. 60 or more per day. The study also found that children contributed 10 per cent of the family income. The study also found that as the work in the gem polishing process was divided into different segments with only some requiring skill and special equipment, the child labour was easily accommodated in all those processes that required no or few skills. Since no special equipment was needed for operations like Kandi Lagana, boring holes in the beads and stringing, such activities were shifted from the workshop to the homes of the labourers. This facilitated the involvement of women and children in their homes. The study also revealed that parents of the child labour were more cynical about the benefits of education and felt that there were better prospectus for their children in the gem industry. The parents viewed that instead of being failure at school, the child could be groomed to be successful in an occupation that he liked to join. The study also revealed that most of the parents, children and even workshop owners were unaware of the various legislations.

Raj and Chauhan (2001) stated that child labour was a multidimensional problem. The study reported both the supply and demand side factors that contributed for the growth of child labour. From the supply side, they specifically focussed on poverty and caste factors. Social, cultural and traditional factors were also responsible for the plight of children in India. On the demand side, determinants of child labour were: as source of cheap labour, less developed egos of children and absence of child labour unions. The study concluded that various circumstances like poverty, low family income, illiteracy, caste and traditions, lack of interest in studies or loss of parents lead to work in early stages. The study also pointed out that it was not enough to have a plethora of laws enacted to provide legal protection to child workers, regulate their working conditions but there was need to install effective administrative machinery to enforce the law.

Sekar and Mohammed (2001) had conducted a study on child labour in the lock industry of Aligarh. The study was based on primary data. The study reported the large scale existence of lock making in Aligarh because it was considered as traditional craft of the Muslims. It revealed that most of the child labourers belonged to poor economic conditions and their households were confined in the income bracket of Rs. 500-2000 per month. It also pointed out that, financial problems of the households were the main cause for the non-enrollment of children as parents preferred to send their children to earn rather than learn at school.

Jeyaranjan (2001) had conducted a study on child labour in the knitwear industry of Thiruppur in Coimbatore. The study revealed that a substantial number of children about 60 per cent were from the age group of 15-18 years. The remaining child labourers were from the youngest age group of 6-11. The study also found that the sample contained a substantial number of backward caste and scheduled caste households. The study also reported that, the parents felt that instead of entering the market at a later date and struggling to learn the work, it is better that the children learn the work now, and earn some wages while learning skills, to emerge as full-fledged workers in a couple of years. These working children were very much happy by the weekly wages that they got. A substantial part of their income was shared at home but their pocket money was enough to go to a movie during the weekends. The study reported that most of the children could afford to go to the cinema- which would be impossible if they had to get the money from their parents. Similarly they could eat out as and when they felt like with the little money that they got for themselves. Many children also pooled their money to hire a vehicle and go for excursions during the weekly holidays. But unfortunately, because of their access to cash, many of them had started drinking at a very early age. Since most of the child labour households had a television at home with a cable connection, many children spent their late evenings before these television sets.

Vidyasagar and Kumarababu (2002) conducted a study on 'Child Labour in the home based match industries of Sivakasi'. The study reported that, the concentration of match industries in Sivakasi was because of pioneering entrepreneurship, close caste cooperation among entrepreneurs, availability of timber from nearby Kerala, drought in the area leading to supply of cheap labour, arid climate facilitating natural drying of match sticks and boxes and low levels of literacy. This heavy concentration had been facilitated by availability of skilled labour, especially child labour in that area. The study also pointed out that female children and adults were employed equally in most of the operations in the match industry, like frame filling, box filling, box making, labeling and so on. The adults (men) were employed as chemical dippers, accountants and supervisors. Women and children constituted nearly 90 per cent of the workforce in the match industry. The study also reported that child labour in Sivakasi's match industry was primarily a demand side creation and the structure of the industry was conducive for garnering such cheap labour. The study revealed that given the nature of organization of production in the hand made match industry and the comparative cost advantage of labour, demand side factors played a primary role for persistence of child labour. However, the supply side factors also provided a fertile ground for the demand for cheap labour to grow and the industry to grow and get agglomerated. The study also found that children's contribution was significant to the families and if children were withdrawn from work, many families would suffer economically.

Singh and Sharma (2002) had conducted a study on child labour in the bangle units of Firozabad. The study found that children were employed only at the household level of bangle production. They were engaged mainly for jhalai, judai, katai and hill chadhana. After the initial making of the glass spirals in the factory, the entire work was transferred to small home based level units. The amount of payment and work done was measured in terms of the tora (312 bangles) and for every tora; payment of Rs. 1.65 was made for Jhalai, Rs. 2.75 for judai and Rs. 1.40 for chaklai. The children earned Rs. 43 per day. The study also showed that 38% of the children belonged to the 6-14 age group and these children entered the job market at the very early age of five and six years old. However, the maximum entry was around the age of 10. The study also found that children contributed about 20% of the family income. It was also found that almost one third of the children were dropped out as their parents could not afford the cost of education.

The study of NIPCCD (2003) conducted in Guwahati reported hazardous working conditions of children and also suggested some measures to prevent child abuse. A sample of 300 child workers upto 14 years were taken from 3 different categories of occupations, namely (i) employed (hotel workers, domestic servants, shop workers, sweepers,); (ii) self-employed (rag pickers, vendors); and (iii) others (helpers). Door to door enumeration, field interviews and observations technique was used to collect data. It was revealed that a majority of the child labourers (79%) were males and only 21% were females. The study also reported that a majority of the respondents belonged to Hindus and Muslims and a very few were Christians. The study also reported that the payment of wages was done both through cash and kind. The working hours of the children varied from 8-12 hours per day. Some of the child labourers were getting free food and first aid facility at the time of need. The study also highlighted the recreational patterns of the children. It reported that, children spent their leisure time playing with friends, watching movies and television. The study also revealed that the employers preferred children as they were trust worthy and could do small jobs. Regarding the future plans of children, a majority of the parents wanted their children to get jobs with a better salary after learning the trade, and some of the parents wanted their children to start a business and become self-employed. The study also reported that a significant number of parents (78%) were satisfied with the child's income.

John and Ghosh (2003) conducted a study of Child Labour in the Zardari and Hathari Units of Varanasi'. The study found that poverty was the main reason behind child labour. In this industry, most of the children were uneducated. Working hours of the children were long and the rooms in which they worked lacked proper ventilation and sufficient light which was harmful to the physical health and well being of the children. As the children were involved in the work from an early age, they neither had time for any physical activity necessary at their age nor were they able to take up any alternative employment, once they grow up. Since most work was piece rated, the pressure to produce more forced children to work for longer hours. This increased fatigue and other psychological problems. It ultimately reduced their working capacity in adult hood. The study also pointed out that television was the most popular household item which was a major source of entertainment. This was perhaps the only medium through which they related to the outside world.

Mishra and Pradhan (2003) conducted a study on 'Child Labour in Transport Sector' in the Ganjam district of Orissa. The study found that due to lack of adequate income of parents, they had to come forward in search of employment and joined in this hazardous sector. These children had no bargaining power, they worked as per the desire of the owner with 'no work no pay' condition. The working hours of these children were not fixed, they resumed their work early in the morning and got relieve till the work is finished which could be midnight. These children were not given any other benefits except the salary. Even when, these children were seriously injured, the owner never took care of them. The study found that economic backwardness was one of the main reasons that forced the parents to send their children to work.

Sekar (2004) had conducted a study titled on 'Child Labour in Urban Informal Sector: A Study of Rag Pickers' in Noida'. The study reiterated the fact that the perpetuation of child labour was inextricably linked to the slow pace of poverty reduction. Intersection of poverty with other forms of disadvantages such as caste and gender complicated its effects on the incidence of child labour.The findings were based on the data elicited from 836 households constituting 4315 members. Children below 14 years in the sample population comprised of 2345 with 1393 males and 952 females and of these 925 children in the age group of 5-14 years were working as rag pickers in various sectors of Noida.The study revealed that 97% of the households with rag picking children were migrants. Almost all the households migrated after 1980s when the city was being constructed. Poverty and unemployment was reported as the most common reason for migration. The study revealed that the living conditions of the rag pickers were extremely poor which hardly had any basic amenities. The study also revealed that a majority of the households were residing in their own houses. These houses were made by using cheap building material and were having only the temporary ceilings which were highly vulnerable to vagaries of weather.

Ghosh (2004) had conducted a study on migration, labour process and employment of brick kiln workers in Noida. The study revealed that most of the workers were migrants from Uttar Pradesh, West Bengal, Chhattisgarh and Rajasthan. The study reported that child labourers were working 11-15 hours per day. These children were contributing 10-20% of their family income. The study also reported that some of the children entered the work force between 5-8 years.

Mishra and Mishra (2004) had conducted a study entitled 'Tiny Hands in Unorganized Sector' in Delhi. The study reported that a majority of children started working at a very young age because of several factors like broken families, alcoholic parents, aversion towards education, a desire to supplement family income and other problems. These children were engaged in various occupations viz, rag picking, dhaba/ road side café workers, domestic help, shoe shine boys, hawkers, cycle/scooter mechanics. Their area of operation was not confined rather spread through out Delhi. Most of the work done by them was monotonous, repetitive and dull in nature. Their wages depended entirely on the work they did. The child was paid much less that what an adult earned for the same work. These children were deprived of health security benefits, and were exposed to extreme weather conditions, traffic hazards, and police beating besides becoming victims of unhealthy habits like smoking, drinking and chewing gutka etc. These children had very little contact with their parents and even those who stayed with their parents had no time to care for them.

The study also revealed that a majority of the children were school drop outs. The study reported that these children had aversion towards education because there was no one to guide them.

The Impulse Net Work (2004) had conducted a study on child labour in Shillong. This study was conducted to understand the psycho-social environment, nature, extent and magnitude of the problem; health and support systems for child labour; and their expectations from the Government and other agencies. A sample of 501 boys, belonging to school going age was taken up for the study. Data was collected through interviews. It was found that these children worked mostly in commercial areas like Bara Bazaar and Police Bazaar, and a majority of them were 11-14 years. Both parents and children were ignorant about the value of education or about the ill effects of child labour. These children were engaged in different types of work, like rag picking, cleaning automobiles, selling betel nuts, shoe polishing, tea boy, domestic help, coolie work, etc. These children worked 8-12 hours a day and on an average earned Rs. 10-50 per day. Most of these children had attended school at one time or the other and a majority of them wanted to go back to school if given an opportunity. Children gave up their studies due to family problems in order to provide financial support to their families. The study also reported that some of the children also did not have interest in studies. Most of the children were found to be weak and undernourished. They were found to be suffering from health problems like cough, tuberculosis, skin disease, anemia, symptoms of deficiencies, physical growth retardation, etc. They lived in unhygienic conditions and slept only 5 hours a day. These children played with friends during leisure, watched movies, and some of the children (20%) took part in gambling. The study reported that a majority of these children ate food from wayside shops or hotels. The study also reported that 6% children were arrested once or twice or more and had a harsh experience with the police. The study also revealed that most of the parents and children were unaware of the existing laws relating to child labour.

Tiwari (2005) in his study "Child Labour in Footwear Industry: Possible Occupational Health Hazards" reported that children between 10 and 15 years old were mainly employed in assembling shoes. Children worked on soling (fixing upper portions of shoes to leather or rubber soles) with glue. The children working in the footwear industry were exposed to physical hazards like poor illumination, noise and poor ventilation, and chemicals like leather dust, benzene that was used as a solvent in glues and p-tert butyl phenols, which was used in neoprene adhesives. Thus, most children suffer from respiratory problems, lung diseases and skin infections through constant exposure to glue and fumes. They were also exposed to risk of nasal cancer, neurotoxicity and adverse physical factors.

Hussain and Sarwar (2005) conducted a study on child labour in Kashmir. The study reported that poverty, population explosion, illiteracy, unemployment, under employment and poor governance were the major causes for child labour. This study reported that most of these children were forced into child labour with a meagre wage of 10-20 rupees and they had to do this because there were no other earning members in their families. They do these activities to take care of siblings and to fulfil the addiction needs of their parents. The study also emphasized for the implementation of policies relating to child labour, introduction of poverty alleviation programmes and joint effort of government and other institutions would be helpful in eliminating child labour.

Singh (2006) had conducted a study on the 'problems of child labour and their working conditions in Agra City'. The study found that majority of child labourers engaged in dhaba and tea stalls, auto workshops; weather and furniture industry had attained ten years of age. Most of the child labourers had come from large families. The study reported that, in most of the cases wages were paid in cash directly to the child labourers and in some cases middle men receive payment. In most of the cases, monthly wages were paid to the children, however daily and weekly payment system was also prevalent in auto workshops and furniture industry. Besides wages, they also got festival gifts. These children did not get statutory benefits like provident fund, pension, bonus etc. The study found that majority of the children worked under miserable conditions amidst lots of smoke, dust and odour.

Shandilya, Kumar and Kumar (2006) conducted a study on 184 child labourers engaged in hotel, restaurants, tea stalls, and dhabas of the Patna town. Their study reported that almost all their sample respondents were male because they had the freedom to enter into this occupation. Almost three out of four children (78.1%) could not even read or write and these children reported that financial constraint of the family prevented them from attending school. Thirty two per cent of the children reported that they disliked studies and hence they did not go to any school. The other reasons given by the children for not studying were the fear of punishment given by class teachers, ill treatment by classmates, failure in studies and frequent shifts in the place of stay. The study also reported that various factors like low education level of the parents, big family size, low income of the parents were the major reasons which played an important role in determining child labour. The study also found that these children worked for more than 13 hours a day with a meagre average wage of Rs. 309/- per month. These children were not provided medical facilities in case of their illness. Most of their employers were indifferent to them or they were provided nominal help. These children had experienced multiple health problems, like fever, headache, cold/cough and even open wounds either on their hands or legs. They were not allowed any rest during the whole course of their work in a day and week. Almost all the children (90.2%) stated that there was no specific period/ day given to them for leave. These children were not receiving adequate quantity of food required for their age and labour. These children also did not enjoy sound sleep, as almost two out of three children were sleeping at the wok place only, that is, in the hotel where they were sleeping in a group along with others.

The study of Sakamoto (2006) on "Parental Attitudes toward Children and Child Labour: Evidence from Rural India," empirically investigated the determinants of child labour in rural India using household survey data. The study reported that parent's attitude was the crucial determinant of child labour. The study used probit model, controlling for individual, household, and community characteristics, and found that children were more likely to work if their parents showed less concern for them. The study also showed that children were more likely to work if their father had greater bargaining power in the household than their mother.

Moreover, the study also indicated that the incidence of child labour was positively associated with household poverty. The study suggested that in order to reduce or eliminate child labour, the government should implement policies to address the various factors causing child labor, such as parents' lack of concern for their children, imbalances in the power structure within households, and household poverty.

Mustafa and Sharma (2008) in their study, 'Child Labour in India-A Bitter Truth' highlighted the working conditions of child labourers in Delhi working in six vocations-tea stalls/dhabas, automobile workshops, domestic child workers and other three of self employed in occupations as shoe shining, rag picking, evening newspaper hawkers. The study reported that, poverty, low educational and occupational status of the parents, inadequacy of legislative system and its enforcements were the important reasons for the persistence of child labour. The study also reported that employers preferred to employ children over adults for their greater benefits and the parents felt that job disciplines the child and protects him against vagrancy and delinquency. Apart from suffering health hazards, the children suffered from the incidence of malnutrition and undernourishment. They were also easy victim to anti social activities, like black marketing, smuggling, theft, drugs de-addiction etc.The study reported that most of the child worked upto 12 hours in a day for a meager wage of Rs. 150 to Rs. 200 per month and about 1/3rd of the children did not receive their earnings themselves, rather the money was sent to their parents or guardians. Despite their hard labour for prolonged hours and minimal wages, these children were not provided with even the basic amenities. These children who got food from their employers were given the left overs of the previous day and were hardly provided with fruits, salads or sweets. The study also reported that some of the children were not treated properly by their employers and/or co-workers. They were neglected, abused and punished over trivial mistakes. More than one third of the children were staying in hutments and a substantial proportion being houseless, were forced to spend the nights either in the night shelters or on the foot paths and did not have private drinking water and sanitation facilities. More than half of the children (56.7%) did not get time to play due to excessive hours of work, fatigue and responsibility towards household chores.

Bhat and Rather (2009) conducted a study on 'Child Labour in the Handicrafts Home Industry in Kashmir: A Sociological Study'. It revealed that the problem of child labour in Kashmiri society had wider ramifications and the situation reflected an extremely cruel social situation which engulfed socially, economically and educationally backward communities. The problem of child labour as existing in Kashmiri society had given rise to multidimensional problems having adverse implications on one's physical, social, emotional, moral and educational development. It was not only social apathy towards child labour but the government in this regard had also shown lack of interest; thereby the problem had become more complex and dangerous. Moreover, the problem of social control, crime and social conflict emanated from the situation without proper care and response, on the part of government and the society at large. The research findings revealed that the problem of child labour was rooted deeply in Kashmiri society, tremendous growth in population accompanied by poverty, illiteracy and ignorance, lack of quality education were the major causes responsible for child labour. It adversely affected one's personality in terms of its physical, social, emotional, moral and educational development. The study showed that no one was showing concern towards the problem of child labour. Their insecure childhood made them more vulnerable to exploitation. They children suffered at the hands of their employers. They worked in very dirty environments. Though there were various laws to abolish child labour but they always remained confined to papers as reflected by the action of the government. The study also indicated that the total abolition of child labour was neither possible nor desirable so long as there was wide spread poverty, illiteracy and ignorance and unemployment.

Mohapatra and Dash conducted a study in 2011 titled "Child Labour- A Product of Socio-Economic Problem for India, Findings and Preventives- A Case of Bhubabaneswar'. The study reported that many appalling realities like poverty, illiteracy, unemployment, low wages, ignorance, social prejudices, regressive traditions, poor standard of living, backwardness, superstition, low status of women were responsible for the terrible practice of child labour. In many cases, child labour was mainly necessitated by economic compulsions of the parents. The main reason which gave rise to child labour was widespread unemployment and underemployment among the adult poor strata of the population, inter alia, due to sharp growth of population. Large families with low income and often lack of educational facilities, illiteracy and ignorance of parents about the importance of education as well as about the impact of labour on the health of their children were some of the reasons which breed child labour.

Lalsuresh (2011) had conducted a study on rag pickers in the Warangal city of Andhra Pradesh. This paper focussed on the health aspects, spending and earning pattern of child rag pickers in Warangal city of Andhra Pradesh, India. The finding showed that majority of rag pickers were suffering from ill health and were having bad habits such as tobacco-chewing and consumption of alcohol. Nearly all the rag pickers were earnings below Rs. 1200 per month and their entire major spending was on unproductive items. Illiteracy, poverty, indebtedness of their family was the main causes for the poor children opting for rag picking activity.

Dhar and Joshi (2008) conducted a study on "Child Labour in the Restaurants and Eateries: A Case Study of Pune City." The different aspects of the working conditions that were outlined in this study clearly indicated that the worst forms of child labour prevailed in Pune. Child labourers were exploited by the restaurant and eatery owners, dictated their payments and working conditions. Children below the age of eighteen years were involved in different work activities related to the eatery sector. They were not only given false promises by the employers, but were also deprived of their basic rights. The study also reported that children worked for long hours with little time to rest or play, that caused great amount of strain. They worked in hazardous conditions predisposing them to a number of health problems including exposure to various chemicals which was used for washing plates and sweeping floors. The study reported that the most prominent reasons for child labour were the poor economic status of the family and the inability of parents to provide basic needs for their children. Children had to mostly drop out of school due to lack of funds to support their education and had to work in this industry. It was noted that children who either dropped out of school or had completed their primary education were now mostly engaged in this industry. It was further noted that children received payments, mostly in cash, mostly at the whims of the owners. They were forced to use their incomes to either support their families or to support themselves for their survival.

The review of the above studies revealed that, most of the studies conducted during this period emphasized on traditional occupations viz. carpet industry, gem polishing, diamond industry, match industry, bangle units, transport sectors, brick kiln work, foot wear industry and rag picking. Only a few studies were conducted on hotel/restaurants/tea stalls/dhabas, garage during this period. These studies had also focussed on working conditions of child labourers, the terms of employment and had also identified the factors leading to child labour.

OVERVIEW OF THE REVIEW

The literature review undertaken by the researcher revealed the following insights:

- The review of literature revealed that most of the studies conducted during the designated chronological period revealed that a majority of studies focused on single and traditional occupations and were conducted in the context of the carpet industry, beedi industry, glass making, lock industry, gem polishing, knit wear industry, match industry and foot wear industry. These empirical studies mainly covered the following aspects: the background characteristics of child labourers; their working conditions with an emphasis on problems arising out of their occupations; the determinants of child labour; educational status; recreational activities; and the adverse consequences of child labour.

- It also revealed that only four studies were conducted on hotels/restaurants/dhabas/tea stalls and garages during the period 2000 and beyond. So, it can be said that service sector informal occupations like tea stalls/ dhabas, shops, garages and vegetable markets (subzi mandis) have been given less importance. Few studies focusing on children working in subzi mandis, shops, dhabas & restaurants and garages have not focused on the changing patterns of jobs assumed by the children and the reasons thereof; the nature of their aspirations; their health seeking behavior, their consumption patterns and several other significant aspects pertaining to their life. These studies also did not highlight the coping mechanisms adopted by children as well as their families to cope with the rigours of the hard lives they face.
- Most of the studies focused on a quantitative analysis. There were only few studies that assumed a qualitative stance in data collection and analysis. Narrative analysis of children engaged in work was not undertaken in any study.
- Most of the studies were based on the views of a single stakeholder i.e. child labour. Few studies have incorporated the view points of parents. There were few studies which incorporated employers also as respondents in the study.
- The review of literature also revealed that there were many studies on child labour in general, but specific studies pertaining to child labour in vegetable markets, dhabas, shops and garages were limited. Moreover, no such studies have been conducted after the employment of children was banned in dhabas (road side eateries), restaurants, hotels, motels, tea shops, resorts, spas or other recreational centers in the year 2006.

3

Research Methodology

INTRODUCTION

Research aims at describing, explaining, and understanding of various phenomena, which involves systematic and critical investigation. Therefore, every research activity needs a particular type of methodology. According to Berger et al (1989), Research methodology offers a guidance that directs the research action, which reduces time and cost. It also offers a systematic approach to the research operation, so that all steps are executed in the right sequence.

The present chapter incorporates the research methodology pursued by the researcher and thereby focuses on providing the statement of the problem, rationale for the study, operational definitions, research design, research objectives and associated research questions, sampling procedure, sources, methods and tools of data collection, difficulties encountered during field work/data collection, and the chapterisation plan.

STATEMENT OF THE PROBLEM

Over the years, several legislations have been passed for the elimination of child labour, but still child labour is on an increase as per the statistics given by census data. As far as all the metropolitan cities of India are concerned, the emergence of the urban informal sector as a major source of employment and income is primarily a manifestation of increasing population pressure combined with inadequate growth of employment in rural areas and in the formal and government sectors of the economy on the other (Shukla &Shukla,1993). Due to rapid industrialization and urbanization there is an unprecedented flow of the poor from villages to cities, mostly in search of gainful vocations. Such migrant families often concentrate in urban slums and squatter dwellings and have to struggle for their existence. People who migrate to these areas find it difficult to make their both ends meet. The cost of living in metropolitan cities is very high. Many of them are compelled to work in various unorganized sectors and are made to earn for themselves a livelihood and sometimes, even to support their families, through hard, strenuous and hazardous jobs. So in order to meet the survival needs, children are put to work. The nature of child labour in urban areas is very complex, particularly in India, because most of the child labourers in urban areas are found in unorganized manufacturing and service sectors. In urban India, there are "maids-of-all-work' whom professor Boudhiba described as "Virtual Slaves" (Boudhiba, 1982 cited in Shandilya et.al, 2006). Most of the children fall prey to evil habits due to bad company and environment. Their number is swelling unabatedly and the problem has acquired dangerous dimensions. But unfortunately the child labourers are suffering a lot, subjected to toil some work without having opportunities to grow. They are living miserable, cheerless lives, toiling endlessly to ward off starvation totally deprived of all comforts and opportunities.

RATIONALE

An overview of review of literature undertaken in the earlier section shows that there are large number of studies conducted in the fields of traditional occupations like carpet industry, gem polishing, diamond industry, match industry, bangle units, transport sectors, brick kiln work, foot wear industry and rag picking. However, there is little empirical research on the child labour in specific settings like automobile garages, dhabas, and subzi mandi (vegetable markets) and shops particularly in the metropolitan cities. Moreover, no such studies have been conducted after the employment of children were banned in 2006 in dhabas (road side eateries), restaurants, hotels, motels, tea shops, resorts, spas or other recreational centers. So, the present study is basically an attempt to fill this gap. Therefore, the researcher decided to undertake a comprehensive study on the various dimensions and determinants of the child labour in a metropolitan city like Delhi. It is also equally important to analyze the frequency of change and changing patterns of jobs taken by child labour, their desire for education, their aspirations, as also their present conditions including health conditions, employment conditions, adopted by children as well as their parents for fulfillment of basic needs. The present study focused on living and working conditions of children, coping mechanisms adopted by children, as well as critically examined the various provisions of all legislations prohibiting child labour. It will enable the planners, policy makers, academicians, researchers, non governmental organizations to have a right perspective of the problems of child labourers engaged in small scale commercial establishments.

OPERATIONAL DEFINITIONS

Child labour: Those children below 14 years of age who are engaged in occupational pursuit with wages in Delhi.

Determinants: Determinants refer to factors contributing to taking up a job.

Dimensions: Dimensions for the purpose of the study refer to the various aspects of the living and working conditions, educational interests, and aspirations, frequency of changing jobs, attitudes of parents, guardians and employers for working children.

Small Scale Commercial Establishment: The establish-ments which employ less than 10 people, and characterized by low labour productivity and include particularly the four categories of establishments i.e. shops, tea stalls/dhabas, subzi mandi (vegetable markets) and motor garages.

Employer: An employer is a person who operates enterprises or engages independently in a profession of a trade and pays some other persons to help him.

Nature of Employment

Regular: This refers to stable or permanent employment or employment for an indefinite period.

Temporary: This refers to employment for a fixed period or of less than one year's duration.

Causal: This refers to intermittent employment on daily or weekly basis.

Full time worker: A full time worker is one who works for full day work constituting of 8 hours or more.

Part time worker: A part time worker is one who works only for a part of the day.

OBJECTIVES

- To prepare a demographic profile of children employed in small scale commercial establishments as well as their parents and employers.
- To study the factors contributing to the incidence of child labour.
- To critically examine the various provisions of all legislations prohibiting child labour.
- To examine the living conditions of children working in small scale commercial establishments.
- To examine the working conditions of children in small scale commercial establishments.
- To extend suggestions for social work intervention for mitigating the problems faced by child labour.

On the basis of these objectives, the present research has answered the following research questions.

- What is the socio-economic background of the children who are involved in various occupations?
- What are the major causes for the incidence child labour?
- Which are the places from which the child/family migrated to NCT of Delhi?
- What is the role of family in making the child undertake occupational pursuits with wages?
- What is the educational level of the children and their parents?
- What are the aspirations and future plans of child labourers?

- What is the frequency of change and changing patterns of jobs by child labourers in a year?
- What are the trends in the incidence, participation in economic activities, and nature of occupational pursuits followed by child labourers (past and Contemporary)?
- What is the duration of work undertaken by children?
- What are the employment conditions under which children are put to work?
- What kinds of health and safety measures are provided to children by their employers?
- What kind of attitudes parents/employers have towards child labourers?
- What is the consumption pattern of child labourers?
- What is the nature of illness/diseases faced by child labourers due to their employment?
- Where do the child labourers procure the requisite treatment/ required medicines for their treatment?
- What is the nature of living conditions which prevail for the child labourers.

RESEARCH DESIGN

The study is descriptive in nature in that it seeks to describe the working and living conditions of child labour, factors contributing to child labour, and coping mechanisms adopted by the children and their families for the fulfillment of their basic needs. It also seeks to study the reasons of migration, recreational pattern, a future hopes and aspirations.

SAMPLE

According to Manheim (1977), "a sample is a part of the population which is studied in order to make inferences about the whole population". In order to get comprehensive idea of the problems, the responses of various stakeholders viz. children, parents and employers were studied. The sample comprised of:

1. Child labourers
2. Employers
3. Parents/Guardians

1. *Child Labourers:* For the selection of respondents, the Quota Sampling method of the Non- probability type was adopted. The sampling was done in two stages.

   In the first stage, the population was divided into four strata: Children working in shops, subzi mandis, motor garages and dhabas/tea stalls in Delhi.

   In the second stage, equal numbers of children i.e. 30 were selected from each stratum. The total samples of working children derived were 120. Besides these respondents, the qualitative data was collected using narrative analysis as a method of data collection. Ten cases were identified from all the four strata.

2. *Employers:* Forty employers constituted the sample size selecting 10 from each stratum. This was done to study their views/perspectives on the reasons for employing child labourers, their working conditions and other components associated with work performed by these children.

3. *Parents:* Forty parents of child labourers constituted the sample size. The parents of those children who were working in Delhi and become the sample of the study.

Thus, the sample size included:

Total number of child labourers	120
Total number of employers	40
Total number of parents/guardians	40
Lawyers/Social Workers/Social Activists	15
Total size of sample	215

The researcher ensured that the respondents were selected from the different parts of Delhi. He tried to cover as many areas as possible to make samples more representative.

The zone wise distribution of the respondents is listed in the following table.

Table 3.1: Zone wise Distribution of the Respondents (Child Labourers)

Sl. No.	Place of Stay	Frequency	Percentage
1.	East Delhi	48	48
2.	West Delhi	19	15.83
3.	North Delhi	21	17.5
4.	South Delhi	32	26.66
Total		**120**	**100**

The areas included were Seelampur, Zama maszid, Tis Hazari, Indira market, R.K. Puram, Kashmiri Gate, Govindpuri, Wazirpur, Palam, Dakshinpuri, Azadpur, Ashok Vihar, Ambedkar Nagar, Giri Nagar, Sarai, Loni, Sanjay Gandhi Transport Nagar, Anand Vihar, Nand Nagari, Sunder Nagari, Shahdara, Loni border, Jhilmil, Harsh Vihar, Mansarover Park, Meet Nagar, Adarsh Nagar, Ashok Nagar, and Welcome.

4. The researcher has also interviewed a select group of lawyers, social workers, social activists working in the field of child labour, selecting 5 respondents from each category to collect their views on the abolition in the incidences of child labour with the help of a small guideline. The purpose of interviewing them was to suggest recommendations for mitigating the problems faced by child labourers.

INCLUSION CRITERIA

The study was limited to children between the ages of 7 and 14 years. The lower age limit of 7 years was set based on the assumption that younger children would not be able to provide requisite information to the researcher. All children between the age of 7-14 years employed in either of the specified occupations with wages, and working more than four and half hours in a day for a minimum period of 6 months in Delhi were included in the sample.

SOURCES OF DATA COLLECTION

The data were collected both from Primary and Secondary sources (documentary sources). The primary sources of data comprised the child labourers, parents, employers and other significant persons (lawyers, social workers and social activists) for gaining first hand information from the respondents. The secondary sources were tapped and informations procured from them was analysed. This primarily pertained to the constitutional provisions, various legislations, Census data, NSSO reports, ILO reports, relevant reports of Ministry of Labour, Government of India, Reports of Government of Delhi, Books, Journals, Periodicals and Reports of Voluntary Organizations.

METHODS AND TOOLS OF DATA COLLECTION

The effective use of different methods to elicit information generally rests upon the problem, its dimensions and areas under the study. In the present study, the data was collected by using both qualitative and quantitative methods of data collection. The methods of data collection included interviews, observation, and using narrative analysis. The following tools were used for the three categories of respondents to be covered by the study.

1. *Interview schedule for child labourers:* An interview schedule was used to collect in-depth information from child labourers which covered I) demographic profile of child labourers such as age, education, caste, nature of family and native place II) Working conditions and terms of employment such as place of work, hours of work, payment of wages, over time, etc. III) Present living conditions like housing, basic facilities available at home like bath room, toilet facilities etc. Besides that, the schedule also contained questions regarding the factors contributing child labour, their educational level, awareness about child labour legislations, their future aspirations etc.
2. *Interview guide for parents of child labourers:* The schedule for parents was prepared with a view to gather some information which was considered to be difficult to be gathered from the child labourers because of their relatively limited understanding and knowledge, and

also to verify the information given by the child labourers. It was used to understand the socio-economic condition of the household, purpose of migration, reasons for allowing children to work, their living conditions and other relevant aspects,

3. *Interview guide for employers of child labourers:* The schedule for employers was also prepared with a view to understanding their motives and feelings in employing children and also to know their awareness about the labour laws and perceptions about child labour. It was used to understand the working conditions of child labourers, leisure period provided, hazards associated with the performance of the job, recruitment policy for appointing child labour, payment to the child labour, attitude towards employment of child labour etc.
4. *Narrative guide:* Ten cases using narratives were undertaken to generate qualitative information for an in-depth knowledge of the research questions and to support quantitative data. Narrative inquiry is concerned with the production, interpretation and representation of storied accounts of the lived experience (Shacklock and Thorp, 2005). Ten cases for narrative analysis were selected by purposive sampling of non probability type. These narratives have basically highlighted their demographic profile, reasons for migration, their life as a child labour, life at home and working place, educational and health status, work responsibility and leisure time, future hopes and aspirations and other relevant aspects.
5. *Observation guide:* An observation guide was developed to study the living and working conditions of child labourers.
6. *Interview guide:* A small interview guide for the lawyers/ social workers/social activists was developed to elicit their views/suggestions regarding mitigating their problems and reducing their problems. Diagrammatically, the methods employed in collecting data are given in the following figure.

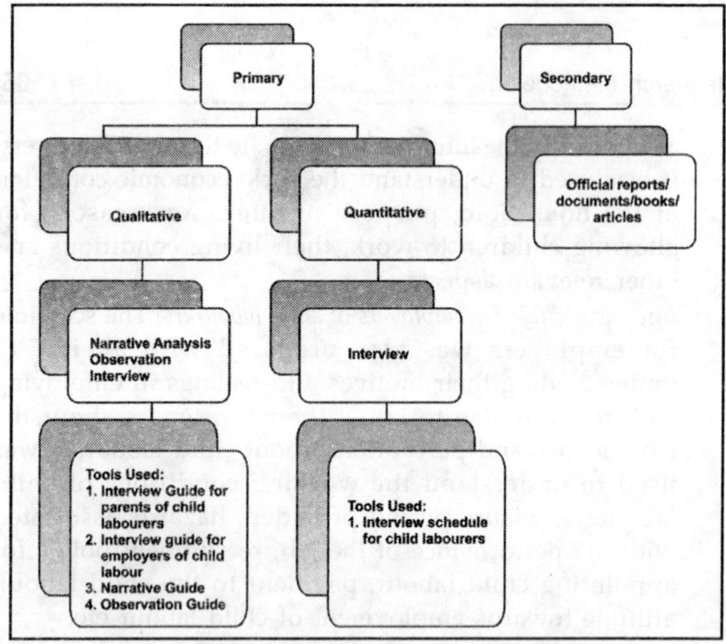

Fig. 3.1: Methods and Tools of Data Collection

DATA ANALYSIS AND INTERPRETATION

Data was processed both manually and through the use of computer programmes. Quantitative information has been used substantially in the analysis to interpret the findings. The process of analysis involved categorizing the qualitative raw data (obtained through administering interview schedule) under some common headings and then coding the same. The quantitative data was pre-coded. The codes were then transferred to the master charts and then to the SPSS spread sheet. This whole procedure was very tedious and time consuming. But once this was accomplished, the data was analyzed descriptively. Through SPSS, univariate tables were made. Tables were used to add to the descriptive data and for easy understanding and viewing. Diagrammatic representation of data was also attempted to provide clarity and easy comprehension. Data analysis was done as per the objectives of the study. The chapterisation plan which was followed for report writing was in accordance with the objectives of the study.

ETHICAL CONSIDERATIONS

The researcher has obtained verbal consent as part of ethical considerations for conducting research. The consent of child labourers, parents and employers were obtained for the purpose of data collection .The researcher has taken very special care before asking any questions which could hurt their sentiments. The permission was asked for from each respondent before interviewing him and a commitment was made to keep their names and responses confidential.

DIFFICULTIES ENCOUNTERED DURING FIELD WORK/DATA COLLECTION

Fieldwork is a personal experience for it involves close interaction with the subject of one's research. Every field worker has therefore to arrive of his own equation with his informants. There can be no clear cut prescribed formula for handling any given field situations, for each situation is in some way unique. While there are certain standardized research techniques, the manner in which they are used and the results that they yield depend on the rapport which the observer is able to establish with his informants. In the ultimate analysis each field worker must face his own challenges and experience his own triumphs and tribulation (Srinivas, 1979). During the present study, too, some problems were faced for data collection.

- As the respondents are children, aged below the age of 14, it created typical problems to establish rapport with them.
- Besides, children working in industries/informal sector have hardly any free time. Therefore, interviews with them under such circumstances were cumbersome.
- The child respondents demonstrated initial hesitation, reluctance and mid way refusal to answer.

In this connection, it appears pertinent to refer to the observation made by Elizabeth, 1972 "The obstacles to scientific study are ubiquitous and sometimes almost insurmountable, of the many obstacles the most common and the most difficult to cope with are: securing children for scientific research finding suitable and scientifically accurate methods for studying children, controlling the accuracy of the material obtained and establishing rapport with children. The children also usually took more time to understand the questions and whenever certain questions related to recreation and income were put, many tried to evade. Another difficulty was the way in which a number of other children surround the child respondents and prompt them, and make them answer the way they wanted. Though the schedule and interview guides were prepared in English, the questions were put to respondents in Hindi. Care was taken to put the questions in a descriptive manner which would make the child respondents understand properly and furnish the needed answers. Before conducting the process of data collection, the researcher had moved to various parts of Delhi and tried to locate the children engaged in various informal sector settings. The researcher had sincerely tried to make the sample, a representative sample and present a realistic picture. Though the researcher had to cross many a hurdles during field work, particularly obstruction by the employers of the children but he was able to succeed in his mission. Some times it so happened that the person who had engaged the child did not allow the researcher to talk to the child. The researcher also faced difficulty in getting information from the employers. They did not provide the complete information as desired by the researcher. However, the parents showed some interest in providing information and insisted to the researcher to keep the information secret and confidential. On the whole, the child respondents and their parents/ guardians were cooperative and willingly agreed to respond in course of time.

CHAPTERISATION OF THE STUDY

The present research has been organized in nine chapters. As usual, the *first chapter* 'Introduction' provides a conceptual understanding of the concept of 'child', 'child labour', global and national magnitude of child labour as well as the magnitude of child labour prevalent in Delhi. It has also highlighted the important factors contributing to the persistent presence of child labour in the present context.

The *second chapter* 'Review of Literature' presents a comprehensive review of the empirical studies on child labour conducted in India after 1986, arranged in a chronological manner. It also discusses the findings of the review process.

The *third chapter* 'Research Methodology' highlights with the methodology adopted in the study. It has included the statement of the problem, rationale of the study, the objectives of the study, research questions, operational definitions, sampling details, methods and tools of data collection and data analysis, as well as field work experiences of the researcher.

The *fourth chapter* 'Child Labour Legislations in India: A Critical Analysis' provides a detailed depiction and critical analysis of child labour legislations in India. It has highlighted the various conventions relating to child labour, the constitutional provisions and the legal protection of children at work and its limitations.

The *fifth chapter* 'Demographic Profile of the Respondents' presents the demographic profile of the respondents viz. the child labourers, parents and employers.

The *sixth chapter* 'Determinants of Child Labour' has outlined the important factors contributing to the prevalence of child labour in the study context.

The *seventh chapter* 'Dimensions of Child Labour' has explicated the working conditions, terms of employment and the living conditions of the child labourers.

The *eighth chapter titled* 'Narratives- A Qualitative Analysis' presents a narrative analysis of the child labourers.

The *ninth chapter* 'Conclusions, Recommendations and Implications for Social Work Intervention" is devoted to the summary of the research work and has provided various recommendations for social work intervention regarding policy framework and action plans for the prevention/ mitigation of child labour.

Besides the *nine chapters,* the thesis also includes the list of detailed bibliographic references. The formats of interview schedule of child labourers, Interview Guide for parents, and Interview Guide for Employers, observation guide.

4

Child Labour Legislations in India
A Critical Analysis

CHILD LABOUR – HISTORICAL PERSPECTIVES

The study of child labour in historical perspective discloses to us that the child labour was prevalent even in ancient period even before 321 B.C. (Tripathy, 1985). Mostly, children were engaged in different occupations by the rich landlords to carry out activities directly or indirectly related to agriculture and domestic services. In fact, in many instances, it was commonly believed that children of slaves were born as a slaves, lived as slaves and died also as slaves unless the master was pleased to manumit them. According to Kautilya, a slave's child could be purchased and sold like a commodity and parents could sell the services of their children to earn their livelihood. Kautilya, during the regime of the Mauryas (321 BC-185 BC) codified some rules in a sprit of abolition of child slavery. Four important codes were as follows:

- Children under eight year's of age were banned from carrying out low and ignoble works.
- Purchase and sale of children below eight years of age was prohibited.
- Provisions were made to relieve oneself from slavery either by paying the dues or other wise.
- Wages were to be paid according to time, work and/or according to the contacts made. Wage of labourers

including the child labourers were to be settled upon the work was actually done (Kautilya cited in Hazarika, 2004).

India, through its medieval period (during the regime of Mughal Kings, 1200-1700 AD) was no exception to this social evil and it remained in existence in large scale. Although, due to sweeping socio-cultural and political changes the practice of child labour and child slavery had a declining trend during the post Maurya era. The continuing, increasing pressure on land compelled the poor parents to use their children to contribute to the household's earning.

The practice of employing children for work was prevalent during medieval period mainly due to: (i) increasing human population pressure; (ii) recurrence of famines; (iii) the fact that the rulers did nothing for the improvement of the condition of common people and those of child labourers, in particular. Child labour was found in the form of child slavery and the rulers did not endeavour to weed out this practice and hence the result was that the child continued to be exploited during this period.

During the British Period (1757-1947 A.D.), under the patronage of the East India Company, certain specific industrial organizations grew in the 18th and 19th centuries and they involved the employment of large number of artisans especially in weaving, carpentry, silk and other sectors. The new sets of industrial organizations replaced the earlier family based farm economy and opened up opportunity for wage paid employment, formation of labour unions, labour markets and a new socio-economic order. But prolonged scarcity of food and extreme poverty caused by famines, lack of education and absence of compulsion for education of children as also, large scale unemployment of adult workers resulted in the introduction of children into the labour market. In the 19th century, employment of children in jute and cotton mills, mines, factories work grew without any consideration of age bar, working hours and gender. Due to lack of adequate regulations regarding wages, working hours and age limit, the child labourers suffered limitless abuse and exploitation by their employers.

During the British period, some changes occurred with regard to the phenomenon of child labour. The new economic forces unleashed by capitalism and the uneven development of industrialization brought a change in the socioeconomic order. This destroyed the family-based economy and a large number of labourers were displaced due to mechanization of agriculture. The farmers were alienated from their home based work place and they became wage earning labourers. Extreme poverty made possible a situation in which the child had to be introduced in the labour market. Under the new order of things, the work-place was separated from the family environment and work exposed the child to unhealthy environment. The hours of working started from morning to night but the earnings remained quite meagre. As a result, the child's ability to grow and develop into a mentally and physically sound adult was severely restricted. The employers' monopoly to bargain freely with the child labourers produced an environment of exploitation.

The phenomenon drew the attention of the public leaders, philosophers and the social activists who shared their views with the British government in India. The factory workers too, for the first time united together in 1875 for securing better working conditions in factories and consolidated a trade union movement opposing dangerous working condition in factories, specially for women workers and children. As a result of these developments, several laws were introduced by the British government in India regulating the employment of children (Hazaria, 2004). These took the shape of a few protective legislations for the child labour in India. The Indian Factories Act, 1881, Mines Act, 1901, Factories Act, 1911, Factories (Amendment) Act, 1922, Indian Factories Act, 1931, Children (Pledging of labour) Act, 1933, Indian Mines (Amendment) Act, 1935, and Employment of Children Act, 1938 were enacted with a view to forbid the employment of children in factories carrying out hazardous work.

These legislations endeavoured to improve the working conditions of child labourers in the factories. However, it was seen that these legislations could not make any significant improvement in the working conditions of the child labourers.

The result of this was that the child labour continued to exist as a means of providing cheap labour. The Labour Investigating Committee, in its report in 1946 has pointed out that the main cause of this was the inadequacy of the inspecting staff to enforce the provisions of those welfare legislations.

LEGISLATIONS BEFORE INDEPENDENCE

The movement to prevent child labour started in India while it was still a part of the British Crown. The first legislation restricting child labour was the Indian Factories Act 1881. The Act prohibited the employment of children below the age of seven years and limited the working hours to nine hours a day. It also provided four holidays in a month and banned the employment of children in two separate factories on the same day.

The Factories Act (1881) had to be modified several times till 1948 on the basis of the recommendations made by the Factory Commission 1884, the Freer Smith Committee 1906, the Factory Labour Commission, 1907 and the Royal Commission on Labour (1929-1931).

The major amendments affecting child labour, which were incorporated in the Factories Act, 1881 till the year 1947 were as follows:

- By its amendments in 1922, the minimum age for employment of a child in factories was raised to 12 years in order to give effect to the ILO (1919) Convention.
- Under the modified Factories Act (1922), a child was defined as a person who has not completed 15 years of age.
- By its 1911 and 1922 amendments, an employer was required to submit age and fitness certificate of the child labourers employed in her/his factories.
- By the amendment in 1923, working of children at night was banned and employment of women below 18 years of age in certain processes was also prohibited.
- By its amendment in 1926 and 1931 certain penalties were imposed on parents and guardians for allowing their children to work in two separate factories on the same day.

- Under the amendment of the Factories Act, 1934, the maximum working hours for a child labour in the age group of 12-15 years were fixed at five hours in a day. The Act was further amended in 1935, 1936, 1940, 1941, 1944, 1945, 1946 and 1947. In the post independence period this Act was again amended in 1948.

After two decades, the Mines Act 1901 was passed, which prohibited the employment of children less than 12 years of age and employment dangerous to their health and safety. The subsequent amendments to the Mines Act (1901) brought about the following improvements:

- The Mines Act was first amended in 1923. Under this amendment the minimum age for employment of a child in a mine was raised from 12 to 14 years.
- The working hours were fixed at 60 and 54 hours a week for the over ground and the under-ground child labourers respectively.
- The working days were limited to six days a week.
- Another amendment to this Act was made in 1925 in order to improve the working conditions of the labourers and the safety in the mines. The other amendments of the Mines Act were made in 1928, 1929, 1935, 1936, and 1937 and after independence in 1952.
- Through its amendment in 1955, the age of child labourers in mines was further raised to 15 years. The concept of "Young Person" was introduced and such young persons were allowed to work who possessed the usual fitness certificate. (Vaid, 1970).

Reporting in 1929, the Royal Commission on Labour, under the chairmanship of John Henry Whitley, had a significant impact on the recognition and legislative treatment of the child labour. It reported widespread prevalence of child labour in a range of industries including carpet, bidi, textile, match, and plantations. A series of laws followed.

The Indian Ports Act of 1931 set twelve years as the minimum age for handling goods in ports. The Tea Districts Emigrant Labour Act of 1932 provided that no child below sixteen years be employed, or allowed to migrate, unless accompanied by parents or close relatives (Ramanathan, 2009).

The Children (Pledging of Labour) Act, passed in 1933, is the first acknowledgment of the problem of child bondage. In 1929, the Royal Commission on Labour in India was constituted as an attempt to survey and report the existing labour conditions in the country. One of the main concerns of the Royal Commission was that of the pledging of children to employers in return for small sums of money. Based on the recommendations of the report, the Children Pledging of Labour Act, 1933, which prohibited parents or guardians from the "pledging of children to employers in return for small sums of money," was passed. The other legal provision made on the basis of the report was the Employment of Children Act of 1938. This was also followed from the twenty-third session of the International Labour Conference, held in 1937, which adopted a special article exclusively on India, recommending that children below thirteen years be prohibited from work in certain categories of employment. The objective of this Act was to prevent the evils of child employment in workshops and factories not covered by the Factories Act. The Employment of Children Act (1938) was amended in 1939 and 1942. The 1938 act set the minimum age of employment in certain industries at fifteen and in the transport of goods on dock and wharves at fourteen.

In spite of various legislations, the child labour laws regulating and prohibiting the employment of children in various economic activities failed to achieve their cherished goals. According to the Labour Investigation Committee Report (1946) the main reasons of it, interalia, were the inadequate machineries, inspecting staff and their inefficiency to ensure the implementation of the provisions of the laws. (Saxena and Saxena, 1992).

The British introduced legislation restricting the employment of children in pre-independent India. The major thrust of these laws was on regulating the conditions and hours of work of children. Moreover, these laws were mainly confined to factories and mines. Also, there was no effective process of verification and strict enforcement rules. It is also important to note that no unified attempt was made by the

British to prohibit child labour as such. The large number of unregulated factories and the informal sector did not come under the purview of the Factories Act of the country and others (Hazaria, 2004).

LEGISLATIONS AFTER INDEPENDENCE

India gained independence in 1947 and the Indian Constitution came into existence on November 26, 1949. Provisions were made within the Constitution to protect children from exploitation and early employment. Various articles intended for the welfare of children, protecting their freedom and dignity against exploitation, were also included in the Constitution.

The prevalence and problems of child labour was made a focal point of government policy after independence. The Preamble of Constitution unequivocally stated that social, economic, and political justice, liberty of thought, expression, belief, faith and worship, equality of status and opportunities and fraternity, assuring the dignity of individual and unity and integrity of nation will be secured to all citizens. Further, it recognized the need for the granting special protection to children. It was intended by the founding fathers of the Constitution that children should have their distributive justice free India.

Child Labour Welfare under Fundamental Rights

Keeping in view the intentions of the founding fathers of the Indian Constitution, numerous provisions ensuring justice to children have been envisaged in Part-III and Part-IV of our Constitution.

Part III of the Constitution contains a long list of fundamental rights which are equally applicable to children also. The children enjoy all the fundamental rights which are granted to the citizens of India under Articles 14-18, 19, 21 and so on. Besides, there are also some fundamental rights exclusively provided for children. These are:

- Article 15(3) enables the state to make special provisions in its law to give favourable treatment to children. Preferential treatment is expected on the consideration of inherent weakness of children.

- The State shall provide free and compulsory education to all children of the age 6 to 14 years (Article 21 (A).
- Article 23 of the Constitution prohibits the traffic in human beings, beggar and other similar forms of forced labour and exploitation.
- Similarly, Article 24 prohibits the employment of children below the age of 14 years in factories, mines or hazardous employment.

Child Labour Welfare Philosophy under Directive Principles of State Policy

Part IV of the Indian Constitution provides certain principles for state policy. Though these directives are not enforceable by court, yet these have been declared fundamental in the governance of the country. It is the obligation of the state to apply these principles in making child welfare legislations.

Article 39(e) and (f) direct the state to evolve a policy eliminating the abuse of tender age and to free children from the circumstances forcing them to enter into avocations unsuited to their age of strength. The state has also been directed to create social and economic conditions and infrastructure for the healthy development of children and to provide facilities and climate for the exercise of freedom and maintenance of dignity. The state is further directed to protect the children against exploitation and moral and material abandonment.

Under Article 45, a duty is imposed upon the state to provide free and compulsory education within a period of ten years of the commencement of the Constitution for all the children until they complete the age of 14 years.

Article 46 provides that the state shall promote with special care, the educational and economic interests of the weaker section of the people, and in particular of the Schedule Castes and the Schedule tribes, and shall protect them from social injustice and all forms of exploitation. The implementation of this principle, while promoting the economic and educational interests of the weaker section of the people, particularly those of Schedule Castes and Schedule Tribes, will indirectly promote the welfare of the children of these sections of the society.

Keeping in view the constitutional philosophy pertaining to child labour, many legislations have been enacted by both the central and the state governments, laying special emphasis on the responsibility of nation for the physical, mental, moral and social development of children. Some of the enactments like The Factories Act, 1948, The Minimum Wage Act, 1948, The Merchant Shipping Act, 1958, The Motor Transport Workers Act, 1966, The Plantations Labour Act, 1951, Beedi and Cigar Workers (Condition of Employment) Act, 1966 and Child Labour (Prohibition and Regulation) Act, 1986 have been enacted in line with the progressive outlook of the state for improving the working conditions of the child labourers. The main objective behind these legislations is to eradicate the evil of child labour to the extent possible and to improve their working conditions so as to allow them to develop into meaningful citizens. The basic aim of all these enactments is also to prohibit the employment of children in certain employments and regulate the conduct of the employers of child labourers in such a way that they are not exploited.

To uphold the provisions made in the Constitution, several legislations were enacted in the years following independence. These have focused on regulating the various aspects of child labour. Several committees, sub-committees and commissions have also been appointed from time to time by the government to find out ways and means to prevent child labour. Similarly, more than twenty acts enacted in this regard have provisions for safeguarding the rights of child labourers.

Besides that, the government had also appointed a 'Task Force on Child Labour' which was set up on the recommendation of the Central Advisory Board on Child Labour. On the recommendations of this Task Force, the government formulated the National Policy on Child Labour in 1987. Also the Supreme Court passed orders on December 10 1996, banning the employment of children in hazardous occupations with action to be taken against those employing children. All these efforts were directed towards the well-being and proper development of children.

As mentioned earlier, the first step in restricting child labour in the post independent era was made in 1948 by the passing of the Factories Act. The Factories Act, 1948 prohibited the employment of children below the age of 14 years. An adolescent aged between 15 and 18 years can be employed in a factory only if he obtains a certificate of fitness from an authorized medical doctor. The Act also prescribes four and a half hours of work per day for children aged between 14 and 18 years and prohibits their working during night hours. Even with the latest amendment to the Factories Act in 1987, the Indian Factories Act, 1881 has not undergone any substantial changes in its character.

The Minimum Wages Act, passed in 1948, specified that the expression "adult", "adolescent" and "child" had meaning assigned to them. It defined "child" as a person who has not completed his 15th year. However, this definition did not have any particular significance since the Act did not contain any important regulatory or prohibitory provision applicable only to child labour, except that it provided the fixing or revising minimum rates of wages, for adults, adolescents, children and apprentices (Kulshreshtha, 1978,). This act of 1948 was a landmark in the domain of child labour legislation in the country for it recognized that wages can not be left to be determined entirely by the market forces. The wages of the children working in various sectors/activity came to be regulated by the Minimum Wages Act, 1948. The Act empowered the union and the state governments to fix minimum rate of wages payable to the employees, including the child labourers (Singh, 1998).

The Amendment to the Employment of Children Act (1938) was done in 1949 introducing a few new provisions in it. The amended provisions were:

- The minimum age for employment in workshops was raised from 12 to 15 years.

- The Act also prevented the employment of children below 15 years of age in hazardous and unhealthy occupations connected with transport of passengers and goods by railways and/or port authority.
- Children between 15-17 years of age had been permitted to work/ employed; if they were allowed 12 hours rest at night and in case of railways and ports, their authorities had to maintain a register showing their names, rest intervals and date of birth of the children employed.
- The labour inspector was empowered to refer the matter to the prescribed medical authority for verification of age incase of dispute arising between the employer and the labour inspector.
- The provision of the Act were extended to cover all the factories employing young persons but not covered by the factories act.

The Plantation Labour Act was enacted in 1951. The employment of children between the ages of 12 years was prohibited under the Act. However, the act permitted the employment of child between the ages 12 years and 18 only on a fitness certificate from the appointed surgeon. The Act also prohibited night work for children. After the repeal of the Tea Districts Immigration Act (1932) in 1970, the scope of the Plantation Labour Act was broadened by amending the Plantation Labour Act in 1981.

The Mines Amendment Act, 1952 states that no child shall be employed in any mines nor shall any child be allowed to be present in any part of mine, which is below ground, or in any open cast working in which any mining operations being carried on. The Act was also further amended in 1984.

The Merchant Shipping Act, 1958 prohibits employment of children below the age of 14 years in a ship except a training ship, home ship or a ship where other family members work. It also prohibits employment of young persons below the age of 18 as trimmers and stokers except under certain specific conditions.

The Shops and Establishment Act, 1954 defines a child as a person below 12 years (in some states the minimum age is

14 years) and prohibits their employment in shops, commercial establishments, restaurants, hotels etc. The hours of work are 7 per day in Andhra Pradesh, Bihar, Tamilnadu, Tripura, Pondicherry and West Bengal, 6 per day in Gujarat, Maharashtra, Jammu and Kashmir, Uttar Pradesh and Delhi, 5 hours per day in Himachal Pradesh, Madhya Pradesh, Karnataka, Orissa and Punjab, 3 hours per day in Rajasthan. Night work for children is also prohibited under the state laws relating to shops and commercial establishments. It varies from 6 a.m. to 7 a.m. in the morning up to 7 p.m. to 9 p.m. at night. The various State Governments have passed the Shops and Establishment Acts which are applicable within their states. The Act has often been amended to suit the given situation.

The Motor Transport Workers Act of 1961 prohibits employment of children below fifteen "in any capacity in any motor transport undertaking."

The Apprentices Act, 1961 come into existence after repealing the original act of 1850. The Act states that no person shall be qualified for being engaged as an apprentice to undergo apprenticeship training in any trade, commercial, industrial, private or government establishment unless he is 14 years of age and satisfied such standards of education and physical fitness as may be prescribed. The Act also provides severe penalties with imprisonment up to six months, or with fine up to Rs.500 or with both for violating the provision of the Act. But the Act has been found to be self defeating for it permits apprenticeship training under section-4, if guardians/ parents of the children enter into a contract for apprenticeship with the employer.

The tobacco industry, where child labour has been rampant and the handling and inhalation of tobacco have been recognized as hazardous, was drawn into the law in 1966, in the Beedi and Cigar Workers (Conditions of Employment) Act. The Act prohibits the employment of children under fourteen in any industrial premises, and "young persons" between fourteen and eighteen years were not to be engaged in work except between 6 A.M. and 7 P.M. A significant exception placed "self-employed persons in private dwelling houses" outside the purview of the Act. This provision expressly allowed the "assistance of the members of his family living with him in such dwelling house and dependent on him." This provision, along with the practice of subcontracting to "out-workers" who are paid piece rates for the finished product, has kept a space open for children to be engaged in bidi manufacture.

The Mines Act of 1952, the Merchant Shipping Act of 1958, the Motor Transport Workers Act of 1961, the Apprentices Act of 1961, and the Beedi & Cigar Workers Act of 1966 were concerning child labour in specific occupations. They were aimed at addressing the different sectors of the economy where child labour existed.

The Bonded Labour System (Abolition) Act of 1976 was a response to a customary system of usury under which a debtor or his descendants or dependents have to work for little or no wages in order to extinguish the debt. The 1976 Act abolished the bonded labour system and extinguished the liability to repay bonded debt. Identification, release, and rehabilitation of the bonded labourers' form the nucleus of the 1976 Act.

The Child Labour (Prohibition and Regulation) Act (CLPRA) of 1986 prohibits employment of children in a scheduled list of occupations and a scheduled list of processes. The Child Labour (Prohibition & Regulation) Act 1986 was the culmination of efforts and ideas that emerged from the deliberations and recommendations of various committees on child labour. Significant among them are the National Commission on Labour (1966-69), Gurupadaswamy Committee on Child Labour (1979), and the Sanat Mehta Committee (1984). A Child Labour Technical Advisory Committee has been tasked with advising the central government on additions to the list of prohibited occupations and processes. When enacted in 1986, the schedule concentrated on occupations and processes considered hazardous. The list grew from five to fifteen occupations and from eleven to fifty-seven processes so far. The Child Labour (Prohibition and Regulation) Act, 1986 stipulates the following:

- Bans the employment of children i.e. those who have not completed their 14th year, in specified occupations and processes;
- Lays down a procedure to decide modifications to the schedule of banned occupations or processes;
- Regulates the conditions of work of children in employment in violation of the provisions of this act, and other acts which forbid the employment of children;
- Lays down enhanced penalties for the employment of children in violation of the provisions of this act, and other acts which forbid the employment of children; and
- Brings about uniformity in the definition of the child in related laws.

Through a notification dated 26.5.1993, the working conditions of children have been regulated in all employments, which were not prohibited under the Child Labour (Prohibition and Regulation) Act, 1986. In an another notification dated 10.5.2000, child labour has been banned in six more processes, thereby bringing the total to 13 occupations and 57 processes. On 10th July, 2006, two more occupations have been added, thereby bringing the total to 15 occupations. The two sections which were added in 2006 had banned the employment of children in dhabas (road side eateries), restaurants, hotels, motels, teashops, resorts, spas and other recreational centers. It purports to regulate the hours and the conditions of child labourers and to prohibit child labourers in certain enumerated hazardous industries. The 1986 Act aimed to achieve uniformity in the definition of child labour, prescribing a uniform age of fourteen years in the definition of a child. In pursuing the objective of uniformity, the 1986 Act actually reduced the minimum age for employment in merchant shipping and motor transport from fifteen to fourteen years. Further, the Act repealed the prohibition of child labour on plantations. In 2001, the Act was amended to restore the minimum age of fifteen in merchant shipping and motor transport and to restore the prohibition of child labour on plantations.

An analysis of the aforementioned legislations reveals that they focus on a number of aspects as follows:

- Ban/prohibition of work in certain employments/sectors/dangerous processes.
- Prohibition of work for children below certain stipulated ages.
- Regulation of working hours/working conditions
- Provision of rest hours, medical facilities, entertainment hours, schedule of weekly, monthly and yearly holidays, minimum wages, mode of payment and other related aspects.

Limitations of the Child Labour Legislations

It is an irony that, despite the number of acts that have been enacted for protecting the rights of the children, the problem of child labour continues to grow alarmingly in India. A plethora of additional protective legislations have been put in place. There are distinct laws governing child labour in factories, in commercial establishments, on plantations and in apprenticeships. The acts aim to minimize the exploitation of this most vulnerable group of society. There are various legislations which have regulated and prohibited the employment of children below the age of 14 years in factories, mines and hazardous employments and have intended to regulate the working conditions of children in other employments. However, experience shows that the employers without any fear flout the provisions of these legislations and therefore, it is only on very seldom occasions that they have been punished for the violation of these provisions.

It is noteworthy that despite the fact that laws exist to regulate and prohibit employment of children in hazardous employments there is neither blanket prohibition on the use of child labour, nor is there any universal minimum age that has been set for child labourers. This provides avenues for employment of child labour. Therefore it would not be fallacious to say that inadequate legislation, as well as insufficient enforcement. is responsible for the continuation and perpetuation of the phenomenon of child labour.

The following table summarizes the child labour legislations in India starting from 1881.

Table 4.1: History of Legislation Relating to Child Labour in India

Year	Legislation	Age that Regulations Apply	What it says
1881	The Factories Act	7	Working hours limited to 9 hours
1891	The Factories Act	9	Working hours limited to 7 hours
1901	The Mines Act	12	Specifically for mines
1911	The Factories Act	9	Work in certain dangerous processes Prohibited
1922	The Factories (Amendment) Act	15	Working hours limited to 6 hours
1923	The Indian Mines Act	13	Raised the age to 13 years
1926	The Factories (Amendment) Act	15	Working in two separate factories on same day prohibited
1931	The Indian Ports Act	12	Related to child labour handling goods At ports
1932	The Tea District's (Emigrant Labour) Act	16	Migration was prohibited without Parents
1933	The Children (Pledging of Labour) Act	15	First law against bonded labour
1934	The Factories (Amendment) Act	12-15	Employment prohibited in certain areasAnd employment hours restricted to 5 hrs.
1935	The Mines Amendment Act	15	Working hours regulated to 10 hoursAbove ground and 9 hours below.

(Contd...)

Year	Legislation	Age that Regulations Apply	What it says
1938	The Employment of Children Act	13	Handling of goods allowed for 12-14 age
1948	The Factories Act	14	Concerning employment in government Establishments
1951	Employment of Children (Amendment) Act	17	Prohibited working for 15-17 at ports And railways
1951	The Plantations Labour Act	12	Prohibited working of children under 12
1952	The Mines Act	15	Required medical certificate forUnderground work
1954	The Factories (Amendment) Act	17	Prohibited work at nights
1954	The shops and Establishment Act	14	Prohibits employments in shops, establishments
1958	The Merchant Shipping Act	15	Prohibits work on ship except in certain Areas
1961	The Motor Transport Worker Act	15	Prohibits working in any motor transport Undertaking
1961	The Apprentices Act	14	Prohibits apprenticeship/training
1966	The Beedi and Cigar Workers (Conditions of Employment) Act	14	Prohibits working in tobacco factories
1978	Employment of Children (Amendment) Act	15	Prohibits working on and near railway Premises
1986	The Child Labour (Prohibition and Regulation) Act	14	Most comprehensive Bans employment in specified industries Regulates the working condition where Not prohibited Uniformity on definition of child in Related laws

As a consequence, despite the various measures undertaken by the Government to tackle the exploitation of children, India has the dubious distinction of having the largest child labour force in the world.

A major criticisms of the legislation on child labour is the lack of uniformity. The various acts define child differently. These legislations do not conform to a single agreed minimum age. The minimum age differs from Act to Act, state to state and industry to industry. This is not only true of the definition of minimum age, but also of the working hours, rest periods, night employment and even where legislations apply, the employers do not employ them. There is also hardly any case of government taking employers to courts for disregarding the various stipulations. Even if they were caught violating the provisions of the child labour laws, the judicial punishment to them is limited and is most often nominal. As a result, the legislation does not act as a deterrent and the tendency to employ children continues. Besides, the administrative authorities have no powers to suspend licenses of a factory violating law. This conveniently ensures that no effective steps are taken to alleviate the presence of child labour.

Another major defect of child labour related laws is that they prohibit employment of children only in hazardous occupations. However, a large number of working children do not come under the term "hazardous labour" as they work in unorganized sectors like agriculture, cottage industries etc. All these are in inferior conditions and are unsuited to their physical development (Weiner, 1996). The legislation also fails to include new hazardous occupations and are unclear about the criteria that shall be used for defining what is hazardous (Burra, 1986; Fernandes, 1986).

The Child Labour (Prohibition and Regulation Act, 1986) represents a half hearted attempt by the Government of India to deal with the massive problem-its aim is not to abolish child labour but only to prohibit its use in hazardous industries. Numerous investigations make it clear that, in fact all employment is hazardous for children, and that they are regularly maimed, tortured or killed by accident or ill-treatment, even in supposedly non hazardous occupations such as garment manufacturing, food production and domestic labour (Hensman 2001). The Child Labour (Prohibition and Regulation) Act of 1986 emphasizes regulation rather than prohibition of child labour. The legislation bans the employment of children in factories, but children are otherwise permitted to enter the labour force at any age. They can be legally employed in small workshops. They are free to work in numerous fields. For example, rag picking is not classified as hazardous, though thousands of children collecting scraps of iron, glass, paper and rags often pick up bits of food to eat and are prone to tetanus and skin diseases. It is important to note that the legislation for child labour in the so called 'non-hazardous' occupations without regard for age is a violation of Articles 24, 39 and 45 of the Indian Constitution, which ban child labour and call for compulsory schooling. Incidentally, in the *Unnikrishnan and others* Vs *the State of Andhra Pradesh* (1993) case, the Supreme Court has argued that free and compulsory education should be considered as a Fundamental Right.

Again Section I1 of the 1986 legislation stipulates that a register must be maintained of all children employed in the establishment and this register should be scrutinized by inspectors. But the stipulation only applies to children employed on regular basis. Since 70 per cent of child labourers are employed on casual basis, these children do not show up in the official registers. Also, the provisions do not apply 'to any establishment wherein any process is carried on by the occupier with the aid of his family' and this somewhat subjective phrase provides a convenient loophole.

Again a major chunk of the girl child labourers do not come under the definition of child labour because according to these laws there must be an identifiable employee and an identifiable employer. But most of the girl child labourers are mainly confined to domestic sphere and this is normally invisible. And also children working as part of the family labour do not come under the purview of Child Labour (Prohibition and Regulation) Act.

Additionally, the governmental machinery to implement these laws is inadequate. Inspectorate system does not work at all and partly as a result of this, children are often not aware of their rights. For example, under section 12 of the 1986 legislation, every establishment where children are employed is supposed to prominently display some of the provisions of 1986 legislation through notice, both in the local language and in English. Virtually no establishment complies with this provision. To add to it, the employers are not punished, as inspectors never turn up. This jurisdiction of individual inspectors is also too extensive for them to keep a regular watch on activities within their purview. The labour inspector, whenever he gets a chance to book any violation, has difficulties in collecting evidence for proper prosecution.

The parents of child labourers are opposed to enforcing such laws when poverty forces them to send their children to work in hazardous industries and when the alternative to hazardous employment is hunger and malnutrition. In spite of the Constitutional directives and multiplicity of enacted laws, millions of children have been working in India in a variety of occupations, the laws remaining placidly in bound volumes without a sign of implementation (Sundarajan, 1993).

The government in the act of 1986 gives itself the timeframe of ten years in which, it claims that it will abolish the serious problem of child labour. The government has had enough power to deal firmly with employers violating the provision of the Children Act of 1938, Factories Act of 1948, Minimum Wages Act, etc. for the past forty years, and yet this abhorrent exploitation continues. The enforcement of the new legislation has again been left in the hands of inspectors who have proved rather ineffective through all these years (Shandilya and Khan, 2003).

The new act does not specify how the welfare, health and safety of working children is to be protected. The government has taken upon itself the task of providing all welfare measures, leaving the employers rather free of this responsibility.

Committees and Commissions on Child Labour

Along with legislations, a series of committees and commissions have been appointed by the Government of India, either specifically on the question of child labour or on labour conditions in general to enquire into the causes or consequences of the problem and to suggest measures to reduce the incidence of child labour and to ameliorate the conditions of the child labourers. These are the Royal Commission on Labour, 1929, the Labour Investigation Committee, 1944, The National Commission on Labour, 1966, Gurupadaswamy Committee on Child Labour, 1966 and Santa Mehta Committee 1986 which deserves special attention.

The Royal Commission on Labour (1930) also known as Whitley Commission observed that the employment of children continued to be a problem since the early days of industrialization and in many cities large number of young boys were employed for long hours and the employers imposed corporal punishment and other disciplinary measures of reprehensible kind even against the small children in order to compel them to do work in their establishments. (GOI, 1936). In the comprehensive report of the Commission, it was observed, interalia that the most noteworthy effect of the 1922 Act was that the employment of children in the mills, cotton spinning and weaving industry had reduced. In its occasional references about the working conditions of children, the report mentions, "Children usually work for five hours a day without any intervals.

The Labour Investigation Committee was appointed by the Government of India under the chairmanship of Mr. D.V. Rege to collect data relating to wages and earning, employment, housing and social conditions of labour in India, and to investigate the risks which bring about insecurity, the need of labour to meet much risks and the methods suitable to meet them and the housing and factory conditions (Nongia, 1987).

The Labour Investigation Committee 1946, submitted in its report in the year 1946, observed that in various industries, especially smaller industries, the statutory prohibition of employment of children was not seriously enforced and the employment of children continued.

The Committee suggested to simultaneously adopting positive measures to wean away child labour from industrial employment. It also suggested enforcing the legal provisions through proper inspection and the provision of educational and other facilities.

The National Commission on Labour was appointed in 1966 by the Ministry of Labour, Employment and Rehabilitation under the chairmanship of Dr. P.B. Gajendragadkar and suggested measures for the improvement of the child labourers. According to the National Commission on Labour, "the employment of children is non-existent in organized industries. It persists in varying degrees in the unorganized sector. The employment of children below the prescribed age was also reported to be continuing in far off places in rural areas where the enforcement of statutory provisions was more difficult. It brought to notice that, quite often it is the feeling of sympathy rather than the desire to exploit, which weigh with employers in employing child labourers. Ironically, it is the same feeling, which makes the inspecting officers take a lenient view of breaches of the legal provisions in this respect". In the context of' employment of children, the Commission was of the view that it was indeed more of an economic problem than anything else and it amounted to denial of' opportunity to children for their proper physical development and education. 'The National Labour Commission in its report submitted to the Union Government in 1969 recommended combination of work with education and flexible employment hours which would not inhibit education. (Tiwana, 2000)

The Guruprasadswamy Committee was appointed in 1979 by the Ministry of Labour under the chairmanship of M.S. Guruprasadswamy to look into detail, the causes leading to end the problems arising out of employment of children in India. The Gurupadaswamy Committee, in its 1979 report, identified the sectors of the economy with substantial number of working children. The report highlighted that it was a common fact that children at the age of 7 or 8 years work in various unorganized industries at meager wage, these children work for prolonged hours and develop many physical problems. These children also handle dangerous chemicals and are also employed on machines with sharp edge and blades. The Committee "summarizes the situation of children in India as one of continuing drift," The Committee also emphasized that a minimum age of 15 years should be laid down for the employment of children for the sake of uniformity. It also stated that enactment of the statute is not the only consideration to prevent exploitation of child labour and the purpose will not be served if there is no effective administrative machinery to enforce those statutory provisions. The Committee nonetheless urged the government to strengthen its enforcement machinery and to make use of voluntary organizations and trade unions. Indeed, the Committee pressed for the enforcement of minimum wage laws for adults. Though the Committee supported primary education for children it also stressed that the present system of education does not prepare children for future occupations. Therefore, the educational curriculum must be geared to bring the maximum of skill and competence in the child. Also, the Committee called for a strengthening of non-formal education facilities for the child labourers. The Committee examined in detail the anomalies in various legislations that deal with children and recommended a single model legislation of child labour in India (Kothari, 1983).

The Committee in its report recommended:

- Setting of child labour advisory boards
- Fixation of minimum age of entry to any establishment
- Strengthening of enforcement machinery
- Formulation of effective educational policy with emphasis on integration of educational equipment with local crafts.

The Child Labour Cell was set up in 1979 is now a part of the Ministry of Labour. It formulates, and coordinates and implements policies and Programmes for the welfare of child labour. It provides grants to voluntary organizations which run action oriented projects for child labour as such as non-formal education, health care and supplementary nutrition. Grants are also released to conduct seminars and research to identity future areas for taking appropriate action.

Following the recommendations of the Gurupadswamy Committee on Child Labour, the Government of India established a special Central Child Labour Advisory Board in March, 1981 with the following objectives.

- Review the implementation of existing laws
- Suggest legislative and administrative measures for child labourers
- Review progress of welfare measures
- Recommend industries where child labour should be eliminated

During the 1980s the Government of India initiated several action oriented programmes to withdraw children from work and prevent them entering the labour market. Towards this objective, several projects have been sanctioned both by the Ministry of Labour and the Ministry of Welfare, Government of India at the grass roots level (Jains, 1996).The most significant step in this direction was the adoption of National Child Labour Policy, 1987.

The Report on Child Labour in Indian Industries, 1981 was the result of a rapid survey conducted by the Labour Bureau in certain organized and unorganized sectors of Indian industries. The report presents an account of the various aspect of child labour e.g. employment, wages and earning, working conditions, welfare facilities etc. The report found that in most factories the hours of work, as prescribed under the act were not being strictly adhered to. The report therefore emphasized the need to strengthen the enforcement machinery to make the employers fully conscious of their obligations towards child employees. The report also revealed that children of very tender age more found working in certain industries, such as match box, handloom, bidi, fishing, hotels and restaurants, repair shops etc. The wages paid to children varied from state to state and from industry to industry, from less than one rupee in plantations and match and fire work units to a maximum of five rupees in cashew processing and textile manufacturing units. In most of the cases, the payment was on piece rate basis. The report stated that the majority of child labourers come from poor families to supplement their family income. They were compelled to discontinue their studies as there was no provision of night schools for those who wanted to continue studies. The report emphasized the need to strengthen the enforcement machinery to make the employers fully conscious of their obligations towards child labourers.

National Child Labour Policy

It was realized that legislation alone cannot bring an end to child labour. The main reasons for this are lack of adequate enforcement machinery, lack of political will, deliberate attempt by employers to flout the legal provisions and lack of consciousness within the minds of parents themselves who obtain false age and medical certificates to enable their children to work in different undertakings. The number of labour inspectors as enforcement officers is far from satisfactory. They can barely visit all the factories in their jurisdiction. Keeping in view the pitiable condition of child labour in India, the Government of India implemented the National Policy on Child Labour (Das, 2011). The National Policy on Child Labour was formulated in conjunction with the legal measures to address the socio economic issues and to provide a framework for a concrete programme of action. The policy encompasses action in the field of education, health, nutrition, integrated child development and employment (Bequele, 1988).The National Child Labour Policy aimed at successfully rehabilitating child labour withdrawn from employment and at reducing the incidence of child labour.

The action plan under the National Child Labour Policy comprises:

- A legislative action plan;
- Focusing of general development programmes for benefitting children wherever possible; and
- Projection based action plans in areas of high concentration of child labour engaged in wage and quasi wage employment.

Within the framework of the National Child Labour Policy, some concrete steps have been taken to implement the project based plan of action through National Child Labour Projects. The projects were launched for the first time in 1988.The project envisaged a large number of activities. The major activity undertaken under the NCLP is the establishment of special schools to provide non formal education, vocational training, supplementary nutrition, stipend, health care etc. to children withdrawn from employment. The actual implementation of various schemes under the projects is being carried out by the local non governmental organizations.

Considering the complexity and the magnitude of the issue, the National Policy on Child Labour announced in 1987 emphasized the need for strict enforcement measures in areas of high child labour concentration. In order to translate the above policy into action, the Government of India initiated the National Child Labour Project Scheme in 1988 to rehabilitate the child labourers starting with 12 child labour endemic districts of the country. Under the Scheme, child labourers were identified through child labour survey, withdrawn from work and put into the special schools, so as to provide them with enabling environment to join mainstream education system. In these Special Schools, besides formal education, they were provided a stipend @ Rs. 100/- per month, nutrition, vocational training and regular health check-ups. In addition, efforts were also made to target the families of these children so as to cover them under various developmental and income/employment generation programmes of the Government. The Scheme also envisaged awareness generation campaigns against the evils of child labour and enforcement of child labour laws. The NCLP Scheme was implemented through a district level Project Society, headed by the District Collector. This Project Society included prominent Non Governmental Organizations and Trade Unions of the district, in addition to the State Government officials from Education, Health, Rural Development, Labour, Social Welfare and Women & Child Development Departments, etc. The involvement of different departments in the Project Society was to ensure better convergence with these Departments for implementation of the Scheme. As far as possible, running of special schools for child labour was entrusted to NGOs. It could, however, be taken up by the Project Society itself, if competent and experienced NGOs were not available in the district for this purpose. The funds under the Scheme were sanctioned by the Ministry directly to the District Collector, who in turn, disbursed them amongst the NGOs for running these Special Schools for child labourers. The funds were also provided under the Scheme for conducting regular child labour surveys, awareness generation programmes and training of instructors/teachers, etc. The coverage of the NCLP programme, which started with 12 districts, has been thereafter progressively increased to cover much larger number of districts in the country. In fact, major thrust to the programme came with the landmark judgment of the Hon'ble Supreme Court in December 1996 in the case of M.C. Mehta Vs. State of Tamilnadu.The Hon'ble Supreme Court gave certain directions regarding the manner in which the children working in the hazardous occupations were to be withdrawn from work and rehabilitated, as also the manner in which the working conditions of the children employed in non-hazardous occupations were to be regulated and improved upon. The Hon'ble Court specifically ordered withdrawal of children working in hazardous industries and ensuring their education in appropriate institutions. It also prescribed employment of at least one adult member of the family of the child so withdrawn from work, a contribution of Rs. 20,000/- per child was ordered to be paid by the offending employer into a corpus of fund set up for the welfare of child labour & their families. Failing which, the State Government to contribute to this Welfare Fund Rs. 5,000/- per child. The interest earnings of this corpus were to be used for providing financial assistance to the families of these children. The Hon'ble Court also ordered regulation of working hours for the children engaged in non-hazardous occupations, so that their working hours did not exceed 5-6 hours per day and that at least two hours of education was ensured. It further directed that the entire expenditure on education of these children be borne by their employers.

In pursuance with the directions of the Hon'ble Court, fresh child labour surveys were conducted in child labour endemic districts of the country and the States were directed to step up enforcement measures. The Hon'ble Supreme Court is monitoring the directions issued in this judgment continuously since then. Based upon the reports received from the State/U.T. Governments, the Ministry of Labour & Employment has been regularly filing Affidavits to apprise the Hon'ble Court of the progress in this regard. The progress of implementation of the NCLP Scheme is monitored in the Ministry through the prescribed periodical reports & regular visits from the officials of the Ministry, State Government and audit departments. A Central Monitoring Committee on Child Labour headed by the Union Secretary (Labour & Employment) and consisting of State Labour Secretaries and representatives from various Ministries connected with the implementation of the project has been set up to look into the important issues faced in implementing the Scheme. The Central Monitoring Committee had recommended setting up of State Monitoring Committees for monitoring the implementation of the Scheme at the State level, which is yet to be set up in most of the States. However, as per the directions of Hon'ble Supreme Court in 1996, in the case of M.C. Mehta vs. State of Tamil Nadu, a Child Labour Cell has been formed in most of the States to implement the directions of the Hon'ble Supreme Court. This Cell has also been instrumental in monitoring the scheme.

In a related judgment on 7th May, 1997, the Supreme Court in Writ Petition Civil No. 12125/84 and 11643/85- Bandhwa Mukti Morcha, etc. (Petitioner) V/s UOI & Ors. (Respondents) has also given a number of directions on the identification, release and rehabilitation of child labour. The Court, inter alia, directed Government of India to convene a meeting with the State Governments to evolve principles/ policies for progressive elimination of employment of children below 14 years in all the employments consistent with the scheme laid down in Civil Writ Petition No. 465/86. These directions were given by the Court in the context of employment of children in the carpet industries in the State of Uttar Pradesh. In this case, the Court issued the following directions to the Government of Uttar Pradesh:

- Investigate into the conditions of employment of children.
- Issue such welfare directions as are appropriate for total prohibition of employment below 14 years of age.
- Provide facilities like education, health, sanitation, nutritious food, etc.

The implementation of the directions of Supreme Court is being monitored by the Ministry of Labour and compliance of the direction reported to the Hon'ble Court on the basis of information received from the State/UT Governments from time to time.

An assessment of the projects revealed that no suitable mechanisms have been evolved for monitoring the implementation of the project either at the district level or at the state level. Also a number of defects were found at the implementation of the project. The task of progressively eliminating child labour calls for an effective mechanism. Setting up a Child Labour Cell in the V.V. Giri National Labour Institute in 1990 made a modest beginning in this regard with the assistance of Government of India and UNICEF. Later the cell was upgraded to the National Resource Centre on Child Labour (NRCCL). The NRCCL was set up in March, 1993 with financial support of Ministry of Labour and UNICEF. The NRCCL has established a network with various NGOs and is assisting them in various ways in implementing child labour programmes.

Indus Child Labour Project (INDUS)

INDUS is a technical cooperation project jointly funded by the Government of India and the Government of the United States of America. It was developed within the framework of the Joint Statement on Enhanced Indo-US Cooperation on Elimination of Child Labour signed between the two governments on 31 August 2000. The project is a collaborative effort to provide programme support in a coordinated manner to ongoing efforts undertaken by the Government of India, through the NCLPs, towards a progressively child labour free country. The project focuses on selected districts within the states of Uttar Pradesh, Madhya Pradesh, Maharashtra and Tamil Nadu, and targets

80,000 children at risk of hazardous employment in the following sectors: brick manufacturing, stone quarrying, bidi manufacturing, footwear manufacturing, fireworks manufacturing, manufacturing of matches, silk manufacturing, lock making, brassware and glassware production. The selected states have some of the highest rates of child labour, as well as a high proportion of children working in these sectors. The project also addresses the employment generation and skills development needs of 10,000 parents. The overall approach of the project is to create an enabling environment where children will be motivated to enroll in schools, induced to refrain from working, and households provided with income generation alternatives that will not make it necessary for them to send their children to work. It seeks to work with two major programmes of the Government of India: the NCLPs and the Sarva Shiksha Abhiyan. The intervention strategy of the project consists of developing a comprehensive child labour elimination model for India by integrating four components. These are:

- strengthening public education as a measure to prevent child labour;
- providing vocational skills training to adolescents in the age group of 14-17 years;
- Monitoring the impact of child labour elimination efforts by tracking each beneficiary on the one hand and developing a child labour monitoring system on the other, to capture the shifts in child labour across different sectors;
- Providing income generating opportunities to the families of child labour. In addition, it seeks to support various initiatives aimed at ending child labour through social mobilization and awareness raising. This is combined with the building of capacities and training of government agencies and civil society partners. The project seeks to develop this model by working in partnership with the NCLP scheme of the Government of India. Several initiatives are being implemented to develop a model which can be replicated in all the NCLP districts.

The child labour programme in India is national in character and involves the Government of India, the Governments of the States and the Union Territories of India, as well as such tripartite for as the Indian Labour Conference and the Standing Labour Committee. A massive national and regional media campaign has been launched to sensitize society against child labour. Funds have been allocated to districts identified as child-labour endemic for surveys to identify child labour, and for awareness generation programmes among employers, parents and the child labourers themselves.

Contribution by National Institutions

A number of national institutions such as the V.V. Giri National Labour Institute (VVGNLI) and the National Institute of Rural Development (NIRD) and some state level institutes have played an important role in the areas of training and capacity building of government functionaries, factory inspectors, and officials of panchayati raj institutions, NCLP project directors, and heads of NGOs. These institutions have also made a significant contribution in the areas of research and surveys, awareness raising and sensitization, thus bringing the discussions on this issue to the forefront.

INTERNATIONAL LABOUR ORGANIZATION (ILO) AND CHILD LABOUR

Besides the various legislations and welfare programmes for the welfare of children, India had also ratified the Conventions which put focus on three main issues: (a) minimum age of employment; (b) medical examination of the working children; and (c) prohibition of night work done by children.

The international instruments on child labour may be divided into the following parts:

- International Convention and Recommendations adopted by the International Labour conference and ratified by member states.
- Convention on the Rights of Child adopted by the General Assembly of United Nations in 1989 and ratified by 191 countries.

The following table summarizes the details of ILO Conventions.

India has also ratified on December 2, 1992, the Convention on the Rights of the Child which came into force in 1990. This ratification implies that India will ensure wide awareness about issues relating to children among government agencies, implementing agencies, the media, the judiciary, the public and children themselves. The Government's endeavor is to meet the goals of the Convention and to amend all legislation, policies and schemes to meet the standards set in the Convention.

Table 4.2: ILO Conventions

Sl. No.	Title of the Convention	Aim	Status of Ratification by India
I	Convention no. 5: Minimum age (Industry) 1919	To prohibit employment of children under the age of 14 in any public cr private industrial undertaking	Ratified on 9.9.55.
II	Convention no. 10: Minimum age (Agriculture) 1921	To provide that children under the age of 14 may not be employed or work in any public or private organizational undertaking or any branch thereof, save outside the hours fixed for school attendance.	Not ratified
III	Convention no. 33: Minimum age (Non-industrial employment) 1932	To provide that children under 14 or those over 14 years who are still required by national laws or regulation to attend primary school shall not be employed in any mployment to which this convention applies.	Not ratified
IV	Convention no. 59: Minimum age (industry) (revised) 1937	To prohibit employment of children under the age of 15 in any public or private industrial undertaking.	Not ratified

(Contd...)

Sl. No.	Title of the Convention	Aim	Status of Ratification by India
V	Convention no. 60: Minimum age (Non-industrial employment) (Revised) 1937	To provide that children under 15 years or children over 15 years who are still required by national laws or regulations to attend primary school shall not be employed in any employment to which this convention applies.	Not ratified
VI	Convention no.123: Minimum age (Underground work) 1965	To provide that person under 16 years of age shall not be employed or work under ground in mines.	Ratified on 20.3.75.
VII	Convention no.138: Minimum age 1973	The convention relates to the abolition of child labour. The minimum age for admission to employment or work shall be not less than the age of completion of compulsory schooling (normally not less than 15 years). Developing countries may, however, initially specify a minimum age of 14 years.	Not ratified
I	Night Work Convention no. 6: Night work for young person (Industry) 1919	Abolition of night work for young person in any public or private industrial undertaking. The provisions of the convention have been modified for India.	Ratified on 14.7.21.

(Contd...)

Sl. No.	Title of the Convention	Aim	Status of Ratification by India
II	Convention no. 79: Night work for young persons (Non-industrial) 1966	To provide that children under 14 years of age who are admissible for full time or part time employment and those over 14 who are still subject to full time compulsory school attendance shall not be employed nor work at night during a period of at least 14 consecutive hours including an interval between 8 p.m. and 8 a.m.	Not ratified
III	Convention no. 124: Medical examination of young person (Underground work) 1965. Seafarers conditions for admission for employment.	To provide that a thorough medical examination and periodic reexamination at intervals of not more than one year for fitness for employment shall required for the employment or work in underground mines of persons under 21 years of age.	Not ratified
I	Convention no.15: Minimum age (Trimmers stokers) Convention 1921.	To prohibit employment of young person of below 18 years as trimmers and stokers in port. If persons of over 18 years are not available then young persons between 16 and 18 can be employed. Trimmers/stokers below 16 years can be employed, subject to medial fitness, in the coastal trade of India.	Ratified on 20.11.22
II	Convention no.16: Medical examination of young persons (Sea) Convention 1921.	Young persons under 18 years of age can be employed on any vessel on the production of a medical certificate attesting fitness for such work.	Ratified on 20.11.22.

India is also a signatory to the World Declaration on the Survival, Protection and Development of Children. In pursuance of the commitment made at the World Summit, the Department of Women and Child Development under the Ministry of Human Resource Development has formulated a National Plan of Action for Children. Most of the recommendations of the World Summit Action Plan are reflected in India's National Plan of Action.

Limitations of ILO Efforts

Most of the conventions and recommendations of ILO shows that though a few of them are relating to agricultural and non-industrial occupations, they are mainly concerned with industrial employment. In other words, they are more relevant to industrial employment. In a country like India where the bulk of the work force is in agriculture their relevance is limited. It may not be wrong to say that these conventions and recommendations have been framed and adopted with reference to the condition prevalent in the industrialized countries and not much thought have been given to the needs of child labour in non industrialized countries.

Moreover, the mere adoption of recommendations does not mean that these are enforced in all the member countries. These conventions can come into force only after their ratification by the concerned national governments. A state may enforce them fully or partly or may not enforce them all. The Indian Government has not adopted and ratified all the conventions of ILO, which is also one of the important reasons for the unbridled growth of child labour in India.

5

Demographic Profile of the Respondents

INTRODUCTION

Child labour is an important area of concern both nationally and internationally. Millions of children worldwide start working at a very young age. These children are exposed to various forms of exploitation and abuse. Children continue to work in large numbers in various sectors of the economy. There has been a continuous influx of children into urban informal sector labour market than the formal sector. A number of factors explain the concentration of child labour in this sector such as absence of any statutory minimum age for employment, easy entry and exit or there are no barriers to entry for new enterprises in this sector, there seems less competition among job seekers, absence of any minimum requirement of education or training; easy nature of work and absence of any minimum wage requirement.

In this chapter an attempt has been made to present the demographic profiles of the respondents (Child labourers, Parents, and Employers) covered under the study.

The demographic parameters include the place of origin, caste, religion, parental occupations, present status of children, their parents as well as employers. It also includes population composition, migration pattern and distribution of population according to region, age, sex, education and occupation.

This chapter has been divided into three sections, Section I deals with the demographic profile of the child labourers, Section-II deals with the demographic profile of the parents and the third section presents the demographic profile of employers.

SECTION - I

DEMOGRAPHIC PROFILE OF CHILD LABOURERS

The demographic features of child labourers are based on interviews with 120 child labourers in the age group of 7 to 14 employed in small scale commercial establishments viz; subzi mandi, garages, dhaba/tea stalls, and shops. The child labourers are spread throughout Delhi. For the present study, the areas that have been selected include, Seelampur, Zama masjid, Tis Hazari, Indira market, R.K.Puram, Kashmir gate, Govindpuri, Wazirpur, Palam, Dakhinpuri, Azadpur, Ashok Vihar, Ambedkar Nagar, Giri Nagar, Sarai, Loni, Sanjay Gandhi transport Nagar, Anand Vihar, Nand nagari, Sundernagari, Shahdara, Loni Border, Jhilmil, Harsh Vihar, Mansarover Park, Meet Nagar, Adarsh Nagar and Ashok Nagar. The variables comprised age, native place, religion, place of stay in Delhi, educational qualification, nature of family, number of siblings, position of the respondents, parents' occupations, some basic information about the child's family in terms of number of family members, education of the parents, their working status and monthly income of the family. These variables are, likely to have an implication on the working status of the child.

A. Socio-Economic Profile

Age

Age is an important factor which shapes one's personality and enables to determine the work responsibilities and occupation one wishes to join for economic independence. It is one of the most important determinants of the mental and physical development of the children. So far as, the age of the child labourers is concerned, for the present study, the children between the age group of 7-14 have been chosen. The table 5.1 shows the age wise classification of child labourers.

Table 5.1: Age of the Child Labourers

Sl. No.	Age (Years)	Frequency	Percentage
1.	7-9	8	6.7
2.	9-11	13	10.8
3.	11-13	47	39.2
4.	13-14	52	43.3
Total		120	100

From the above table, it is clear that more than 50 per cent of the child labourers i.e. 52(43.3%) were in the age group of 13-14 years followed by 47(39.2%) children whose age was 11 to 13 years. The next in number were the child labourers in the age group of 9 to 11 years i.e 13(10.8%). The least number of child labourers were 8 (6.7%) in the age group of 7 to 9 years.

Thus, it can be concluded that that in a metropolitan city, few children at the tender age of seven also start working in the unorganized sector. The possible reasons for opting to work could be due to poverty or lack of parental care, apart from others.

Religion

Religion exercises control over human beings and binds them within certain codes of ethics. It also specifies the values, attitudes and modes of behaviour of the people. In the present sample, children belonged to two religious groups i.e. 73(60.8%) were Hindus and the remaining 47(39.2%) practiced Islam.

Table 5.2: Religion of the Respondents

Sl. No.	Religion	Frequency	Percentage
1.	Hindu	73	60.8
2.	Islam	47	39.2

Thus, it can be concluded that children, both from the Hindu and Muslim community are predominately engaged in small scale establishments in Delhi.

Caste

Indian society is divided and stratified into a well established caste system evolved over thousand of years.

Caste determines a person's social status and also one's own perceptions and expectations from life. In this highly stratified society, the domineering so called 'upper castes' have always reaped the benefits of economic growth and all development programmes. The so called 'lower castes' remain suppressed and hence access to resources, whether natural or developmental are generally denied to them. The exploitative socio-economic structure results in the marginalization of poor, belonging mainly to the lower caste, who have no option but to put their children in the labour market for their survival.

Table 5.3: Caste of the Respondents

Type of Caste	Frequency	Percentage
Upper Castes	29	24.1
OBCs	23	18.3
SCs and STs	21	17.5
Religious minority group (Muslims)	47	37.5
Total	**120**	**100**

The above table reveals that 29(24.1%) respondents belonged to upper castes, 23(18.3%) respondents belonged to other back ward castes and 21(17.5%) respondents were scheduled castes and scheduled tribes. The study also revealed that 47(37.5%) respondents were Muslims. So the study revealed that child labour is uniformly prevalent in all the types of caste/social groups.

Occupation of Parents

The occupation of the parents and their monthly earnings has significant impact on the family and particularly on the status of child. So, the child labourers were asked about the occupation of their parents. It has been a general observation that the parents of the child labourers were employed/ engaged in occupations that were not remunerative and that the occupational status of these persons was rather low.

Table 5.4: Occupation of Parents

Occupation of Parents	Frequency	Percentage
Employed in petty jobs	30	25
Self employed	68	54.16
Truck driver/auto rickshaw driver	2	1.66
Unemployed	17	14.16
Employed in private company jobs	2	1.66
Do not know	1	0.83
Total	**120**	**100**

The study revealed that a majority of the parents of the respondents were engaged in variety of activities in the informal sector, mostly in dhabas/ restaurants, tea stalls, garages, shops and construction work. The study also found that a large number of them 68(54.16%) were self employed and were engaged in selling fruits and vegetables, were hawkers and were also working as auto rickshaw drivers. The study also found that a significant per cent of parents were unemployed.

Parent's Income

Table 5.5: Monthly Income of Parents

Earning Per Month	Frequency	Percentage
Less than 1000	1	8
1000- less than 2000	4	3.3
2000- less than 3000	15	12.5
3000- less than 4000	23	19.2
4000- less than 5000	49	40.8
5000-more	8	6.7
Don't know	3	2.5
Nil	17	14.1
Total	**120**	**100**

The above table reveals that 49(40.8 %) respondents revealed that their parents earned between Rs. 4000- less than Rs. 5000 followed by 23(19.2%) who earned between Rs3000-Rs. 4000 per month. 15(12.5%) respondents reported that their parents earned Rs. 2000-Rs. 3000 per month. A few respondents pointed out that their parents earned even less than Rs. 2000 per month. 17(14.1%) of the respondents revealed that their parents were unemployed.

B. Family Related Profile

Nature of Family

Family plays a very important role in shaping the child's personality. Accordingly, the researcher wanted to know from the respondents what type of family they belonged to? In this study, nuclear family refers to a household consisting of a father, a mother and their children. The joint family refers to a social group in which the father, mother, their children, their brothers and parents live together. Extended family for the purpose of the study consists of parents and their children's families and includes multiple generations in the family. The Table 5.6 reveals that 79(65.8%) respondents belonged to nuclear families, followed by 31(25.8%) belonging to joint families. The least number of child labourers 10(8.3%) belonged to extended families.

Table 5.6: Nature of Family

Sl. No.	Nature of Family	No. of Respondents	Percentage
1.	Nuclear family	79	65.8
2.	Joint family	31	25.8
3.	Extended family	10	8.3
Total		**120**	**100**

Size of the Family

The large families with a comparatively less income are not likely to have the happy notions in their mind. They fail to meet even the basic needs of the family like good food, shelter and education to their children. As a consequence, it seems that they are left with no alternative but to send their children into labour market. It is in view of these facts that information was gathered from the children and the same is presented below.

Out of 120 respondents, 56.6% respondents stated that at least two to four family members were staying in the village. Thirty three (27.5%) respondents informed that none of their family members were staying in villages. Eight respondents reported that more than five family members were staying in villages. However, 64.9% of the total respondents opined that they were having 2 to 4 family members staying along with them in Delhi. Sixteen (16) respondents revealed that they were having 5 to 10 family members in Delhi. Only 5 (4.2%) of the children reported that they were staying alone in Delhi.

Thus, the size of the family did not seem to have any relation with the employment of the children. Depending on the circumstances, some family members were continuing to stay in the village whereas others had migrated to the city.

Number of Siblings

The researcher had also asked about the number of siblings of the respondents. The study revealed that 61(50.8%) were having 3 or more than 3 siblings followed by 37(30.8%) having 2 siblings and only 18(15%) were single children. It is significant to note that four respondents could not answer about their siblings as they did not know about their families.

The researcher also asked the respondents if their siblings were also engaged in petty jobs like them. The study revealed that in the case of 75 respondents, their siblings were also engaged in jobs out of which 23 respondents reported that their siblings were engaged in the same kind of job.

The main reasons given by the respondents for being occupied in jobs were because of parental pressure or due to the poor economic strata to which parents belonged.

Position of the Respondents

The study reported that 31(26%) respondents were younger in the family, whereas 34(28%) were the eldest child in the family. The remaining 33(27.5%) respondents occupied the middle position. 18(15%) respondents reported that they were the only child of their parents.

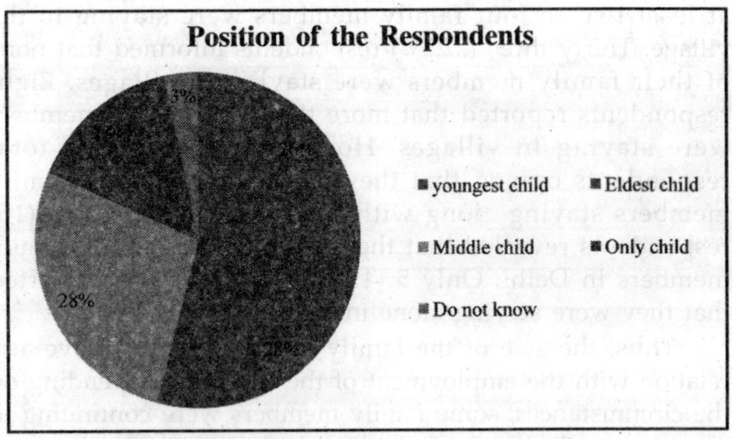

Fig. 5.1: Position of the Respondents

Again it is important to note that 4 respondents did not have any idea about their siblings.

Parent's Status

One of the reasons for child labour is a depleted family, particularly the loss of the adult male earning member, i.e. the head of the family or his disability. Presence of both parents in a family is always beneficial for the children. Single parents find it difficult to manage the family. Single parenthood is associated with multiple adversities like economic, social and psychological. Children are prone to receive less care and attention when they do not have a father or a mother. Children's upbringing is sure to suffer in this situation. Single parent families, as a coping mechanism and survival strategy, may engage children in employment to make up for the loss of income caused by death or disability of either parent. The researcher thus intended to uncover the status of their parents at the time of the study.

A large majority of the respondents (103 out of 120) reported that both their parents were alive, thereby disputing the assumption that the death of one or both the parents probably compelled these children to take up employment. Twelve respondents viewed that only their mother was alive. In two cases it was found that only father was alive.

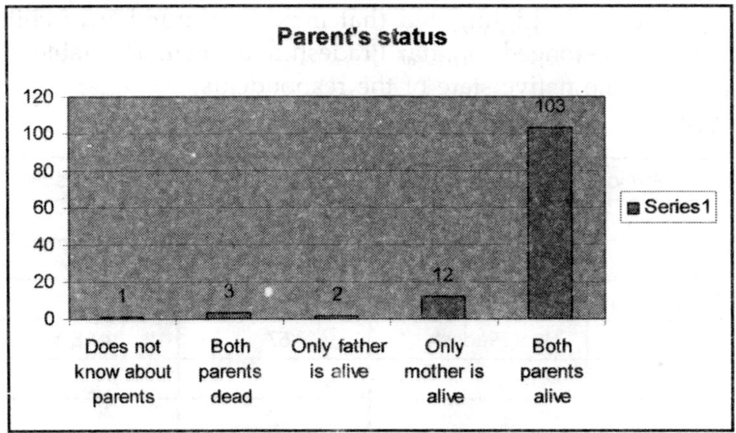

Fig. 5.2: Parent's status

The study also revealed that, three respondents reported that both their parents had died. Thus, the study found that the children were found engaged in jobs for various reasons and absence of parent was one such cause.

Place of Stay

The study revealed that child labourers are widely dispersed throughout Delhi.

Table 5.7: Place of Stay in Delhi

Sl. No.	Place of Stay	Frequency	Percentage
1.	East Delhi	48	48
2.	West Delhi	19	15.83
3.	North Delhi	21	17.5
4.	South Delhi	32	26.66
Total		**120**	**100**

The areas where the children resided included Seelampur, Jama Maszid, Tis Hazari, Indira market, RK Puram, Kashmiri Gate, Govindpuri, Wazirpur, Palam, Dakshinpuri, Azadpur, Ashok Vihar, Ambedkar Nagar, Giri Nagar, Sarai, Loni, Sanjay Gandhi Transport Nagar, Anand Vihar, Nand Nagari, Sundernagari, Shahdara, Loni Border, Jhilmil, Harsh Vihar, Mansarover Park, Meet Nagar, Adarsh Nagar and Ashok Nagar.

Native Place of Respondents

The study highlighted that maximum number of child labourers belonged to Uttar Pradesh and Bihar. The Table 5.8 presents the native state of the respondents.

Table 5.8: Native Place of the Respondents

Sl. No.	Native State	Frequency	Percentage
1.	Bihar	52	43.3
2.	Jharkhand	01	0.8
3.	Delhi	03	2.5
4.	Uttar Pradesh	57	47.5
5.	Madhya Pradesh	02	1.7
6.	West Bengal	02	1.7
7.	Rajasthan	03	2.5
Total		**120**	**100**

The table reveals that the maximum number of child labourers 57(47.5%) hailed from Uttar Pradesh, followed by Bihar 52(43.3%). An insignificant number of respondents 11(9.16%) also hailed from other states including Jharkhand, Madhya Pradesh, West Bengal, Rajasthan and Delhi.

C. Education Related Profile

Educational Qualifications

Education plays an important role in one's life. It helps in shaping the right kind of life style in the human beings. Education, formal or informal helps in acquiring knowledge, improving work skills, efficiency, building personality and enhancing the capability of the children. It helps them in identifying their potentialities. Accordingly, the child labourers were asked to state their educational qualifications/ background. The table 5.9 presents the educational qualifications of the respondents.

It is evident from the table 5.9 that out of the 120 child labourers, 58(48.3%) were illiterate and 25(20.8%) respondents were literate. It was only one respondent who had passed middle school.

Table 5.9: Educational Qualification of the Respondents

Sl. No.	Educational Qualifications	No. of Respondents	Percentage
1.	Illiterate	58	48.3
2.	Basic Literacy	25	20.8
3.	Upto Primary	36	30
4.	Upto Middle	01	0.8
Total		120	100

Literacy Level of the Parents

Literacy level of the parents has a strong correlation with the incidence of child labour. Thus, parental illiteracy is also a significant contributory factor for existence of child labour in that it undermines the value of education in one's life, thereby pushing children into the work context, rather than in schools. A majority of the child labourers hailed from illiterate families.

Table 5.10: Literacy Level of the Parents

Literacy Level of the Parents				
Literacy Level	Frequency		Percentage	
	Father	Mother	Father	Mother
Illiterate	67	55.83	103	85.83
Basic Literacy	4	5.83	1	0.83
Up to Primary	22	18.33	7	5.83
Up to Middle	10	8.33	1	0.83
Up to Higher School	1	0.83	2	1.66
Not Aware of Parents education	13	10.83	6	5
Total	120	100	120	100

The Table 5.10 reveals that in most of the cases parents were found to be illiterates. The fathers of 67(55.83%) respondents were illiterates and for 103(85.83%) respondents, their mothers were illiterate. Further, the study also reported that 22(18.33%) of fathers had attained education up to primary, followed by 10(8.33%) who had education up to middle classes. It is also significant to note that 13(10.83%) of children were not aware of their father's education. This reflects a poor educational attainment of the parents of the children covered by the study.

Summary

An analysis of the demographic profile of child labourers in Delhi reveals that nearly 43 per cent of the children were 13 years or above, the remaining i.e. 57 per cent were less than 11 years of age at the time of data collection. It is significant to note that 7 per cent of the respondents belonged to 7-9 years age group also.

The sample comprised of a mix of children from Hindu and Muslim families, though a majority of them (60.8%) were Hindus and the rest (39.2%) were Muslims. The findings of the study are in contrast with the study of Patil (1988). His study revealed that a large percentage of children were from Muslim and Christian families. This reflects that children from all religions/strata of society are compelled to work. The phenomenon of child labour is delinked from religious background.

The study found that while 24.10 per cent children belonged to the Upper Castes, 18.3% belonged to Other Backward Classes, 17.5% Scheduled Castes and Scheduled Tribes. So, it can be said that children, irrespective of religion and caste, were engaged in menial jobs in various small scale commercial establishments in Delhi.

As far as the occupational status of the parents of the child labourers is concerned, a majority of the children reported that their parents were wage labourers and were engaged in jobs which were by and large covered in the unorganized sector. In few cases parents were found to be self employed. Seventeen children reported that their parents were not doing any job and mostly dependent on their earnings.

In keeping with the nature of occupation in which parents were involved it was noticed that the monthly earning of parents was also very low. A negligible number of respondents

(3) reported that their parents earned more than Rs. 5000/- per month. The low income of the parents could be a major reason for migration of children in search of jobs in metropolitan cities to work in small scale commercial establishments.

The study revealed that 65.8% belonged to nuclear families, whereas the remaining belonged to joint families or to extended families. In the study context, a large percentage of the child labourers came from nuclear families. The study also found that only 16(13.3%) respondents were from families with seven or less members. This is contrary to the common belief that larger families contribute more to the child labour.

The study found that 37(30.8%) of the respondents had two siblings followed by 31(25.8%) respondents having more than 3 siblings. Thirty (25%) had three siblings and only 18(15%) were single children. The study also reported that 4 children did not have any information regarding their families at native places.

The study found that 34(28%) respondents were the eldest among the siblings, whereas the rest 33(27.5%) were in the middle position. Thirty one (25.8%) were youngest in the family. It is significant to note that 18(15%) were the only child in the family. Despite the fact that they were the only child in their families, they were engaged in petty employment. Poverty seems to be an important contributory reason for children's compulsion to work.

The study reported that, a majority of the respondents 103(85%) had both parents alive. The remaining 14(11.6%) respondents had only one of their parents. It was in three cases that both the parents were expired.

The demographic profile of child labourers shows that a majority of the children were from outside Delhi and belonged to the states of Uttar Pradesh and Bihar. Regarding migration of the respondents it was found that a majority of the respondents migrated before the year 2009. However, it also reflects that immigration to Delhi is a continuous phenomenon for the people belonging to lower economic class.

The educational qualifications of child labourers, as found in the study, revealed that 58(48.3%) of the respondents were illiterate, 36(30%) had studied up to primary level, 25(20.8%) had only basic literacy. Thus, most of the children in the study had studied up to primary level or less than that. The study also found that a majority of the child labourers were from illiterate families.

SECTION – II

PROFILE OF THE PARENTS OF CHILD LABOURERS

In this section, the focus has been on the demographic profile of the parents covered by the study. The family/parents background of the respondents assumes more significance because it is the family where the child learns the basic social skills. It has its own pattern of interpersonal relations which acts as an agency for socialization which in turn is affected by the socio-economic conditions of the family. The parents are the dominant actors in the children's life course. The parents decide all matters for the best interests of the family, particularly for the child. Their actions and inactions have a bearing on the life of their children. The earning of parents affects the well being of the children. If the father is a poor earner and the meagre income is the only source of living, children's well being is the first casualty. Low income is the cause of multiple adversities for children. So, the present study has encompassed 40 parents for the collection of relevant facts about their socio economic status. The demographic characteristics of parents/guardians are discussed here.

Table 5.11 reveals that a majority of the parents 16(40%) were in the age group of 30-35 years followed by 10(25%) in the age group of 35-40 years. Six parents (15%) were in the age group of 40-45 years. The study also revealed that only 2 respondents were older than 45 years. So, the study revealed that a majority of the parents were young and had married at an early age.

A. Socio-Economic Profile

Age wise Distribution of the Respondents

Table 5.11: Age of the Father/Guardian

Age of the Father/Guardian	Frequency	Percentage
Below 30 years	6	15
30-35 Years	16	40
35-40 Years	10	25
40-45 Years	6	15
45-50 Years	1	2.5
50-55 Years	1	2.5
Total	**40**	**100**

Religion

Table 5.12: Religion of the Respondents

Religion	Frequency	Percentage
Hindi	29	72.5
Muslim	11	27.5
Total	**40**	**100**

Religion helps to understand one's personality especially customs and values. In concurrence with the India's population (where the majority are Hindus), the above table reveals that a majority of the respondents 29(72.5%) were Hindus, followed by 11(27.5%) who belonged to Islam. This is in line with the larger demographic profile of the country.

Caste

Caste system is a predominant feature of the social structure in India. It is a descriptive system of status and hierarchy. The traditional Indian caste system was based on traditional occupations. The SCs and STs who belonged to the lower castes in the Indian caste hierarchy are more marginalized. It is believed that, from this category, the majority of the child labourers come.

Table 5.13: Caste of the Respondents

Type of Caste	Frequency	Percentage
Upper Castes	12	30
OBCs	9	22.5
SCs & STs	8	20
Muslims	11	27.5
Total	**40**	**100**

The above table reveals that 12(30%) respondents belonged to the Upper Castes, 9 (22.5%) were from Other Backward Classes, 8(20%) respondents belonged to Scheduled Castes and Scheduled Tribes and 11 (27.5%) respondents belonged to the minority group. So, it may be concluded that persons belonging to different caste/groups are involved in informal sector work and it is not exclusively any one caste which compels children to undertake employment in cities. In stead, it is a situation of poverty which forces them to migrate to cities in search of employment at a tender age.

Year of Migration

Due to the attraction of urbanization and industrialization in the urban centres and the relatively less scope of finding a job at the native place, people migrate to these city centres in search of employment.

Table 5.14: Year of Migration

	Frequency	Percentage
Before 2003	17	42.5
2003-05	3	7.5
2006-08	15	37.5
2009-11	5	12.5
Total	**40**	**100**

The above table reveals that except in 5(12.5%) cases where families of respondents migrated to Delhi after 2009, the remaining migrated to Delhi before 2009. Hence, it is for the past many years that families were surviving in the city on their own with their children.

Occupation of Parents

The occupation of the parents is also likely to impact the life of their children. The occupation of father, its nature and earning opportunities have a significant influence in the enjoyment of childhood by the children. More so, it has close relation with the practice of child labour in our country. Parents engaged in better occupations are likely to be interested in better care and rearing of the child, whereas, parents with low paid occupation may demonstrate chances of child neglect, abuse and child labour.

Table 5.15: Occupations of the Parents

Occupation	Frequency	Percentage
Employed in Petty jobs	19	47.5
Self Employed	18	45
Truck Driver	1	2.5
Unemployed	2	5
Total	**40**	**100**

It has been a general observation that the parents of the child labourers are employed/engaged in occupations that are not remunerative and that the occupational status of these persons is rather low. The researcher had also asked the respondents regarding the profession of their parent i.e. father/guardian and mother.

The study reported that most of the respondents' father worked as labourer/farmer in agricultural/farming activities. The families of child labourers who were staying in Bihar and Uttar Pradesh were mostly working in the fields. Those families who had migrated to Delhi, their parents were found to be engaged mainly in petty jobs or self employed. An insignificant number 2(5%) were unemployed at the time of the study. It may be perhaps the inadequate wage/income that they earn forces them to get their child employed. This may suggest that parents are more concerned about the future of their children; hence they have secured jobs for them in small scale commercial establishments.

Monthly Income

Inadequate or intermittent family income or no income in most cases is one of the important causal factors of child labour.

Table 5.16: Monthly Income of the Parents

Monthly Income in Rupees	Frequency	Percentage
Less than 2000	9	22.5
2000-3000	11	27.5
3000-4000	15	37.5
4000-5000	5	12.5
Total	**40**	**100**

The study revealed that a majority of the parents i.e. 26(65%) earned between Rs. 2000-4000/ per month followed by 11(27.5%) respondents who earned between Rs. 2001-3000 per month. In case of nearly one fifth (22.5%) respondents the monthly income was less than Rs. 2000/.

This indicates that due to low income of the family, children were deprived of the facilities which were essential for the proper growth and development and on the contrary, they were put to work to supplement their family income. As the parents of the child labourers had jobs with low wages, it was very difficult for them to educate their children. Thus, poverty emerges as a major reason for compelling these small children to undertake menial jobs in cities.

B. Family Related Profile

Family Structure

Gore (1968) points out that ideally, the joint family consists of a man and his wife and their adult sons, their wives and children and younger children of the paternal couple whereas a nuclear family is a family consisting of at most a father, mother and dependent children. It is ordinarily believed that large families with poor resources contribute to the problem of child labour.The present study indicates that majority of the respondents live in a single nuclear family. The above study also reveals that a majority of the respondents 36(90%) belonged to nuclear families and only 4(10%) belonged to a joint family.

Table 5.17: Family Structures of the Respondents

Type of Family	Frequency	Percentage
Nuclear Family	36	90
Joint Family	4	10
Total	**40**	**100**

Size of the Family

It is important to study the size of the families because it has its bearing on the economic standards affecting their level of income and consumption.

Table 5.18: Size of the Family

Size of the Family	Frequency	Percentage
1-4	34	85
5-8	6	15
Total	**40**	**100**

X=4

A majority of the respondents 34(85%) revealed that their family size comprised of one to four members in Delhi whereas 6(15%) opined that five to eight members of their families were staying in Delhi. The mean size of the family (residing in Delhi) was found to be 4.

Number of Siblings Engaged in Jobs

Table 5.19: Number of Siblings Engaged in Job

	Frequency	Percentage
0 Sibling	2	5
1 Sibling	31	77.5
2 Sibling	7	17.5
Total	**40**	**100**

The above table shows that for a large majority of the families i.e. 31(77.5%) it is not only the respondent who was working; instead he had more siblings who were simultaneously associated in employment.

C. Education Related Profile

Literacy Level

Undoubtedly, education plays an important role in the development of an individual, society or the nation. Education is considered to be an investment for developing desirable qualities in human beings. It is an important indicator of social development. It is education which makes a person capable of living a socially acceptable life and enables him/her to become fit to survive in the society at large. The educated parents plan their families; provide the best possible education and recreational facilities to their children. They are cautious about the nutritional and health requirements of their children and give them love and affection which is essential for their growth, development and preparation for the future life.

Table 5.20: Educational Qualifications of Parents

	Frequency	Percentage
Illiterate	25	62.5
Basic Education	11	27.5
Primary	3	7.5
Middle	1	2.5
Total	**40**	**100**

It is evident from the above table that a majority of parents 25(62.5%) were found to be illiterate and 11(27.5%) had only basic education. A few parents studied up to primary and middle levels. So, it can be concluded that most of the child labourers' parents were not much educated. Thus, it seems from the findings of the study that poor education of parents also contributes to the prevalence of child labour.

Summary

The age wise distribution of respondents showed that a majority of the parents were found to be less than 45 years. Moreover, the children were primarily the Hindus (72.5%) and Muslims (27.5%) who were engaged in small scale commercial establishments. The caste wise distribution of the respondents reported that caste did not play a major role in determining the status of the children. It was mainly the economic background which broadly compelled children to undertake menial jobs. Regarding migration of the respondents it was found that a majority of the respondents migrated before the year 2009. However, it also reflects that immigration to Delhi is a continuous phenomenon for the people belonging to lower economic classes. The parents of the respondents were either self employed in petty professions like hawking, rickshaw pulling and fruits and vegetable selling or they were engaged in menial jobs like working as construction workers or employed in dhabas, tea stalls and garages . The study revealed that most of the children came from a poor economic background. None of the families had a monthly earning of more than Rs. 5000/. The family structure of the respondents revealed that a majority 36(90%) belonged to nuclear families. The mean size of the family members was found to be 4.As far as the number of siblings is concerned, a majority of the respondents reported that their other children were also engaged in job. However, only 2 parents reported that they are not sending their children for work. The educational status of parents also presented a very dismal picture as 25(62.5%) of father had no education and 11(27.5%) had only basic education, 3(7.5%) had studied up to primary level and only one respondent was found to have studied up to middle level.

SECTION - III

PROFILE OF THE EMPLOYERS OF CHILD LABOURERS

In India, a large number of child labourers are found to be working in different hazardous and unhazardous occupations. Some of the studies have highlighted that employers find it easier to employ children than adults, as they feel that children do not join labour unions to fight for their rights and they can be paid a minimum wage to work for long hours, at times without any rest interval. Therefore it is imperative to understand the view points of the employers regarding various issues of the child labourers. The present study has encompassed 40 employers for collection of relevant facts on child labour. The demographic characteristics of employers are discussed in this section.

Age

Table 5.21: Age of the Employers

Age of the Employers	Frequency	Percentage
Less than 30 years	2	5
30-35 years	6	15
35-40 years	14	35
40-45 years	11	27.5
45-50 years	4	10
50-55 years	3	7.5
Total	**40**	**100**

The above table reveals that except 8(20%) employers, the rest of them were above 35 years of age.

Caste

Caste structure is an important index to determine the social and political consciousness of people. In India, the economic and social status of the people is closely linked with the caste structure.

Table 5.22: Caste of the Respondents

Type of Caste	Frequency	Percentage
Upper caste	22	55
OBC	7	17.5
Muslims	11	27.5
Total	**40**	**100**

The above table reflects that 22(55%) of the employers belonged to the Upper Castes, 7(17.5%) belonged to OBCs. 11(27.5%) of the employers belonged to Muslim Community. The study found that most of the employers belonged to Upper Castes and OBCs among the Hindu category and the rest of the respondents were Muslims.

Educational Qualifications

Table 5.23: Educational Qualifications of the Employers

Educational Qualification	Frequency	Percentage
Illiterate	2	5
Basic Education	5	12.5
Primary	24	60
Middle	7	17.5
Any other	2	5
Total	**40**	**100.0**

The above table reveals that a majority of the employers 24(60%) had studied up to primary level and 7(17.5%) of the respondents had studied up to middle classes. Only 5(12.5%) of the employers had only basic education and only 2(5%) employers were illiterate. However, the study also revealed that 2 respondents had also studied above middle level.

Religion

Table 5.24: Religion of the Respondents

Religion	Frequency	Percentage
Hindu	29	72.5
Islam	11	27.5
Total	**40**	**27.5**

The above table reveals that a majority of the respondents 29(72.5%) belonged to the Hindu religion followed by 11(27.5%) in Islam. The study reveals that only the two religious community people i.e. Hindu and Islam were mostly engaged in running small scale commercial establishments in Delhi.

Summary

The age wise distribution of employers reveals that a majority of employers were above 36 years and below 45 years. Majority of the employers who belonged to Hindu religion were from Upper Castes and OBCs. As far as the educational qualification of the employers is concerned, a majority of the employers 24(60%) had studied up to primary level and a few of the respondents 2(5%) had studied up to middle level.

6

Determinants of Child Labour

INTRODUCTION

Child labour is a multi-dimensional problem. Several factors are responsible for the engagement of children in economic activities. There are several reasons which compel children to join in the work force. The various reasons include poverty, illiteracy, economic backwardness of the family, employer's preference to employ children, parent's desire to be free from children's responsibility as early as possible, and use them as labour to supplement the family income.

Thus, there are several factors which seem to be responsible for the early entry of children in the labour force, but all of them can't be qualified. This chapter will highlight the important factors which emerged from the present study that have contributed to their joining workforce in their childhood.

This chapter has been divided into three sections. Section-I describes the factors responsible for the incidence of child labour as reported by the child labourers. In this section, besides children's' responses on determinants of child labour, their views on reasons of school drop out, age and education at the time of migration, reasons of migration, aspirations of child labourers, and their awareness about compulsory education and legal provisions were studied as these seem to be important factors responsible for the entry of the children into the labour force. Section-II describes the factors contributing to child labour as reported by their parents. In this section, other important factors, poverty and inadequate income of the parents, illiteracy of the parents and occupation of the parents were studied separately as these variables were responsible for the growth of child labour. Section III describes the responses of employers regarding the reasons for appointing them in their establishments.

SECTION - I

The children were asked to narrate various reasons which compelled them to engage in remunerative jobs at a tender age. It was found that the reasons put forth by them were overlapping. The researcher tried to classify them according to the responses given by the respondents. This resulted in multiple responses as each respondent was free to give more than one response.

CHILDREN'S RESPONSES

Determinants of Child Labour

Table 6.1: Determinants of Child Labour

Determinants of Child Labour	Number of Responses	Percentage
Supplement family income	62	51.66
Family Pressure	59	49.16
Poverty	48	40
Lack of interest in studies and school drop outs	41	34.16
Migration of parents	36	30
Self-desire to work	8	6.66
Death of parents	3	2.5

N= 120(Multiple Responses)

The above table reveals that the most important factor which led them to work was to supplement their family income. More than half of the child labourers (52%) child labourers started working only because their parents wanted them to work owing to the poor economic background. They joined work so that they could provide extra income to the family. Some of the respondents also responded that their fathers did not get jobs throughout the year and hence they had to face financial crisis. So, in order to support the family, they joined in a remunerative job. Almost 40% of them also mentioned an associated compulsion arising out of sheer poverty that compelled them to opt for work. The fact that they were facing a situation of absolute poverty did not give them any other option. Another related factor was the unemployment of parents. Again 59(49%) child labourers reported that they started work due to the family pressure only because their parents wanted them to work. This was due to the illiteracy and ignorance of the parents. Around 41(34%) respondents reported that they had less interest in studies and had dropped out from schools and did not want to study further. Some of the respondents 36(30%) also pointed out that, they dropped out from school because of the migration of their parents and hence got engaged in jobs. Only 8(7%) child labourers said that they started working because of their own desire for having a better living standard and to earn some pocket money. Still another factor was death of parent in some cases. Loss of parents or bread winner of the family, chronic illness of family members, drinking habits and other social evils among adults also, forced some children to enter employment at a tender age.

In some families children are the main bread winners. Often orphans and children from broken families run away to big cities and work as child labourers. These children viewed that they had no other option and started working in remunerative jobs.

So, the present study revealed that a majority of the children joined the labour force because of poverty and need to supplement family income; family pressure as also a lack of interest in studies, which attracted them to engagement in work. The data sheds light on the fact that a majority of the children were engaged in jobs for fulfilling the basic economic needs of the family.

School Dropouts

Another important cause for the perpetuation of child labour is the dropping out of children from schools because of various reasons. The dropping out of children from schools is associated with the pressing needs for the childrens' earnings as well as with low perceived advantages of schooling. Child labour is believed to be closely related to the children dropping out from schools. Wherever dropout rates are high at the primary levels, incidence of child labour is also very high. If a dropped out child does not enter the labour force, then there is a tendency for him to drift into crime and other illegitimate activities.

Sociologists consider school dropping out of school as an important reason for the persistence of child labour. But as regards, the reason of school drop outs, there is a difference of opinion between those who argue poverty as the paramount reason and those who attribute factors within the school system as the cause. According to the National Council for Educational Research and Training (NCERT), the inability of the school system to retain children who have enrolled in the primary level education- *"the push out"* has been the single greatest reason responsible for the existence of child labour (Weiner, 1991). This may suggest that poverty cannot always be argued to be the only important reason of school drop outs and supply of child labour. It is poverty simply a classical defense offered by sociologists till date (Basu and Van, 1998).

Table 6.2: Reasons of Dropping out of School of Child Labourers

Reasons of Drop out	Frequency	Percentage
For supplementing family income	65	54.16
Lack of interest in studies	46	38.33
Parental Pressure	54	45
Migration	38	31.66
Death of parents	3	2.5

N=120 (Multiple Responses)

One of the important reasons that forced children to drop out of their educational institutions was their poor economic condition. The data reveals that about 54% of the drop outs were those whose parents could not afford to send them to schools due to financial constraints. These children reported that they had been pulled out of schools in order to supplement the family income. Thus, the poor income of the parents is an important factor for dropping out of children from schools. It was also found that 46(38.33%) of the total drop outs were not interested in studies and considered work more beneficial than study. A majority of these child labourers 54(45%) dropped out because of parental pressure to get engaged in either remunerative jobs or in family occupations/ employment. A significant number of respondents 38(31.66%) also dropped out due to the migration of their parents to Delhi.

However, the study reported that 16 (13.3%) respondents of the respondents expressed unhappiness due to dropping out from school because they wanted to continue their study and wanted to stay on their village. In contrast, 25 (20.80%) respondents opined that they felt very much relieved after dropping out. These respondents reported that they became economically independent, in the process.

It can be concluded that supplementing family income, migration and parental pressure mainly because of poverty were responsible for the dropout of those children. The study of Achari, 1986 reported that children belonging to poor families for supplementing family income were sent to work and were not allowed to complete their schooling. Castle et.al (1997) in their study reported that low quality of education and lack of access to educational facilities were also some of the reasons for the existence of child labour.

Age at the Time of Migration

The details of age at which these children migrated to Delhi is given below.

Table 6.3: Age at the Time of Migration

Age of Entry into Job	Percentage	Frequency
Less than 7	8	6.7
7-9	27	22.5
9-11	64	53.3
11-13	21	17.5
Total	120	100

The above table shows that as high as 64(53.3%) child labourers joined work force between the age group of 9-11 years, followed by 27(22.5%) between 7-9 years and 21 (17.5%) at the age of 11-13 years and only 8 (6.7%) started work at the young age of less than 7 years.

Education at the Time of Migration

Education plays an important role in one's life. Education aims at developing positive qualities in the children and helps them realise their potentialities. Accordingly, the child labourers were asked to state their educational qualification at the time of migration.

Table 6.4: Education at the Time of Migration

Educational Standard	Frequency	Percentage
Illiterate'	58	48.3
Upto 2nd standard	25	20.8
3rd to 5th standard	36	30
6th to 7th standard	1	0.8
Total	120	100

The data show that a majority of the respondents 58(48.3%) had never attended the school at the time of joining their work followed by 25(20.8%) who had schooling up to 2nd standard and 36(30%) had education up to 5th standard. Only a single child labourer was found who had studied up to 7th standard at the time of joining the work force.

So, it can be concluded that lack of education is one of the significant factors that contribute to children being compelled to join the workforce.

Migration

The increasing industrialization since India's independence brought about migration to the cities, where rural poor found greater opportunities for earning a livelihood. Migration is caused by various forces that encourage an individual to leave one place (*push*) and attract him to another (*pull*) place. For each migration, however several push and pull forces may be operating and interacting, so that the migration can not be attributed wholly to a single force. In modern times it is the movement of families and, still more of individuals seeking economic settlement and transient work in other lands. Migration is a shift from the place of residence to the urban areas mostly because of economic opportunities. Perloff (1960) argues that localities with attractive economic conditions can draw sizeable numbers of migrants from other localities, though only a small number may come from any single locality. On the other hand, what is very important in determining out-migration from a locality suffering from economic distress is the percentage of the labour force that is willing to leave in order to search for opportunities elsewhere. The better income opportunities and attraction of city life are some of the other factors which were responsible for rural urban migration. On the other hand, lack of work opportunities available in the village is among the push factors responsible for migration. In many cases, it has been seen that it is the parents who leave in search of better economic prospects and with them the child is forced to migrate.

Migration from rural areas to urban areas also encourages child employment. With growing population, small or no agriculture holdings, greater mechanization of agriculture and in general, inability of the agriculture sector to absorb everyone in labour force, a large number of farm workers (who are unemployed or underemployed) are forced to migrate to cities. Most of these workers are engaged in low paid work. Coupled with unfamiliar environment and deprivation, children of these migrant families are forced to join the work force.

Table 6.5: Reasons of Migration of Respondents

Reasons of Migration	No. of Responses	Percentage
Financial problem	59	49
Family problem	47	39
Natural disaster	16	13
Peer pressure	9	7.5
Self-desire	8	7
Family migration	59	49

N=120

The above table shows that 59(49%) children reported that financial problems of their families was the most important reason of migration. 47(39%)children reported that they had come to Delhi because of the family problems. These parents reported that their parents used to quarrel and the child felt neglected and uncared for. Eight per cent children said that they were allured by city's charm and better job prospects, so they migrated from their home town. The above table reveals that the main reasons for migration was financial problems, family problems, natural disasters and family pressure to migrate to Delhi in search of better livelihood opportunities.

This aspect has been dealt with in some of the reviewed studies. The study of child labour in Bombay by NIPPCD (1978) revealed that 58.2% of the child labour was the exclusive result of the internalization of the urban slum culture, as their families had migrated to cities before their birth. In all, there were 90 per cent of them who belonged to migrated families. The study of Gangrade (1978) in Delhi found that there were a substantial number of migrants among child labourers, particularly in the field of domestic services. Besides, domestic work they were working in tea stalls, dhabas, hawking evening newspapers and in rag picking. Most of the child labourers had migrated from Uttar Pradesh and Bihar. Khandekar (1972) revealed that low socio-economic status of family and migration from rural areas was some of the main factors which had forced their children to join the Mumbai labour market.

Aspirations of Child Labourers

The early engagement in work checks the intellectual development of a child and confines his vision only to the periphery of the occupation he is engaged in. He hardly knows about the professions/vocations beyond his territory and this, as well as the lack of education limits his aspirations to a great extent. It was found that the children who had acquired some education or were still continuing it had better aspirations. Since, it is difficult for child labourers to pursue schooling, they can not develop mental faculties in a proper way, as a result of which their aspirations get confined to low levels of aspiration.

The study reported that a majority of the respondents 94(78.3%) had never thought about their future. Their major concern was only to fulfil their immediate basic needs. Besides that, a significant number of respondents had very low ambitions.

So, it may be concluded that lack of future aspirations was also an important factor for forcing them to become child labourers and remain in the same context. This was again because of the poor socio economic background of respondents, lack of awareness about alternate avenues for engagement and having no/little idea about how to improve their life chances/opportunities.

Table 6.6: Aspirations of Child Labourers

Level of Aspirations	Frequency	Percentage
To continue in the same work	8	6.66
Low ambitions (Earn some money)	7	5.8
High ambitions (owner of hotel, doctor, actor etc.)	9	7.5
To get engaged in skilled job	2	1.7
Never thought about the future	94	78.3
Total	**120**	**100**

Awareness about Compulsory Education and Legal Provisions

The National Policy on Education (1986) and the Right to Education Act (2009) recommended free and compulsory education for all children below 14 years of age. Prior to it, for compulsory education provision was made in the Indian Constitution (Article-45), for all children up to the age of 14 years. Besides that, the Government of India implemented the Child Labour Prohibition and Regulation Act, 1986. In spite of this, the government has not yet been able to make primary education compulsory and ensure that all children in the stipulated age group get enrolled in schools. As a result of it and because of massive poverty, children of poorer families get employed at early ages.

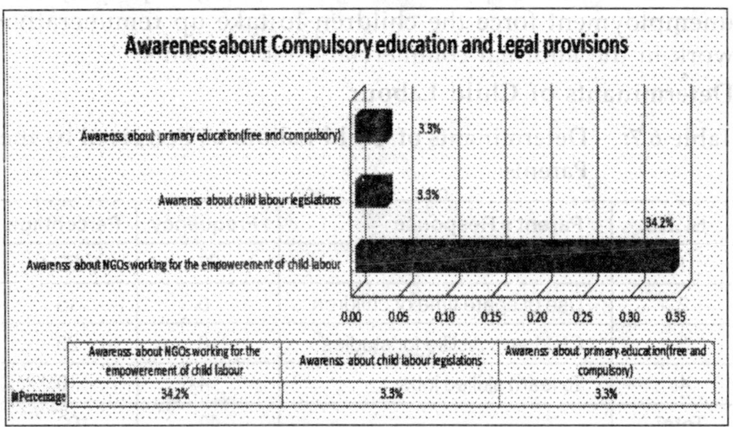

	Awarenss about NGOs working for the empowerement of child labour	Awarenss about child labour legislations	Awarenss about primary education(free and compulsory)
Percentage	34.2%	3.3%	3.3%

Fig. 6.1: Awareness about Legislations and Compulsory Education

The above diagram reveals that a very few respondents (3.3%) were aware of child labour legislation which bans employment of children below 14 years. These children also did not have knowledge about free and compulsory education being provided. However, a significant number of children (34.2%) were aware about various non-governmental organizations working nearby for the education and empowerment of child labourers.

SECTION – II

PARENTS' RESPONSES

In this section, the determinants of child labour as reported by their parents have been presented. In addition to this, other important factors, poverty and inadequate income of the parents, illiteracy of the parents and occupation of the parents were also discussed separately as these variables were responsible for the growth in the incidence of child labour.

The parents also play a pivotal role in the incidence of child labour. The low income of the parents which is not adequate to meet the basic needs of the family, forces the parents to send their children to work and supplement the family income. Thus, poverty propels parents to send their children to distant places to work. The abject poverty and unemployment force the children to take up remunerative work in the informal commercial establishments.

Determinants of Child Labour

Table 6.7: Determinants of Child Labour as Perceived by the Parents

Sl .No.	Parent's Response	Frequency	Percentage
1.	Poverty	22	55
2.	Use of spare time of children	6	15
3.	Children's dislike for studies	8	20
4.	To learn skilled jobs	4	10
Total		40	100

When parents/guardians were asked to state their reasons for sending their children to the labour force, the study revealed that 22(55%) sent their children because of the poverty. Six (15%) parents reported that they sent their child to job as he was wasting his time. Eight (20%) parents reported that their child was not interested in studies, followed by 4(10%) who viewed that children were sent to jobs to learn skilled job so that in the future they could be employed in the market easily.

So, again poverty seems to emerge as the important reason which compelled the parents to send their children to remunerative jobs.

Poverty and Inadequate Income of the Parents

There are a number of factors at the household level that determine whether a child should be sent to work or not. It is often believed that it is the poverty that is the main cause of child labour. The association between household poverty and child labour is beyond dispute. The intergenerational cycle of poverty and child labour persists and that cycle continues for generations. If the households do not have enough money to meet the basic needs, children are usually sent to work to earn money for the fulfillment of the basic needs of the family. So, the most important cause of child labour is widespread poverty. In India, which is a developing country, poverty forces the parents to send their children to seek employment. Diseases and other contingencies may need extra money and the employment of children is resorted to as an easily accessible method to bring in partial money.

Table 6.8: Poverty as a Crucial Determinant

Sl. No.	Poverty as a Crucial Determinant for Child Labour	Frequency	Percentage
1.	Children	48	40
2.	Parents	22	55
3.	Employers	6	15

In the present study forty per cent of child labourers reported poverty as the main reason for their engagement in the occupations, whereas fifty five per cent of parents and fifteen per cent of employers also reported that poverty was the prime cause of child labour.

While poverty is one of the leading factors resulting child labour, there is a reverse effect too, such that it remains locked in a vicious circle. When the parents send their children to work, particularly to hazardous work, their potential to work may be declined by the age of 30 to 35 years as they are early starters of work. Hence it is like a *vicious cycle*, wherein when they become parents, they again send their wards to work when they reach their forties and this continues as a never ending process and poverty continues. This is due to the inability of the parents who began their life as child labourers.

Poverty of the households may be due to several factors: inadequate income of the family, due to unemployed adults, absence of schemes for family allowance, large family etc. Child labour actually creates and perpetuates poverty. It not only displaces adults from their jobs but also condemns the child to a life of unskilled, badly paid work. Ultimately this leads to the same impoverished, unemployed fate as their parents. Children become part of the vicious circle of poverty from one generation to another generation.

The study conducted in the Cuttack city of Orissa pointed out that due to poverty, it becomes difficult for the parents to bring up their children but to engage them in some form of economic activity to earn their livelihood and support their families (Mishra and Mishra, 1990). The study of urban working children in Bangalore (Patil, 1988) also reported that economic compulsions were the strong reason forcing 46.33% of child labourers to seek employment. The study of Kulshrestha (1978) also concludes that factors like poverty, lack of education and large family size were responsible for child labour. Ahmed (1999) has concluded after a quantitative cross country empirical study that child labour is basically associated with inequality in society but not with poverty. Both inequality and poverty in the society have been currently found to be the consequence of capability deprivation-deprivation from quality of being able to do something and, hence, the latter is a more responsible variable for the existence and continuum supply of child labour (Foster and Sen, 1998).

The problem of child labour is interrelated to the inadequate wages of the parents. This inadequacy in wages of parents compels them to send their children to do some work in return of some wages in order to fulfill their basic economic needs and the employers also takes the benefit of this weakness by providing work to the children on low wages inspite of the various protective laws. The present study also shows (Table 5.16) that for none of the parents the income is more than Rs. 5000 per month.

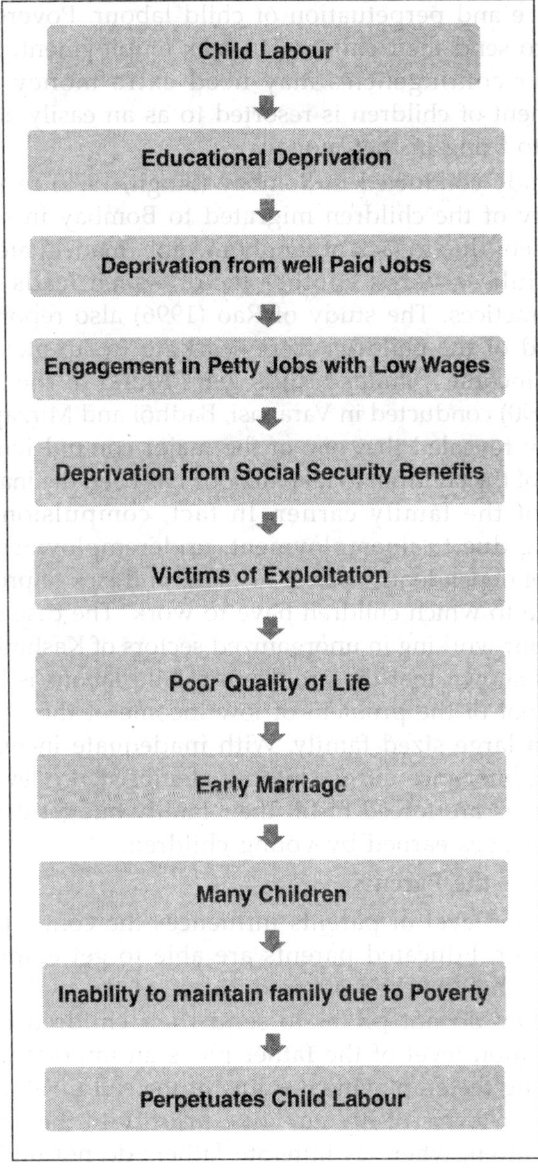

Fig. 6.2: Vicious Cycle of Poverty and Child Labour

Chronic poverty is the largest factor responsible for the prevalence and perpetuation of child labour. Poverty forces parents to send their children to seek employment. Diseases and other contingencies may need extra money and the employment of children is resorted to as an easily accessible method to bring in that money.

A study conducted in Bombay (Singh, 1979) reveals that a majority of the children migrated to Bombay in search of employment due to lack of family income. Inadequate income of the adult earner is another factor which leads to child labour practices. The study of Rao (1996) also reported that one- third of the children were working to supplement the parental income. Similar results were found in the study of Singh (1990) conducted in Varanasi, Badhoi and Mirzapur belt. The study revealed that one of the major compulsions of the majority of the children to take up jobs has been the inadequate income of the family earner. In fact, compulsion is also increasing due to unemployment, underemployment, large number of dependents, little or no skills and lack of productive assets due to which children have to work. The case study of child labour working in unorganized sectors of Kashmir (Shah, 1992) has shown that the problem of child labour is basically an off shoot of the problem of low income of the parents to support a large sized family. With inadequate income even for the maintenance of the children at subsistence level, these poor parents are forced to fill their family budget deficits by the little wages earned by young children.

Illiteracy of the Parents

Literacy level of parents influences the continuation of child labour. Educated parents are able to get employment easily. Further, as they become aware of the evils of child labour, they do not prefer to send their children to work. The education level of the father plays an important role in determining the employment status of the child. Fathers, who have higher levels of literacy give priority to the education of the children, where as illiterate fathers do not understand the importance of education and hence do not send their children for schooling. In many cases, parents particularly in villages and urban slums are themselves illiterate and do not realize the importance of educating their children. They are unaware of the injustice done to the children by making them work instead of sending them to schools. They are ignorant about the rights and needs of children. Some parents, even though they realize the importance of educating their children, are compelled to send their children to work due to economic reasons. A large number of parents of poor families find no meaning in education as it does not guarantee a job in future. They prefer to send children for work at an early age instead of sending them to school with the hope that the children will at least acquire a skill or learn a trade by the time they become adults.

So, the present study revealed that literacy level of the parents has a strong co relation with the incidence of child labour as 25(62.5%) parents were found to be illiterate.

Thus; parental illiteracy is also a contributory factor for existence of child labour. Majority of the child labour comes from illiterate families. Overall the literacy level of the child labourers is very low and as such children are engaged in small scale commercial establishments as a means of survival as this occupation doesn't require prior training or education. The incidence of child labour is found to be more in families whose fathers or mothers are illiterate. Sharma and Sharma (1997) have also come out with a similar result in their study on child labour in the glass industry of Firozabad. The study of George (1977) revealed that most of the children who came to labour force belonged to lower literacy group. His study reported that forty four per cent of child labourer's parents were illiterate.

Table 6.9: Literacy Level of Parents

Literacy Level of the Parents	Frequency	Percentage
Illiterate	25	62.5
Basic education	11	27.5
Primary	3	7.5
Middle	1	2.5
Total	**40**	**100**

Occupation of Parents

Table 6.10: Occupation of Parents

Occupation	Frequency	Percentage
Employed in petty jobs	19	47.5
Unemployed	2	5
Truck driver	1	2.5
Self employed	18	45
Total	**40**	**100**

The above table shows that a significant number of parents 21(48%) were either engaged in petty jobs or unemployed, which is of course an important contributing factor for the incidence of child labour. Lumpkin and Douglas have very rightly pointed out that two-fifth of the children seek work due to the unemployment of adult member of the family. Nearly two-third of the children were at work because the adult member of the family had no employment or had some part time job, and one- third of children wanted to work due to the serious cuts in the pay of the adult(Lumpkin & Douglas, 1938).

The study of Savitri (1985) also stated that poverty, large family, the death of bread winner, physical and mental illness of the parents or unemployment of adult members in the family are some of the reasons which contribute towards child labour. The study undertaken by the researcher supports all the above findings of different researchers.

SECTION - III

EMPLOYERS' RESPONSES

It is not only the children and their parents who are responsible for the early entry of child in the work force. Child labour can be attributed considerably to a segment of the employers who prefer children for various reasons. One of the main objectives of the employer is to get more profit on limited expenditure. Moreover, they are aware of the economic compulsions of the families having extreme poverty.

They watch out for exploiting the parental economic compulsions when they know that children of the backward families are more tolerant, can be put on difficult jobs for long hours, even on lower wages. The employers also understand the productive quality of children who do not raise grievances pertaining to their working conditions.

Many employers prefer child labourers to adult workers for various reasons as follows.

- It is easy to handle the child in factory or at work place
- There are no discipline problems, no unions
- The children have nimble fingers
- The children can do more work than adults
- Children get one-third or one half of wages an adult gets
- Employers need not spend on welfare facilities or pay benefits to child labourers
- Children are obedient and it is easy for the employer to get more work from a child and for long hours but the same is not possible with an adult.

The reasons stated in the report of the committee on child labour(1980) for employers preference for children in work are : " less age and status conscious, lesser affliction by feelings of guilt and shame, no hesitation to do non status even demeaning jobs, activeness, agility and quickness and lesser feeling of tiredness , greater in discipline and control, less expensive to maintain, superior adaptive qualities, lack of organization, moral consideration of employers to help and to provide succour to destitute or forsaken children and acquisition of fitness through initiation in the early age". The National commission of labour (1969) has also pointed out that "quite often it is the feeling of sympathy rather than the desire to exploit which weighs with employers in employing child workers.

The following table describes the various reasons cited by employers in appointing child labour.

Table 6.11: Reasons for Hiring Child Labourers

Employer's Responses	Frequency	Percentage
Very cheap	7	17.5
Obey Orders	9	22.5
Child centric work	4	10
Children's need for job	6	15
Learning trade skills	13	40
Parents request for proving job to their children	7	17.5
Total	**40**	**100**

The table reveals that 13(40%) parents reported that children were engaged in the job only because they wanted to learn the trade. 7(17.5%) viewed that their parents had requested them to give employment to their child. It may be that their parents were financially very weak and are unable to fulfill the basic necessities of the life. 7(17.5%) employers reported that children were very obedient and obey orders. These children never complained on any issues. They work harder and are happy with their salary. However, 6(15%) employers reported them children had approached them directly for job due to family pressure to supplement family income followed by 4(10%) who viewed that the work is basically child centric and the children can do these unskilled jobs efficiently.

So, it can be said that learning the trade skills was the most important reason cited by the employer's for the employment of children in small scale commercial establishments.

A study conducted by Singh (1990) in Varanasi also reported that employers prefers children because they work hard, it is cheaper and can be put on any job and can work for long hours; and lastly children create less troubles in the workplace. These factors establish the importance of employer's willingness to employ children which further becomes an important reason for increasing child labour.

On the basis of the above discussions, case studies using narratives and from review of literature, the following determinants were found which were responsible for the prevalence of child labourers in Delhi. The responses of children, parents and employers of child labourers as well as the various structural factors identified by the researcher are presented below.

Table 6.12: Determinants for the Incidence of Child Labour

Children's Response	Parent's Response	Employer's Response	Structural Factors (Identified by the Researcher)
Poverty	Poverty	Poverty	• Inequality of development between regions leading to migration • Rapid urbanization • Rural urban migration • Bad governance • Lack of effective enforcement of legislation • Social exclusion of marginal groups • Insufficient financial and political commitments to education • Lack of decent work for adults.
Migration of parents	–	–	
Lack of interest in studies and school dropout	Children's dislike for studies	–	
Supplementing family income	Supplementing family income	Parent's request for providing jobs to their children for supplementing family income	
Self-desire	Self-desire	Children's need for job	
Family pressure	–	–	
Death of parents	–	–	
Family indebtedness	–	–	
Crop failure/draught	–	–	
Landless parents	–	–	
Family business	–	–	
Parental abuse	–	–	
Alcoholism of parents	–	–	
Unemployment of parents	–	–	
To learn skilled jobs	–	Desire of child respondents to acquire necessary skills of special trades very cheap and was obedient Child centric work	

7

Dimensions on Child Labour

INTRODUCTION

The present chapter 'dimensions of child labour' is divided into two sections. Section-I describes the work history, working conditions and terms of employment of child labourers while the section-II presents the living conditions of child labourers.

SECTION – I

WORK HISTORY, WORKING CONDITIONS AND TERMS OF EMPLOYMENT

This section deals with the work history, terms of employment and working conditions of child labourers in Delhi. It focuses dimensions like the age of entry of children into work force, monthly wages, hours of work, overtime, rest interval, leave, attitude of employers and others. An attempt has been made to highlight the kind of disciplinary actions taken by the employer, the work satisfaction of children and other allied aspects related with the work life of the child labourers.

The working conditions and terms of employment are two important aspects which determine the employee-employer relationship at the work place. The terms of employment paves the way for personal satisfaction of the workers in terms of wages, over time, bonus, leave, holidays, and medical benefits etc. It also indicates other welfare and social security components linked with the employment. While the terms of work helps the workers to meet their personal needs, better working conditions help them to work effectively, efficiently and productively. The better and conducive working conditions also have a great impact on various aspects of the worker's life like work satisfaction and harmonious interpersonal relationship.

It is a well established fact that age plays a dominant role in shaping personality and values of responsibility to work and to participate in different walks of life. It was against this background that information on age of the respondents was collected.

Age of Entry into the Work

Table 7.1: Age of Entry into the Work

Sl. No.	Age	No. of Respondents	Percentage
1.	Less than 5	3	2.5
2.	5-7	5	4.2
3.	7-9	27	22.5
4.	9-11	64	53.3
5.	11-13	21	17.5
Total		120	100

The above table indicates that a majority 64(53.3%) of child labourers entered the work force between the age group of 9-11 years. 27(22.5%) of children started working between the age group of 7-9 years and 21(17.5%) children started their work at a bit later stage i.e. between the age of 11-13 years. A few children were found who also started doing work before the age of 5 years. Thus, we see that there is no such particular age at which the children started working. Though in the Constitution it is stated that children should not be allowed to work till they attain the age of 14 years, yet they are being employed as early as 5 years of years. The study also revealed that the children of the poor families entered work at an early stage to support the family.

A study conducted by Singh,2006 on the problems of child labourers and their working conditions in Agra city revealed that most of the child labourers that come to the labour market were between the ages of 11 to 13 years. It means that when they were expected to be studying in primary classes, they were forced to enter the labour market. Another study conducted by NIPPCD (1977) revealed that 18.7 per cent of the children started working before they completed an age of 12 years. These children were found to be seen working in small establishments like shops, way side restaurants, brick kilns, garages, construction work, metal workshops, handloom and handicraft industries or as domestic help.

Initial Work of the Child Labourers

Table 7.2: Initial Work of the Child Labourers

Sl.No.	Whether this was their First Job	No. of Respondents	Percentage
1.	Yes	116	96.7
2.	No	4	3.3
Total		**120**	**100**

The table reveals that it was the first work engagement for a large majority 116(96.7%) of children. For a very few number of children 4 (3.3%), it was their second work. These children left their previous work as it was not of their liking and also faced difficulty in adjustment with their employers. One of the children who had changed his work reported that he was being physically abused by his employer. On the whole, it can be said that the once child was engaged in some work, he mostly continued to be in that very work only. Only if the work was not suitable and the working conditions were not good, did the children change their work.

Sources of Getting Work

Regarding means of getting a work, a significant proportion of the child labourers informed that they got their work either with the help of relatives who were already employed or through friends who were working in Delhi.

As can be seen from the Figure 7.1, 19% of the respondents indicated that they were working in family work/vocations. About 6% of the respondents viewed that they got the work through their own efforts. So it can be said that children mostly get work through friends/relatives or parents.

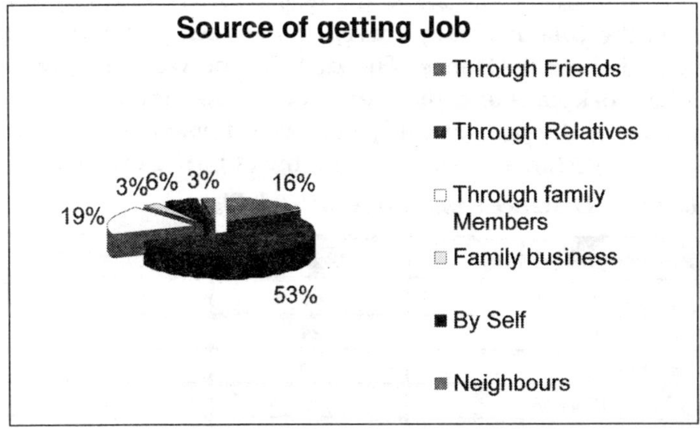

Fig. 7.1: Source of Getting Job

Duration of Work in the Present Context

The researcher had also asked the respondents about the duration of work in the present context.

Table 7.3: Duration of Work in the Present Context

Duration of Work in the Present Job	Frequency	Percentage
6 months to less than 1 year	59	49.2
1 year to less than 2 years	38	31.7
2 years to less than 3 years	17	14.2
3 year to less than 4 years	3	2.5
4 years and above	3	2.5
Total	**120**	**100.0**

From the above table it is clear that 59(49.2%) children were in the present work since the last six months to one year, followed by 38(31.7%) of them who were in it between one and two years. Seventeen children were in the present work for two to three years. The study also reported that the least number of children had worked for more than three years in the present work.

Distance from Home to Work Place

The researcher had asked the respondents (children) how far was the distance they travelled between their place of work and their residence. The distance between residence and the workplace and the means of transportation are also significant in the present study as it would enable us to know how much distance is travelled by the children everyday.

Table 7.4: Distance from Home to Work Place

Distance to Work Place	Frequency	Percentage
Less than 1 KM	69	57.5
1-2 KM	24	20.0
2-3 KM	6	5.0
More than 3 KM	6	5.0
Stay in work place	15	12.5
Total	**120**	**100.0**

The above table revealed that a majority 69(57.5%) of child labourers were staying very near (less than 1 km) to their work place. 24(20%) of the respondents stayed within the distance of 1-2 kms. A few respondents were staying more than 2 kms from their place of work. However, 15(12.5%) respondents stayed at their place of work. These respondents were employed mostly in dhabas/tea stalls and also in garages.

The researcher also tried to find out the means of transportation used to commute from home to their place of work. A majority of the respondents (99) reported that they came to their place of work by walking and only six respondents reported that they used bicycle for transportation. The workplace were thus more often within walking distance. Perhaps, the children and/or their wards preferred a workplace, closer to their living place, unless forced by circumstances. When the child respondents were asked whether they met with any accidents/ injury during the time of transportation, almost all the respondents reported that they did not meet with any such accident.

The study conducted by Kumar and Singh, 2006 on the problems of child labour in urban informal sector (with special reference to Allahabad) reported that nearly two-thirds of child labourers had to cover on an average a daily distance of 3-4 kilometers to reach their place of work and returned to their homes on foot.

Employment Status of the Child

The data on the nature of employment of the child labourers is presented in Figure 7.2. A majority of the respondents (55%) pointed out that they were having full time work. 21% of the respondents viewed that their work was basically part time in nature as they were working only to gain experience as well as to supplement the family income. 8% of the respondents said that their work was permanent in nature. These respondents were mainly working in family work/vocations or in relatives business. Only 4% of the respondents said that their job is casual in nature as they were not compelled by their parents to do the work.

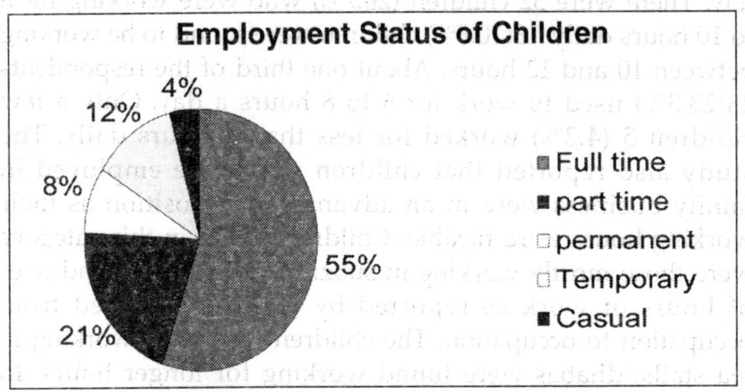

Fig. 7.2: Employment Status of the Child

They were working to earn some pocket money for their personal expenditure. However, some of the child labourers (12%) pointed out that there was no such permanent kind of work. They were employed and paid till the employer desired to take work from them. In case, they did not have work, the children were laid off and payment was done according to the output of each child labourer.

Working Hours

A large number of children were mostly employed in unorganized informal sectors, where working hours were not regulated by any of the statutes, and hence, children had to work for excessively long hours.

Table 7.5: Working Hours of Children

Working Hours	Frequency	Per cent
Less then 4 hours	5	4.2
4 hours - 6 hours	17	14.2
6 hours - 8 hours	28	23.3
8 hours - 10 hours	32	26.7
10 hours – 12 hours	13	10.8
More than 12 hours	25	20.8
Total	**120**	**100.0**

The above table indicates that irrespective of occupation, 25(20.8%) children were working for more than 12 hours a day. There were 32 children (26.7%) who were working for 8 to 10 hours daily. 13(10.8%) children were found to be working between 10 and 12 hours. About one third of the respondents 28(23.3%) used to work for 6 to 8 hours a day. Only a few children 5 (4.2%) worked for less than 4 hours daily. The study also reported that children who were employed in family business were in an advantageous position as their working hours were flexible. Children falling in this category were those mostly working in subzi mandis. The spread over of hours of work as reported by children differed from occupation to occupation. The children who were working in tea stalls/dhabas were found working for longer hours. In dhaba/tea stalls, children were found engaged since early morning to late night. Those children engaged in subzi mandi were found to be working from early morning. In one particular case, a child who was engaged in subzi mandi started his work at 2.a.m. in the morning. In garages and shops children worked from morning to late evening.

Barooch (1977) in his study had also highlighted the unhealthy conditions in which children worked. It had also brought into limelight the long working hours of children in construction work, on tea estates, in dhabas, way side restaurants, cycle and auto repairing workshops and in domestic work. The Report of the National Commission of Labour, (Government of India, 1969) had also reported that in many cities large numbers of young boys were employed for long hours. Even children of five years of age were found in some of these places working without adequate meal, intervals or weekly rest days and worked for at least 10 to 12 hours daily.

Weekly Holidays

Weekly holidays are a must for everybody in order to relax and refresh one self. Whether it is a child or an adult, every one needs weekly holidays. In this background, the researcher wanted to know from the child labourers whether they were getting any weekly offs. The following table shows whether the children got weekly holidays or not.

Table 7.6: Status of Weekly Offs for Child Labourers

Sl. No.	Whether they got Weekly Holidays	No. of Respondents	Percentage
1.	Yes	49	40.8
2.	No	71	59.2
Total		120	100

It was very disheartening to note that a majority of child labourers 71(59.2%) were not getting weekly holidays and had to work on Sundays as well as other holidays. Around 41% child labourers responded positively and viewed that they got one day off in a week. These children were mainly engaged within their family business or in their relative's business. These respondents also reported that besides weekly offs they also got leave on festivals like Diwali, Holi, Id and other important festivals. Only 20 respondents, mostly those working in dhabas/tea stalls and garages reported that they could take leave for two days in a month without pay. So, the researcher found that there was no provision for paid holidays and leave of any kind. Remuneration was based on the principle that the wages would be paid according to the number of days they had really worked. If they were absent, their wages were accordingly deducted.

Rest Intervals

The researcher had also asked the children whether they got any rest intervals during the working hours. In the work situation, it is necessary to make provisions for rest intervals so that the harmful effects of work on health caused by continuous work for long hours may be avoided and worker's efficiency may be restored and maintained.

Table 7.7: Rest Intervals Provided to Child Labourers

Sl. No.	Whether they got Rest Interval	No. of Respondents	Percentage
1.	Yes	115	97
2.	No	5	3
Total		120	100

From the Table 7.7, it is found that a majority of children 115(97%) were getting rest intervals during the course of work. Only 5(3%) children replied that they were not getting any rest interval. These children were engaged in dhabas/tea stalls situated near by Subzi mandi and in bus stops which always remained very busy.

During discussion with the children, it was found that those children who were mostly engaged in dhabas/tea stalls got about half an hour to one hour rest interval. After the rush hour (lunch time) the workers got half an hour or so to relax. After relaxing, they again went for work as it was time for serving tea and snacks.

Those children engaged in shops reported that they get about 1 hour to 2 hours rest interval during lunch time.

The children who were employed in garages reported that, they got rest when there were no customers. Only 4 children opined that, they got rest whenever they wanted as they were working in family business (subzi mandis) .They had the privilege because their parents did not pressurize them to work more, if they felt tired.

Over Time Work

Table 7.8: Over Time Work

Whether Children do Overtime Work	Frequency	Per cent
Yes	73	61.6
No	46	38.3
Total	**120**	**100.0**

In order to earn more money, the child labourers sometimes did overtime work. Keeping this fact in mind, the researcher asked them whether they were working beyond their scheduled timings. The above table revealed that a majority of the children (73 out of 120) were doing over time work and the rest 46(38.3%) were not doing any overtime work. Those who were working overtime work were provided with free food and some pocket money. The children who were employed in tea shops/dhabas and subzi mandi were doing overtime work. So, it can be said that children even in tender ages were forced to do overtime work, beyond their scheduled timings.

Children's Monthly Earning

The children are generally paid their wages either in cash or in kind or in both. The study revealed that most of the children were paid in cash. The respondents (children, parents and employers) were asked about children's monthly earnings. The wages which the working children received was dependent upon various factors like nature of job-skilled, semi skilled or unskilled, duration of working hours, risk involvement in the work, nature of employment etc. The need to earn a wage to supplement the family income in many cases generally forced the children into the labour market. But their employers did not pay them adequate wages, since for them child labour meant economy of labour cost. However, all the employers were silent on the issue and did not exactly mention the children's monthly earning. They only said that wages were given on the basis of their performance in the work. The employers also viewed that these children were kept on 'probation' and were expected to learn the work. The following table presents the parent's as well as children's views about the monthly earning of the children.

Table 7.9: Children's Monthly Earning (Children's Responses)

Children's Monthly Income	Number of Respondents (Children)	Percentage
Less than Rs. 500	18	15
Rs. 500- less than Rs. 1000	51	42.5
Rs. 1000- less than Rs. 1500	38	31.66
Rs. 1500- less than Rs. 2000	7	5.83
Rs. 2000- less than Rs. 2500	4	3.33
Rs. 2500- less than Rs. 3000	2	1.66
Total	**120**	**100**

The above table indicates that a sizeable number of child labourers 51(42.5%) received a monthly earnings between Rs. 500 to Rs. 1000.There were 38(31.66%) children who earned between Rs. 1000 to Rs. 1500. There were 18 (15%) children who reported that they earned less than Rs. 500. Some of these children in this category were employed in family business and received only pocket money less than Rs. 500. Besides that there were few children who earned more than Rs. 1500 per month. Almost all the child labourers received their earning in cash, some on daily basis, some on weekly basis and some on monthly basis, depending upon the type of work they worked in the parents were also asked about the children's' monthly earning. The following table presents the same as reported by the parents.

Table 7.10: Children's Monthly Earnings (Parent's Responses)

Children's Monthly Income	Number of Respondents (Parents)	Percentage
Less than Rs. 500	4	7.5
Rs. 500- less than Rs. 1000	19	47.5
Rs. 1000- less than Rs. 1500	12	30
Rs. 1500- less than Rs. 2000	3	7.5
Rs. 2000- less than Rs. 2500	1	2.5
Rs. 2500- less than Rs. 3000	1	2.5
Total	120	100

A majority of parents 19(47.5%) reported that their children received a monthly earnings between Rs. 500 and Rs. 1000. The study reported that wages of the working children in Delhi ranged from Rs. 500 to Rs. 3000. There were 12(30%) children who earned between Rs. 1000 and Rs. 1500 per month followed by 4(7.5%) children whose earnings were less than Rs. 500 per month. Only 2 parents reported that their children earned more than Rs. 2000 per month. So, it can be said that children received very less income in return to their hard labour. The study revealed that the children working in the informal sectors are generally not protected either by legal restriction or by strong trade unions. So, this deprives them not only of the legal minimum wage but often of other benefits available to these workers working in the formal sector. Thus, the wages of children in informal sectors was very low.

Payment of Wages

The timely payment of wages is an important factor in increasing the productivity of the establishment. A majority of the children 61(50%) told that they got their wages once in a month, 38(31.7%) of children respondents viewed that they got wages on a daily basis and 15(12.5%) children received their wages on weekly basis. Rest of the respondents expressed that they were getting only pocket money. So, it could be said that wages were paid weekly, daily or monthly.

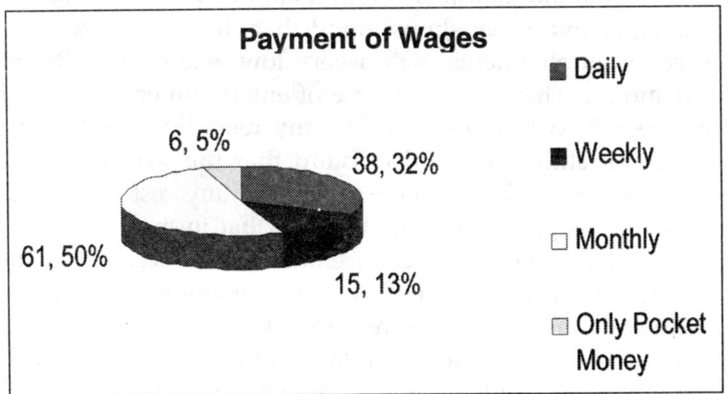

Fig. 7.3: Payment of Wages

Recipients of Children's Earnings

The researcher had also tried to find out the actual recipients of children's earnings. The question of the recipients of the child labourer's earnings is very relevant to the present study as it enables one to gain some insight into certain practices.

Table 7.11: Recipient of Children's Income

Recipient of Children' Income	Frequency	Percentage
Parents/relatives	42	35
Children	59	49
No wages	19	16
Total	**120**	**100**

The data revealed that a majority of the respondents (children) replied that their wages were paid to their parents and relatives. These children were neither aware of monthly earning nor the terms of contract. As many as 42(35%) respondents said that wages were given to them and 59(49%) viewed that the wages were given to their parents/relatives and the rest of the respondents did not receive any wages as they were placed in family business. The practice of receiving wages on behalf of the child labourers was prevalent in almost all sectors included in the study. However, its prevalence was greater in tea stalls/ dhabas.

Mehta and Jaswal (1996) in their study on child labour in tea stalls and sweet shops found that children worked in all sorts of employments with a very low wage below Rs. 350/ per month. They had no source of entertainment and worked between 8 to 15 hours without any rest. Sinha (1994) in his study on child labour also found that the wages were low and they worked continuously without any rest interval. The study by Singh, (2006) also reported that in most of the cases wages were paid to the children. Daily and weekly payment system was also prevalent in auto workshops and furniture industry. The study also reported that mostly wages were paid in cash directly to the child labourers by their employers. About 17 per cent parents received the wages of the child labourers. It was only in 5 per cent cases i.e. only in leather and dhabas where middlemen received the payment from the employers on behalf of the child. Another study conducted by Singh et.al on working children in Bombay (NIPPCD, 1980) revealed that majority of the children(68.2%) were getting salary of Rs. 100 or below per month. The study also reported that the minimum number of hours a child worked was 4 hours and the maximum 14 hours, the average being 8.7 hours.

Basis of Children's Employment

Table 7.12: Basis of Children's Employment

Basis of Children's Employment	No. of Respondents	Percentage
Verbal Contract	32	78%
No Written or verbal Contract	8	20%
Total	**40**	**100**

The above table reveals that 32(78%) of the parents expressed that their children were engaged into the work through verbal contract. These parents informed that they had negotiated with the employers regarding the wage, working hours etc. 8% of the respondents viewed that there was no such agreement as some children got jobs on their own and some children were engaged in family business. So, it can be said that mostly it was parents/relatives, who had negotiated with the employers regarding the terms and conditions of employment.

Nature of Work Performed by Children

The child labourers were ordinarily employed as helpers to do all kinds of unskilled work. Some of them were taken as learners and given independent job assignments in course of time.

A majority of the respondents 87(72.5%) reported that they were doing unskilled work followed by 25(20.8%) who were into semi skilled work. A few children 8(6.7%) said that they were doing skilled work.

The children engaged in dhabas/tea stalls reported that they were mainly doing unskilled work. Their duties consisted of sweeping the premises, dusting and cleaning of chairs, cleaning the vessels such as cups, spoons, plates and glasses and other containers used to prepare and keep food, serving the customers by visiting the nearby shops etc.

Table 7.13: Nature of Work Performed by the Children

Nature of Work Performed	Frequency	Per cent
Skilled	8	6.7
Semi-Skilled	25	20.8
Unskilled	87	72.5
Total	**120**	**100.0**

The children who were employed in garages mostly performed semi skilled and skilled work. Their work consisted of dismantling machinery and parts of the vehicle, cleaning and oiling and also in few cases they refit the nuts and bolts under the supervision of adult workers.

The children employed in subzi mandi mostly did unskilled work. Their duties consisted of collecting vegetables, supplying to the shops and weighing goods etc. Those children engaged in shops only weighed goods and gave it to customers.

So, it can be said that most of the children employed in informal sector were doing unskilled work. Most of the children (except those working in shops) reported that they were working in very unhygienic, congested and dirty places. They also reported that there were no toilet facilities, drinking water facilities. Some of the respondents also reported that they had to work in the open space.

A majority of the employers (25) reported that children mostly helped adult workers at the workplace. These employers were mainly the owners of garage and tea shops/ dhabas and shops. Rest of the respondents (employers) reported that children were also able to work on their own even in shops and subzi mandi.

Level of Work Satisfaction

Work satisfaction is dependent upon several factors such as wages, hours of work, physical condition of the work place, nature of work, employer's behaviour, regularity of payment and other facilities. Keeping these points in view, an attempt has been made to know the satisfaction level of the child labourers.

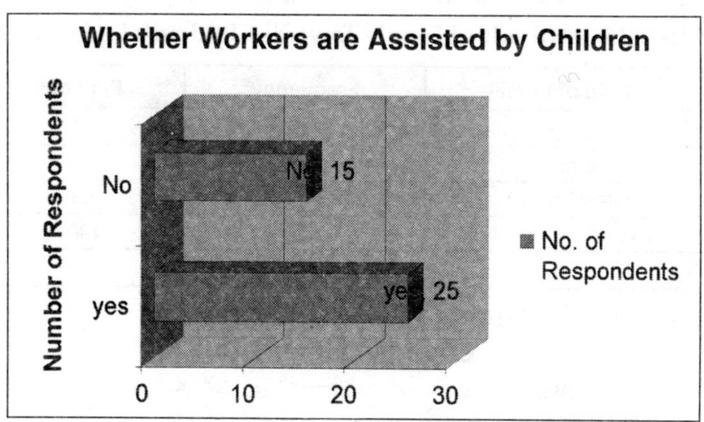

Fig. 7.4: Whether Workers are Assisted by Children

Table 7.14: Level of Satisfaction of the Child Labourers

Level of Satisfaction	Frequency	Percentage
Fully	46	38.3
Partially	27	22.5
Not At All	47	39.2
Total	**120**	**100.0**

The above table reveals that 46(38.3%) children were fully satisfied with their present work. Those who were satisfied reported that they had become economically independent and were able to support their family financially to meet the basic needs. 27 (22.5%) respondents who were partially satisfied viewed that they were getting less pay and worked for longer hours. Only 2 respondents (who were partially satisfied) in this category said that they missed their family members who were staying in villages. 47(39.2%) respondents said that they were not at all satisfied with the present work because of rude behaviour of their employers, temporary nature of work, lower wages and longer hours of work, physical abuses by employers and lack of facilities at the work place etc.

Attitude of Family Towards Children's Engagement

The researcher also wanted to know the attitude of the family towards children's engagement in work from children themselves, their parents as well as their employers.

Table 7.15: Attitude of Family Towards Children's Engagement

Attitude of Family	Frequency	Per cent
Favourable	108	90
Indifferent	8	6.6
Unfavourable	4	3.3
Total	**120**	**100**

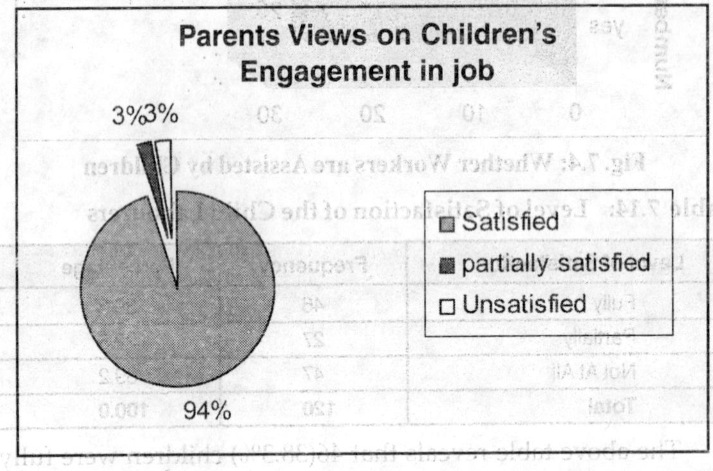

Fig. 7.5: Attitude of Family Towards Children's Engagement in Job

Table 7.15 indicates that 108 (90%) children reported that their family had a positive attitude towards their work engagement. Only 4(3.3%) of the respondents reported that their parents were not happy with their work. In 8(6.6%) cases, children viewed that their parents were indifferent towards their work.However, 38(95%) parents viewed that they were satisfied as their children were engaged in some work and earning some money. Only two parents were not satisfied with the children's engagement and said that their child was not interested in education and was having undesirable peer group and had started drinking alcohol and smoking cigarettes. So, they forcefully sent them to get engaged in work.

The researcher also asked the employers regarding the children's engagement. 28(70%) of the employers reported that children were working with full knowledge of their parents/guardians while 12(30%) employers viewed that their parents were relieved due to the employment of their children as these children would contribute some money for the household expenditure.

The foregoing analysis clearly points out that the children were pushed in a variety of urban informal activities due to the insistence of their parents.

Attitude of the Employers/Co-workers/Customers towards the Child Labour

The children were asked about the attitude of the employers/co-workers and customers as well as the treatment meted out to them during the course of work. A majority of the respondents reported that, the attitude of the employers/co-workers and customers towards the children were cordial and kind. Only a few respondents (as shown in the table) said that they were sometimes harassed by their employers/customers and co workers.

Table 7.16: Attitude of the Employers/Co-workers/Customers Towards the Child

Attitudes towards the Child	Employers Frequency	Percentage	Co-workers Frequency	Percentage	Customers Frequency	Percentage
Very cordial	37	30.8	36	30.0	25	20.8
Kind enough	37	30.8	21	17.5	28	23.3
Indifferent	36	30.0	40	33.33	55	45.83
Hostile	7	5.8	8	6.7	8	6.7
Did not answer	3	2.5	15	12.5	4	3.3
Total	120	100	120	100	120	100

These children complained that their employers/co-workers used to scold them for every small fault and sometimes without any reason. They were also sometimes physically harassed by their employers and co workers. The findings testify that a better understanding and good relations between the employer and child labourers existed in the present study. One of the reasons that employers pretended to be kind to the child labourers was so that they could ensure their stay in the work, use them for long hours and get the work done at low wages. So, one can say that the relationship of the employer, customer and co-worker with the child was satisfactory.

Impact of Work on the Health of Child Labourers

The nature and quantum of work is likely to have effect on physical as well as mental growth of the child labourers. The respondents were asked whether their present work was harmful to their health. Only 14(11.7%) respondents viewed that their present work was not too conducive to their health. These respondents reported that they suffered from fever, tiredness, headache, joint pain, stomach pain, depression, anxiety, tension and sometimes physical injury. A majority of respondents 62(51.7%) reported that no health hazard was associated with their work, whereas 44(36.7%) respondents said that they did not know whether their work was harmful to their health. So, the findings revealed that most of the children did not have any idea whether the work was harmful to their health or not.

A significant number 41(34.2%) of the respondents viewed that during illness, they used to visit private doctors for treatment and consultation. Also significant number of respondents (31) reported that they used to visit local practioners and chemists for medicines. Only a few respondents (8) said that they used to visit the government hospitals for treatment. 101(84.2%) respondents viewed that they did not face any monetary crisis for treatment because of the support of their parents and relatives. However only 18 respondents viewed that their employers supported them for treatment during illness. Nineteen respondents viewed that they had faced monetary difficulties for treatment.

Table 7.17: Impact of Work on the Health of Child Labour

Whether Work is Harmful to Health	Frequency	Per cent
Yes	14	11.7
No	62	51.7
Don't Know	44	36.7
Total	**120**	**100.0**

Disciplinary Actions taken by the Employers

Childhood is a period of socialization. This period is characterized by immaturity, high sensitivity, and impulsiveness. It is only through guidance and loving care that the child learns the normal behaviour which is expected of an adult. It is natural for him to commit more mistakes because of his mental immaturity. The employers were asked about the kind of disciplinary action taken by them when the performance and conduct of the child was not satisfactory. The following table depicts the nature of disciplinary action taken by employers for any mistakes, misbehavior and damages caused by children.

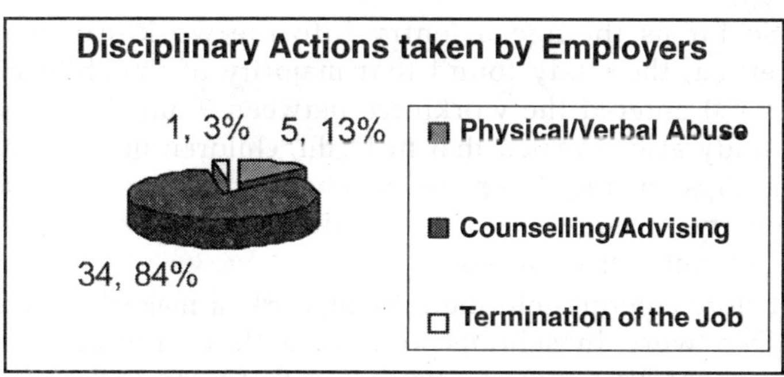

Fig. 7.6: Disciplinary Actions taken by the Employers

Only 5(13%) respondents reported that when the children's performance and behaviour was not satisfactory, he was scolded and given some kind of physical punishment. 34(84%) employers viewed that they counseled the child, advised him to do his work properly if his performance/ behaviour in the work was not satisfactory. Only one employer

(3%) viewed that he had terminated the job of the child for his poor performance and unsatisfactory behavior. So, it can be said, according to the employers that they did not usually harass the children physically and psychologically.

Recruitment System for Engaging Children under 14 Years of Age

The researcher had asked the employers regarding the recruitment procedure for hiring children under the age of 14. 12(30%) of the employers reported that most of the times parents usually approached for the work of their children. In 24 cases, employers said that children approached them directly for work. One employer said that they appointed children only on the recommendations of already working employees. Rest of the employers reported that there was no such recruitment policy. They appointed children when there was more work pressure; they gave employment to children for few months whenever any one approached them. So, it is clear that the employers did not have any such proper policy for hiring children less than 14 years of age.

Analysis

So far as the age of entry into the workforce was concerned, the study found that majority of the children 64(53.3%) entered the workforce between 9 and 11 years. The study also revealed that in Delhi, children in different age groups entered into some or other vocations either due to poverty, or large size of the families, or lack of parental care or some other reasons.

Before entering into the present work, a majority of the children were in schools and once they entered into employment, they were continuing in that very work. So, it could be said that once the child was engaged in one work, he continued to be in that work.

Regarding the source of getting work, a majority of the respondents (53%) informed that, they got their work either though the help of relatives who were already employed or through friends who were working in Delhi. Some of the respondents were also engaged in family businesses or they had got work through themselves. So, it can be concluded that children got work through multiple sources, either through the help of friends/relatives or themselves.

The child labourers views on duration of work in the present employment revealed that a majority of child labourers 59(49.2%) were in the present work since last six months to one year. The children's length of service was found from the six months to three years. In the least number of cases (5%) children were found working for more than 3 years.

A majority of the child labour respondents (57.5%) reported that their workplace was within walking distance (less than 1 km) and used to come to workplace by walking. The study revealed that the distance between home to work place varied from less than 1 km to 3 km. In the least number of cases (5%) children used to travel more than 3 km to reach their place of work.

Regarding working hours of children, the study revealed that their working hours varied from less than 4 hours to more than 12 hours per day. A large number of children worked for more than 12 hours per day. This confirms the general observation that children are put to longer hours of work by the employers.

Regarding weekly off days, it is very disheartening that most of the children (59.2%) did not get weekly offs and even if they got it that was unpaid.

The study revealed that the wages of child labourers were dependent entirely on the work they do. The child was paid much less than what an adult earned for the same work.

A majority of the employers views on whether workers were assisted by children reported that, child labourers mostly help adult workers particularly those engaged in garages/ tea shops/dhabas and a sizeable section of the employers also viewed that children were able to work independently.

Regarding the level of work satisfaction of child labourers, the study found that about 38% of the child labourers were satisfied in the present work because they felt that they had become economically independent and were able to support their family financially to meet their basic needs. Those who were partially satisfied reported that they got less pay and worked for long hours. A significant number of child labourers reported that they were not satisfied with the present work because of the rude behavior of the employers, temporary nature of work, lower wages and longer hours of work, physical abuses by employers and lack of facilities at the work place.

Regarding the attitude of the family towards children's engagement in work, a majority of the children 90(108%) reported that their family had a positive attitude towards children's engagement in work. The study also found that a majority of the parents (95%) were also satisfied as their children were earning money due to their engagement.

The study found that the attitude of the employers/co-workers/customers was very cordial as reported by the child labourers. However, a few child labourers reported that they were sometimes harassed by the employers/co-workers and customers on small faults and sometimes without any reason.

Regarding the impact of work on the health of the child labourers, a majority of the children reported that no health hazards were associated with their present occupation. However, a significant number of child labourers also reported that they had no idea whether their work was harmful to them.

Regarding disciplinary action, a majority of the employers (84%) reported that, they used to counsel the child to work properly if his performance and behaviour was not satisfactory. However a few employers reported that they used to scold and give some kind of physical punishment.

The employer's responses regarding the recruitment procedure for hiring child labour under 14 years of age showed that there was no such strict recruitment processes like the formal sector. Children were hired on the basis of recommendations of internal employees, parent's requests for engaging the child and sometimes on the basis of children's requests and needs.

SECTION – II

LIVING CONDITIONS OF CHILD LABOURERS

The main objective of this section is to explore the living conditions of the child labourers employed in the small scale commercial establishments in Delhi. It has been seen that the quality of living conditions is directly related to the state of economic well being. The people belonging to lower income groups are largely deprived of necessary infrastructure and amenities which are pre requisites for proper living. Child labourers in general belong to the disadvantaged and the low income groups, which do not have the capacity to access facilities for a better living.

In the less developed regions, the living conditions of the child labourers are generally appalling. The abysmal quality the housing is a widespread social problem especially in the urban areas. Sometimes even members of a family are cramped together in the shacks and hovels and are forced to live in a single room, with little or no ventilation.

Such conditions are typical of any developing country with a high rate of population growth (ILO, 1973).

In the course of research, it was observed that child labourers lived in a condition wherein they had no or very little access to proper housing and sanitation facilities, recreation and social support system. In order to study the living conditions of the child labourers, following the variables were taken into consideration:

1. Housing conditions including ownership of the house, monthly rent, nature of dwellings and size of the dwellings.
2. Electrification and domestic electronic items available.
3. Sanitation and civic amenities.
4. Play and leisure opportunities.
5. Recreational facilities available at home.
6. Addiction status.
7. Food arrangement.
8. Social interaction among children.

Housing Conditions

Housing is one of the basic needs and important private rest place for human beings, which not only provides shelter but also keeps its own importance in nurturing and rearing of the children. It provides opportunities to its members to enjoy basic domestic as well as personal needs that one requires to satisfy in the house. Proper housing facility provides a protected atmosphere to the children where their future is guided according to the set of values of the family. Provision of good housing makes significant influence on health, efficiency and social well-being of the people. Therefore, its priority in this sector needs to be emphasized. The housing is very significant in assuring the welfare and developmental services at a common place in an unorganized form to the individual, family and children in particular (Vagale, 1968). Lack of proper housing not only impairs the healthy growth of the children, but also brings them in contact with undesirable conditions which affect their health.

Inferior housing and shortage of housing accommodation is an index of backwardness and poverty of the people. It is therefore, necessary to make an assessment of the housing facilities available to the sample child labourers.

Most of the child labourers lived in slums. Most of the houses in the slums were overcrowded, single room tenements, ill ventilated and in an extremely poor state of habitation without adequate essential services in most of the cities. The living conditions of these slum dwellers were quite deplorable. Most of these dwellings neither had ventilation nor any outlet for filth. In this context, an attempt has been made in this section to study the housing and living conditions of the child labourers.

Table 7.18 shows the type of house in which the respondents live.

The study revealed that nearly 11% of the child labourers stayed in pucca houses, 41(34.2%) in semi pucca houses followed by 60(50%) who lived in kutcha houses and a few respondents 6(5%) who resided on foot paths and parks.

Table 7.18: Types of houses of child labourers

Types of Houses	Frequency	Percentage
Pucca	13	10.8
Semi-Pucca	41	34.2
Kuchha	60	50
Open Space (Street/Park)	6	5
Total	**120**	**100**

Ownership of Houses

Table 7.19: Ownership of the houses

Ownership of the House	Frequency	Percentage
Own house	28	23.3
Rented House	64	53.3
Stay in work place	22	18.33
No houses	6	5
Total	**120**	**100**

The study revealed that 64(53.3%) child labourers were staying in rented accommodation, 28(23%) in their own houses and 22(18.33%) stayed in an accommodation which was provided by their employers at their place of work and only a few 6(5%) respondents reported that they were staying on the foot paths and parks. Those who had their own house, it was mostly Jhuggis and Jhopdis in the slum areas.

The researcher also observed that the housing conditions of these child labourers were quite deplorable. Most of their houses being in the slum environment , almost all the civic amenities like proper drainage system and safe drinking water were absent. Their houses were ill ventilated, overcrowded and suffocating. Mustafa and Sharma (1996) in his study also revealed that the living and working conditions of child labourers were appalling. Their homes were cluster of congested, over crowded, unhygienic houses with water logging, mosquitoes, filth and stench emanating from the open drains. Another study conducted by NIPCCD, 1986 in Delhi reported that a big proportion of the respondents (90%) lived in houses owned by them. Every three out of four lived in kutcha houses with minimum civic amenities.

Monthly Rent

During the discussion with parents as well as with the child labourers, it was observed that the rent paid in slums was more, because the owners did not ask for any identify proof, or rent agreement. Most of the child labourers and their parents were migrants and did not have any kind of identity proof. So, they got rented accommodation easily in the slums.

Table 7.20: Monthly Rent Paid by the Respondents

Amount of Monthly Rent Paid	Frequency	Percentage
Below Rs. 500	10	8.3
Rs. 500- Rs. 1000	29	24.16
Rs. 1000- Rs. 1500	20	16.7
Rs. 1500- Rs. 2000	04	3.3
More than Rs. 2000	01	0.8
Not applicable	56	46.66
Total	**120**	**100**

The study reported that those who were staying in rented accommodation, 29(24.16%) respondents were paying monthly rent between Rs. 500 to Rs. 1000, 20 (16.7%) were paying between Rs. 1000 to Rs. 1500 month, 10(8.3%) were paying less than Rs. 500 and a very few respondents 4(3.3%) reported that they were paying between Rs. 1500-2000 per month as rent. So, it can be said that the monthly rent in the slums varied from Rs. 500 to Rs. 2000 depending upon the size of the rooms, proximity to the market areas and the facilities available in the houses.

Size of the Dwellings

Table 7.21: Size of the Dwellings

No. of Rooms	Frequency	Percentage
One room set	79	65.8
Two rooms set	25	20.8
Jhuggi	7	5.8
Not applicable	9	7.5
Total	**120**	**7.5**

The above table indicates that 79(65.8%) of the respondents lived in one room houses, followed by 25(20.85%) who lived in two room houses and only 7(5.8%) respondents shared that they were staying in Jhuggis. During data collection, the researcher observed that these houses did not have windows and were ill ventilated, and poorly lit. A majority of the respondents reported that they had temporary electricity connections. This type of congestion without proper lighting, ventilation and absence of adequate fresh air naturally poses several health problems.

It can, therefore be concluded that child labourers mostly stayed in slums in single room accommodation which was very unhygienic, congested and therefore quite harmful to their health as also the health of their families. The study by Rao and Mallik (1992) also revealed that the most basic needs of the child labourers were poorly met. Their general health was moderate, though they were undernourished. They did not have adequate clothing. They had no provision for bath, toilet and facilities for education. They also did not get doctors help when it was needed the most.

Domestic Appliances Available

The study also revealed that a sizeable section of the respondents possessed various domestic appliances as shown in the table. The most commonly owned domestic appliances were items like gas stove, bicycles, fans and small stoves.

Table 7.22: Domestic Appliances Available

Domestic Appliances Available	Frequency	Percentage
Gas stove	26	21.66
Refrigerator	4	3.33
Bicycle	44	36.66
Fan	78	65
Small stove (kerosene/gas)	68	56.66
Cooler	16	13.33

N = 120

Water and Sanitation Facility

During the study it was observed that, the child labourers staying in pucca houses could mostly avail water from private connections. Those respondents who were staying in huts and kutcha houses were facing difficulties in procuring water because these houses were illegal constructions on unauthorized land. Therefore they lacked proper water and sanitation facilities.

Table 7.23: Water and Sanitation Facility Available in the House

Facilities Available in the House	Yes		No		Frequency	Percentage
	Frequency	Percentage	Frequency	Percentage		
Water tab facility	42	35	78	65	120	100
Separate bathroom	25	20.8	95	79.2	120	100
Separate toilet	27	22.5	93	77.5	120	100

A majority of the child labourers 78(65%) reported that they had to get water from public tube wells and Delhi Jal Board tankers (which came frequently). They had to stand in big queues to get water. But in the summer season, when the water requirement was more, they faced scarcity in the procurement of water.

Sanitation was also another big problem for the child labourers living in the slums of Delhi. The study revealed that only 27(22.5%) of the respondents had private latrines at their place of residence. A majority of the respondents 93(77.5%) reported that they were using public lavatories mainly Sulabh Sauchalaya as well as MCD toilets situated near their place of living/market areas. Rest of the respondents shared that they were using open space behind the slums for defecation purposes.

A large number of child labourers 95(79.2%) reported that they did not have separate bathroom facility at their place of residence. They used to take bath at the nearby Sulabh Sauchalaya or at the nearby hand pump/ community water tap facility available in the community. Only 25 (20.8%) were having separate bathroom at their residence.

Play and Recreation

Childhood is the time for play and recreation. The need for movement of physical limbs and exercise in the open air is essential for the proper development of the child. So, leisure and recreation is an essential activity for children. All kinds of play, games, entertainment and rest periods form the child's recreation and leisure avenues (Rodgers and standing, 1981).

Table 7.24: Nature of Recreational Activities

Leisure Time is Spent	Frequency	Percentage
Did not have time for play & recreation	84	70
Watching T.V. & Cinema	25	20.8
Wandering/Playing	07	5.8
Sleeping	4	3.4
Total	**120**	**100**

It was very disheartening to note that 84(70%) of the child labourers never got an opportunity to play. This indicates the plight and predicament of the child labourers employed in the informal sector. Any child is expected to play and enjoy the childhood for his/her normal and healthy development. Instead, they were forced to take up remunerative work for supplementing the earnings of the family.

Table 7.25: Recreational Facilities Available in the House

Recreational Facilities Available in the House	Yes		No		Total	
	Frequency	Percentage	Frequency	Percentage	Frequency	Percentage
Television	61	50.8	59	49.2	120	100
Radio	35	29.2	85	70.8	120	100
Tape Recorder	11	9.2	109	90.3	120	100
Carom Board	06	05	114	95	120	100
Chess	–	–	120	100	120	100
Ludo	12	10	108	90	120	100
Playing Cards	11	9.2	109	90.8	120	100
Total					**120**	**100**

These child labourers hardly got any spare time. But whenever they got spare time, they utilised it in the best possible manner. The table revealed that 25(20.8%) of the child labourers watched movies and television during their spare time. Rest of the respondents reported that they used their spare time in wandering/playing with friends, talking to their friends, roaming in the street/market areas and sleeping at home. Only 2 respondents viewed that they spent their time in drinking/smoking along with friends.

Addiction

The child labourers were hesitant and did not take any interest in speaking about their addiction habits. However, during discussions, some of the respondents mentioned about their friends who started smoking or chewing tobacco after getting a work and even some of their friends were addicts since the last three to four years. After long interaction, discussion and rapport building with child labourers, the researcher was able to assess that there were some very young boys who were getting into this addiction.

Table 7.26: Nature of Addiction of Child Labourers

Types of Addiction	Frequency	Percentage
Drinking	12	10
Chewing tobacco	49	40.83
Smoking	36	30
No addiction	23	19.16
Total	**120**	**100**

From the above table, it becomes clear that 49(40.83%) of the child labourers were addicted to chewing gutka, 36(30%) were addicted to smoking and 12(10%) were addicted to drinking liquor. The rest 23(19.16%) of them did not having addiction of any kind. The children who were employed in family businesses and worked under the guidance of their parents reported that they did not have any kind of addiction. It was also observed that some of the children whose place of work was close to their parent's work place or their place of residence were not addicted. The researcher found the family environment, and the surroundings in which they lived and worked the impact of peer group and sometimes curiosity to taste something new were the important factors for their addiction.

The researcher observed that most of them smoked bidi and chewed tobacco which were cheap and easily available. Though observations, the researcher could derive that a major factor responsible for getting child labour addicted to alcohol and smoking was their peer group.

Food Arrangement

Food is the most important ingredient for survival. Children left their houses in the early morning after breakfast, which mainly consisted of tea with roti/bread. They were provided a cup of tea (and sometimes a samosa or pakoda) in the morning by their employers. After a long strenuous work, they were provided lunch by their employers. Most of the children also reported that they took their dinner along with their family members. Most of the child labourers covered under the study also viewed that in special occasions/festivals they got chance to eat ghee, meat, fruits, sweets etc.

Social Interaction Among Children

The need for social interaction is felt by every human being. He is satisfied by interacting with other people and by giving and receiving friendship. The children form their peer groups and usually establish intimate relationship with the children of their age. With this in view, child labourers were asked to state the kind of activities performed by them with their friends. The study revealed that the child labourers in general used to discuss matters pertaining to their work and family matters which helped them to reduce their worries and tensions. Sometimes they also used to talk about movies, cricket etc during the free hours. Nonetheless, the child labourers also reported that they hardly got much free time to spend with their friends. During festivals alone they got an opportunity to interact with their friends.

Analysis

The study revealed that about half of the child labourers were staying in kutcha houses and a few respondents were also staying on foot paths and in parks.

Regarding the ownership of the house, it was found that child labourers in Delhi mostly stayed in the rented accommodation in the slum areas and the monthly rent varied from Rs. 500 to Rs. 2000, depending upon size of the dwellings, proximity to the market areas and the facilities available in the house.

The study also reported that water and sanitation were a major problems faced by child labourers and their families. A majority of the child labourers had to get water from public tube well/community water tap and Delhi Jal board tankers. These respondents also used sulabh sauchalaya and open spaces for defecation/relieving themselves.

Regarding play and recreation, the child labourers hardly got any free time for play and recreation. Some of the respondents spent their leisure time in watching T.V, cinema and sleeping at their homes.

The study also found that a majority of the children were addicted to chewing gutka and smoking which was cheap and easily available. The researcher found that the family environment and the surroundings in which they lived and worked, the impact of peer group and sometimes curiosity to taste something new were important factors for their addiction.

The study reported that the child labourers hardly got free time to spend with their friends. It was only during festivals that they got opportunity to interact with their friends. These child labourers also did not have much opportunity to eat nutritious food which was only available to them during festivals and special occasions.

8

Narratives
A Qualitative Analysis

Narratives are one of the fundamental ways that people organize their understanding of the world (Flick, 2007). In narratives they make sense to themselves of their past experience and they share that experience with others. So the careful analysis of topic, content, style, context, and the telling of narratives will reveal people's understanding of the meanings of key events in their lives or their communities and the cultural context in which they live (Gibbs, 2007). The analysis of narratives adds a new dimension to qualitative research. It focuses not just on what people said and the things and events they describe but on how they said it, why they said it, and what they felt and experienced. Narratives thus allow us to understand how they experience life.

In the present study the researcher had selected ten cases for narrative analysis. On the basis of narratives, the researcher had also developed the grounded theory for generating theoretical ideas.

Narratives 1

Name	:	Amjad (name changed)
Age	:	13 years
Permanent Address	:	Dist-Saharsa, Bihar
Years of working	:	4 years
Place of working	:	Azadpur subzi mandi

Amjad is a native of a village of Bihar which constituted of mostly Muslim families. He belongs to a joint family and has five brothers and three sisters. All his family members including his grand parents stay in village. Only Amjad and his elder brother Rahim (name changed) are putting up in Delhi. They are the only earning members of his family.

Amjad and his brother left their ancestral home in Bihar for Delhi in 2007 to overcome the financial difficulties of their parents. In the earlier days, his father used to work as labourer on daily wages (mostly in agricultural activities). With the growing family he was finding it difficult to make both ends meet. So, in order to meet the requirements of the house, he had to borrow money from villagers and money lenders for the sustenance of the family. Amjad's elder brother (Rahim) also told that his family had lost the small piece of land which they had owned to repay the debt taken by his father. His father was unable to get employment throughout the year as there were minimal employment opportunities in his village and neighbouring areas. The moneylenders/villagers pressurized him to pay back loan in time. So, with very little chances of any other source of employment other than being a landless agricultural labourer, his father decided to move to Delhi with the hope that he would be able to get employment and could earn decent money. At that time Amjad was three years old. While working for few years in Delhi, his father suffered from several diseases and was forced to spend huge money for his medical treatment. Life at Delhi was not easy for him. He remained unhealthy and continued to be sick for a long time and at last returned to his own village. Amir said, his father used to work very hard to feed and sustain the family. Then Amjad and his elder brother (Rahim) decided to work and return all the money borrowed by his father. Rahim (the elder brother of Amjad) was greatly impressed by the information about the opportunities in Delhi given by some members of his community who had earlier migrated to Delhi. It provided him a ray of hope and he decided to provide financial support for the family. Rahim and Amjad are working in Delhi Azadpur subzi mandi since

2007 to reduce the economic burden faced by their parents. In case of Amjad, poverty of his parents is the major cause for his engagement in remunerative job. Poor economic and social conditions forced Amjad and his brother to migrate to Delhi. In case of Amjad, both push (poverty, compulsion of parents, and their interest to earn for the family) and pull factors (availability of easy work in Delhi) forced them to migrate to Delhi. So, Poverty, indebtedness and unemployment was the main reasons for his migration.

His day starts at 4 a.m. in the morning when he directly goes to the Subzi mandi. "*Main subah chaar baje uthtaa hun aur sauch ke baad paanch baje mandee nikal jaataa hun aur sabji mandee mein hi naashtaa kartaa hun, wahaan main ek baje tak lagaataar kaam kartaa hun aur ek baje ghar par lunch karne ke liye aataa hun.*" Both of them used to collect tomatoes (Spoilt tomatoes) and fill in crate and send to the selected hotels/dhabas where they have made verbal contract to send tamatos everyday @ Rs. 150 per crate. In summer (June-August), they do not get sufficient tamatoes from the market and have to purchase Ratlaam and Shimla varieties in a much higher price and send this to hotels. In this time, they had to face financial loss because they used to get only Rs. 150/ per one crate. Amjad said "*Jab Ratlaam aur shimlaa girtaa hai to hamne bahut jyaadaa ghaataa hotaa hai, jiske kaaran hamne kai baar udhaar le kar bhi business mein lagaanaa padtaa hai, is samay ke dauraan hamein pandraa se bees hajaar rupaye tak kaa ghaataa uthaa kar kaam karnaa padtaa hai*". When he was asked by the researcher, why he is bearing such loss, Amjad said "*agar ismein munaafaa na hotaa to hum ye kaam karte hi kyun? Jab ismein do paise bachte hain tabhi to hum ye kaam kar rahe hain, aur isi ke bal par hamne apnaa do lakh rupaye kaa karj chukaa diyaa hai.*" Amjad also said if we do not supply tomatoes regularly, they give contract to others. The hotel/ dhaba owners often used to tell "*Kar nahin sakte to chhod do, hum koi aur dekh lengen.*" With this continuous threat hanging, they used to supply tamatos even with a huge loss. Amjad and his brother feel proud that they are able to return about Rs. 50,000/ out of the total 2 lakhs of rupees loaned by his father. Every month they save about Rs. 5000/ after fulfilling their minimum expenditure. From the saved money, they send some amount of money to their father every month through money order. They are also saving money for the marriage of their sisters. Amjad also said "the entire burden of running the family is on their shoulders".

Amjad and his brother stay in a rented accommodation and pay Rs. 1000/ per month for a single room excluding electricity charges. They pay about Rs. 160/ for electricity charges per month. Their landlord only provides drinking water. He collects water from public tap available in the slum cluster for washing of utensils and clothes. Only one water tab is situated near the mosque. Sometimes Amjad has to stand in queue for long time for his turn to get water. In his rented accommodation, they do not have bathroom and toilet facilities. They go to Sulabh Sauchalaya and have to pay for bath and toilet at the rate of Rs. 2 and Rs. 1 respectively. Sometimes they also visit toilet and bathroom in the market which charges Rs. 5 for toilet and Rs. 10 for bath.

Amjad and his elder brother cook food themselves. They have kerosene stove in their house. His elder brother cooks food (lunch and dinner) and Amjad helps in cooking. Amjad purchases kerosene from market at the rate of Rs. 30 per litre because they do not have ration card and can not avail PDS facilities.

Amjad's landlord has provided them a ceiling fan which is used for cooling in the summer. During summer, they can manage but in winter they face lots of problems due to lack of sufficient woollen clothes. They also do not have a room heater and any other things to warm up the room. Both of them manage with only one blanket during winter season.

During the leisure, they see Hindi movies in T.V. (colour television purchased by them) with cable connection. He likes action movies of Bobby Deol and Sunny Deol. He also visits nearby market areas along with his friends. Amjad had many friends in his village like Ruskan, Sabeer and Baseer. But after coming to Delhi, Sahim (name changed) is his only good friend. He also has another friend Faheem (name changed), but their friendship broke down because of Faheem's addiction with drugs. Amjad always tried to motivate him to give up drugs, but Faheem was deeply addicted and dependent on drugs. Due to this reason, Amjad left him alone and broke his friendship. After a gap of long time, again they became friends. Amjad tried to motivate him; spoke to him about its negative consequences. Faheem gave up his bad habits and again became a good friend of Amjad. Amjad also says that Faheem was also influenced by motivational talks delivered by various resource persons organised by various non-governmental organisations. Amjad is very happy as he is instrumental in helping Faheem to get out of these bad habits. In his words, *"Main ek aisaa ladkaa hun, jo ladkaa kisi bhi tarah kaa nashaa kartaa hai main use ekdum sudhaar detaa hun"*. Amjad sometimes eats sweet beetel (meetha pan) and once he was offered beer by his friend Faheem. When his brother came to know about it, he was beaten brutally. Amjad said *"Jab mere ghar mein koi nahin khaataa to main kyun khaaun, Sahin mere jaisaa hai Jo kuch bhi khaataa peetaa nahin hai isi liye wo meraa sabse pakkaa dost hai"*. Amjad says that many people in the mandi take some or other kinds of drugs. In his family, every body is very strict and no body takes any kinds of drugs.

Amjad seems to be weak and undernourished. Very often, during the cold season, he suffers from cold, cough and skin diseases. He lives in very unhygienic conditions. In case of sickness, he visits nearby private clinics which charges Rs. 30 for consultation. According to him, his neighbours look upon him with suspicion or indifference. In case of illness, neighbours never come forward to help them.

Amjad has never attended school but expressed that he wants to go back to school given an opportunity. He is not aware of existing laws to protect children or child labour or the available government schemes for free education of children. Amjad is very much interested and keen to study, but he has no scope and opportunity for the same. He says *"Jab kaam karte-karte disturb ho jaataa hun to kaam chhod kar padhaai karne ka mann kartaa hai, magar kyaa karun hamaare is kaam ke alaawaa kamaai kaa koi jariyaa bhi to nahin hai, isi liye main kaam kartaa hun. Jyaadaa padhne ke liye jyaadaa paisaa chahiye, mere poore pariwaar mein koi nahin padhaa hai"*.

Amjad says he doesn't want to go back to his village; however he does go to village at least four times in a year. He doesn't feel comfortable and happy when he visits his village. He feels very happy in Delhi and wanted to continue this job.

The narrative analysis reveals that poverty was the major cause for his engagement in remunerative job. Both the push (poverty, compulsion of parents) and pull factors (easy availability of jobs in Delhi) forced him to migrate to Delhi. The mild comforts being provided by his job have enabled him to feel contented as far as his necessities are concerned.

Narratives 2

Name	:	Raju (Name Changed)
Age	:	13 years
Permanent address	:	Paschimi Champaran, Bihar
Years of working	:	2 years
Place of working	:	Azadpur

Raju is thirteen years old; and has five brothers and two sisters. His family hails from Paschimi Champaran, Bihar. For the past couple of years they have been residing in village Bhadola near Adarsh Nagar metro station. Raju, his elder brother and father are the earning members of his family.

His father had borrowed huge sum of money and invested in sugar cane farming to get more profits. Due to heavy flood, his farm as well as living premises got damaged and his farming land became almost infertile due to deposit of sands carried out by flood water. He said *"Har saal baadh ke Kaaran kheton aur gharon mein paani bhar jaataa hai aur hamein bahut pareshaani hoti hai, kai baar to saari fasal barbaad ho jaati hai"*. Due to heavy loans and losses, his father went to Mumbai in search of work about three years back. He was working there as a labour contractor and was earning well. But unfortunately, after few months of working in Mumbai, again he lost his job and was coming back to village. On his way, he met someone in the train who suggested working in Azadpur Subzi Mandi. Since then, his father continued to work here and sell garlic in Azadpur Subzi mandi. During that time, his father was in financial doldrums and took loan of Rs. 750/ from a lady (whom he called sister) to start garlic business. After few months of working in Delhi, he also brought the entire family to Delhi. Raju said it was poverty that drove them out from the village and the entire family had to migrate to Delhi after that severe flood which was the turning point for his family. So, thus, in case of Raju poverty, recurrence of frequent floods and loss of job of his father were the important reasons for migration.

He starts working since 5 a.m. in the morning and works till 1 p.m. and earns about Rs. 200/ per day. He gives all his earned money to his father. He has been in this work for the last two years. His work place is quite at a distance from his jhuggis. After getting up early in the morning, he starts his way on foot to his work place. He goes to subzi mandi without taking breakfast to find a place for selling garlic. He has no fixed place in the subzi mandi where he can seat and sell garlic permanently. Everyday he has to make request to shop owner/house owner to use a part of his front premise for selling garlic with a payment of Rs. 100/ per day. When asked why he has not been able to secure a fixed place in the subzi mandi, he said then they have to approach the market association and have to contribute a big amount of money for the same. His elder brother has only been able to secure a fixed place, so he used to sell more and earns more as compared to his father also. When Raju was asked why he sells only garlic, he said there is no such extra work like cleaning, storage problem as well as no more fluctuations of price in the market.

His living conditions are extremely appalling. His family though is very poor is also extremely large. Raju is living along with his parents and other family members in a rented house (jhuggis) with a monthly payment of Rs. 1100/ including electricity charges. His home is very much congested and overcrowded without any ventilation or sanitary facilities; even a modicum of essential human needs is not there. The entire eleven members of his family managed to live within the two room accommodation without bathroom and kitchen. The entire basti is unhygienic with water logging, dirt, insects and flies. They collect water from a nearby mosque which is a tough task for his family because they have to wait in queue for long hours. They go for toilet and bathrooms in common premises where they also stand in queue for their turn which charges Rs. 1 for toilet and Rs. 2/for bath for each member. He takes dinner with all his family members and shares his day long experiences during that time. However he takes his breakfast and lunch in the subzi mandi. In the breakfast, he used to take samosa, bread pakoda and tea. During winter he faces lots of problems without any room heating facility and lack of sufficient blanket and woolen clothes.

In the afternoon, he goes to Tamatar wala park to play with his friends. Sometimes he also watches television programme in his home. He also used to go to theatre to see movies along with his friends. He spoke loudly that he had visited Red Fort along with all family members very recently. He has not visited any other tourist place in Delhi except Red Fort.

The health conditions of Raju are more pitiable than other children working over there. He used to sit at a stretch for 9 hours and feels adequate pain in his waist. His feet are swelled up. He takes treatment from a nearby private hospital which charges Rs 40/ per visit. He continuously falls ill due to exposure to extreme weather conditions. His appearance is very dirty and looks very weak. His diet is frugal. He desires to have milk, fruits, sweets and other good eatables which are never purchased. He has always some kinds of apprehension and anxiety in his mind for getting space to sit next day in the subzi mandi. His face shows emotions of fear and distress as he really finds difficult to secure a place.

He is very keen to study and said *"jab mann mein padhaai kaa khayaal aa jaataa hai to kaam mein mann nahi lagtaa hai."* When asked if he would like to continue his study, his eyes lit up with hope. He often watched many children going to school and sometimes he also dreamt of going to school. But at the same time he feels happy in his work. He is interested to learn a trade skill that would fetch him a better job, pay and security like his uncle who is working as a tailor master in Gurgaon.

The child is very interested to study and want to become a doctor. The motivation behind his aspiration is to get rid of poverty and lead a happy and prosperous life. The child feels very uncomfortable and insecure in Jhuggi because he has fear that anybody will physically harm to him for sake of money. There are many drug addicted children who roam around in this area. They can thief and snatch by showing weapon. That he has informed the same to the nearby police station. So he always wants to earn more and can shift to a good housing colony where he can live happily. The narrative analysis reveals that poverty, recurrence of frequent floods and loss of job of his father were the important reasons for his migration as well as engagement in the job at such a tender age. The present living conditions of the child are also appalling. A large family and unlimited resources have added to his problem.

Narrative 3

Name	:	Ruskan (Name changed)
Permanent Address	:	Madhepura district, Bihar
Age	:	12 years
Years of working	:	3 years
Area of working	:	Azadpur Subzi Mandi

Ruskan is a native of madhepura district of Bihar. He belongs to Dhuniya caste in Islam. He stays in Delhi along with his father. His other family members (mother, four younger brothers and one younger sister) stay in village. He has studied up to class three in his village school and presently working in Azadpur Subzi mandi.

Ruskan came to Delhi three years back to help his father who works as a construction worker. Due to extreme poverty, his father wanted him to come to Delhi to join him in the work, so that he can earn something. During that time, Ruskan was nine years old. Ruskan says, his father's income was not sufficient for taking care of the needs of his family. So, the economic needs of his family indirectly put a compulsion on him to engage in strenuous labour. So, 9 years old Ruskan left his home and moved towards Delhi as he was constantly pressurized to work.

He starts working since 6 a.m. in the morning to 11 a.m. (sometimes till 2 p.m.) and in the evening from 8 p.m. to 11 p.m. During this time, trucks carrying tomatoes reach in the market area of subzi mandi. Ruskan's job is only to classify rotten and the fresh tomatoes. He has no fixed place of job. Everyday, he asks for job when goods particularly tomatoes are unloaded at market area of Azadpur. He always remains mobile and asks for job when trucks carrying vegetables come to Azadpur subzi mandi. He also works on Saturdays and Sundays. The only happiness in his job is that he gets the payment immediately after the work is done. Sometimes he gets cash and sometimes tomatoes as remuneration. His residence is very close to the market area. Ruskan earlier used to help his father in selling vegetables, but due to extreme loss, his father started working as a labourer in construction site. Ruskan is not satisfied in his present job, but he realizes his responsibility and his father's financial problems. So he works hard to support the family. Ruskan said, he continues to work even if he is ill because the daily earnings are very important not only for him but also to meet the basic needs of family.

Ruskan stays in a single room rented accommodation along with his father and pays Rs. 800/ per month for rent and Rs. 200/ per month for electricity charges. In his rented accommodation, there are no bathroom and toilet facilities. So, he uses public toilet (Sulabh Sauchalaya) which charges nominal payment. His landlord has provided him a fan and a tube light in his accommodation. Ruskan takes his breakfast and lunch in the market. His father cooks food in the night and both of them eat together and during dinner, he shares his day long experiences with his father. Recently his father has purchased a mobile phone and Ruskan is very happy to speak to his mother over phone at least once in every week. He loves his mother very much and says *"main apni mummy se bahut pyaar kartaa hun"*. His father generally cooks rice or roti and pulses. Once in week, his father cooks either egg or fish in the dinner.

During the leisure time, he prefers to sleep in his home. Sometimes he also plays with friends. He has never visited cinema hall so far. Sometimes he also visits Sahim's (name changed) house to see television. He likes to watch CID episodes on Sony TV or Bhojpuri channels. He happily said *"Khelnaa achchhaa lagtaa hai par T.V. par programme zyaadaa achchhaa lagtaa hai. Ek din main bhi kamaakar T.V. kharidunga aur apne gaon le jaungaa."* He also listens songs in the radio available in his home.

Most of the time, he suffers from headache, fever and takes medicine from the medical store. Sometimes he also visits private clinics nearby which charges Rs. 30/ per visit. His appearance is very untidy and wears old and unclean clothes. He lives in very unhygienic conditions.

He has studied up to 3rd standard before migrating to Delhi. He felt very bad when dropped out from school as he had to be separated from family and friends. He is very happy that he has the ability to read and write and confidently said that no body can cheat him in the market which is reflected in his saying *"Main din ki kamaai aur kharche ka hisaab kar letaa hun."* He is very keen and eager to study but due to hard pressed with time and responsibility, he is unable to attend school. He has no idea about child labour legislations and said *"mujhe iske baare mein koi jaankaari nahi hai."*

He wants to complete his studies till 12th class and wants to do his own business, so that he will be free from tension and uncertainty and will be able to pay back all family debts and take care of his family obligations.

The narrative analysis revealed that poverty of his family and family pressure were the important reasons forcing him to engage in strenuous labour. Again he was also living in unhygienic circumstances and had several health problems too.

Narratives 4

Name	:	Vicky (Name changed)
Age	:	13
Permanent address	:	Darbhanga district, Bihar
Years of working	:	1 year
Place of working	:	Loni garage

Vicky (13years) belongs to Darbhanga district of Bihar. His mother and younger brother stays in village. His three elder sisters have got married before his father's death. He came to Delhi about one year back after his father's death.

His father was an agricultural labourer in the village and was very much addicted to alcohol. After his father's death, there was no body to support them financially. Therefore, his family members and relatives pressurized him to do some work. His mother works as a domestic labour in his village and earns meager wages. So, one of his uncle brought him to Delhi with the assurance of providing him a job and placed him in a garage in Loni. Since then, he is working in that garage.

He has joined the trade one year before and was in the process of learning the trade. His working hour stretches from 8 a.m. to 9 p.m. without any intermittent rest except sparing sometime for lunch. The boy helps the adult mechanic in many ways. He dismantles the different spare parts, tightens or looses the bolts, removes and fits the spare parts of the vehicle, does the oiling and cleaning of the different parts and hands over the different parts to the adult mechanic. He works in the open and thus exposed to Sun and sometimes rain. He gets Rs. 100/ per day as wages besides tea, breakfast and lunch. His duties also consist of sweeping the premises everyday. He brings cigarettes, gutka, tea and samosa for the adult mechanics and owners. Almost everyday, he is verbally abused by the adult mechanics for wrongly putting spare parts in the vehicle. On few occasions, he was thrashed by the adult mechanic as well as the employers over minor mistakes.

He stays with another adult mechanic in the small room situated nearby the garage without any ventilation and sanitary facilities and pays rent Rs. 600/ in a month. He goes to toilet on the road side along with a water bottle. He takes bath in the open near the hand pump situated very close to his garage and also collects water from hand pump for drinking purposes. His employer has provided them a table fan. They do not have bed or any other furniture. Even the space is not sufficient to place table, chairs or beds. They sleep in the floors with mats and bed sheets. All their things are kept in boxes. During night, he along with his room partner cooks food in stove and most of the time; he cooks eggs in his dinner as it is very easy to cook.

His health is very poor. During the cold days he often falls ill. He is also suffering from stomach ache and worm trouble. In the evening, he feels pain in his body. He has also health hazards connected with his occupation such as headache, tiredness etc. His clothes are very old and unclean and it looks dirtier due to the nature of his work, cleaning the vehicle, oiling, dismantling machinery and parts of the vehicle under the supervision of adult mechanics.

He is very quiet in nature and says he has no time for playing and to do rest. He is addicted with gutka and consumes at least 4/5 gutkas in a day. He has no other source of enjoyment and said *"Paise ke liye kaam karnaa padtaa hai."*

He is very much interested to study and wants to have ability to write letters. After being fully trained in this work, he wants to be a good mechanic and wants to establish his own garage.

It was revealed from the narratives that after the death of his father, there was no body to support them financially. Therefore, he was pressurized by his family members and relatives to get engaged in work to earn money.

Narratives 5

Name	:	Susheel (Name Changed)
Age	:	12
Permanent Address	:	Manjoura, Bihar
Years of Working	:	2 years
Place of Working	:	Azadpur

Susheel along with his three brothers are staying in Bharolla, Delhi. Ravi (name changed) and Ramu (name changed) are his elder brothers and Rajesh (name changed) his younger brother. His parents, sisters and his elder brother's wife and sisters stay in village.

Susheel came to Delhi two years ago along with his younger brother due to the pressure of his parents and eldest brother. His eldest brother came to Delhi five/six years back in search of employment in order to fulfil the domestic needs of his family. His father was also working in Azadpur Subzi mandi for a long time but due to an accident, he was disabled and unable to work anymore. So, he left for the village and started staying with his mother and sisters. Susheel came to Delhi two years ago along with his younger brother due to the pressure of economic reasons and started working in Azadpur in a tea stall. Susheel said *"Hum Sab bhaai yahaan ek saath rehte hain, kabhi-kabhi bade bhaai log pitaai kar dete hain, par unke saath rehna achchhaa lagtaa hai, wo meraa bahut khayaal rakhte hain"*. So, poverty and loss of job of his father was the main reason for his migration.

Susheel has been working in the tea stall for the last two years. He starts his work in the morning since 5 a.m. to 8p.m. in the evening. He also works even on Saturday and Sunday. There is no specified holiday for him. Sometimes if he asks for leave to his employer, it is provided to him without much hesitation. His home is 30-40 kilometers away from his workplace. Susheel along with his three brothers come together by bus in the early morning to the subzi mandi. So, he doesn't face any problem in commuting to the workplace. His duties consists of sweeping the premises, dusting and cleaning of benches, cleaning the vessels such as cups, spoons, tea kettles etc. He serves the customers those who come to the shop and also supplies tea to the shop keeper in the market areas. When there is rush of customers particularly during morning and evening, he has to very fast. He gets very tired in the evening; sometimes he is also scolded by his employer if he is late in serving the customers. He is also abused by his employer for reaching late to the work place. His employer gives him breakfast (tea, samosa or pakoda) and lunch (roti, dal and subzi). His elder brother comes in the evening to collect his wages from his employer. He took decision twice to discontinue with this job and search for another job but he was forced by his elder brother to go for work. Sameer said, *"Main khush hun, kabhi mann na bhi kare to bhaai log zabardasti kaam par le jaate hain phir to kaam mein mann lag hi jaataa hai"*.

Susheel along with his three brothers is staying in a one room pucca dwelling with a monthly rent of Rs. 1500/ per month. They do not have toilet and bath room facility in his house. For toilet and bath, they use Sulabh Sauchalaya in Azadpur during day time and use the open space during the night. They have one colour T.V. with cable connection, one mobile phone, one ceiling phone, one tube light in his home. His elder brother cooks food at home in the night. He cooks roti or rice, pulses and vegetables. During the festival times, his brother brings sweets to home and he enjoys a lot in eating sweets. He never takes milk in his diet. Sometimes his brother brings milk to prepare tea if any of his friends comes to house. Susheel likes to have milk if it is left after making tea.

He hardly gets any time for recreational activities. During the leisure time, he only prefers to see television. He said *"hamaaraa chhotaa kamraa hai par T.V. par programme hamesha chaltaa rehtaa hai, dekh ke mann ko bahut khushi hoti hai"*. He has never visited nay cinema hall for watching movies. He said *"bhaai manaa karte hain kehte hain yahaan achchhe log nahi jaate"*. He only gets time during night to see television.

His physical health condition appears good. He wears clean clothes and looks very neat and tidy. He has not witnessed any such health problems after coming to Delhi. He said, his younger brother was suffering from malaria few months back and they had visited government dispensary for his treatment. On minor illness, they purchase medicine from the chemist shop for the treatment of the disease.

He has no knowledge about any child labour legislations. He wants to study at least till 10th class. He has studied up to class II in his village school before migrating to Delhi. After completing his 10th standard, he wants to be engaged either in a Government job or to start his own shop in Azadpur.

It is revealed that poverty and loss of job of his father were the main reasons for his migration and engagement in his job. He is living with his elder brother under threat who collects his wages from his employer every month.

Narratives 6

Name	:	Saroj Kumar (Name changed)
Age	:	12 years
Permanent Address	:	Bhagalpur, Bihar
Years of Working	:	3 years
Place of Working	:	Azadpur

Saroj along with his 6 brothers and father Stay in Bhodala near Adarsh Nagar metro station. Saroj's mother, grandmother and sister stay in the village.

Saroj's father along with the eldest son migrated to Delhi 12 years ago in search of employment. His father at that time was working in New Delhi railway station as a welder and his eldest brother was helping his father in this work. His father worked for two years as a welder and then came to subzi mandi on the advice of a close relative who helped him to start work in the subzi mandi. His father used to purchase fresh vegetables from the market to supply to hotels. In this way, he was able to have a little hike in his income. However, his father was not able to earn sufficient money to fulfil the needs of the family. Moreover, there was also a stiff competition among the suppliers. So, his father quit the job and started to work as a Rickshaw puller. Since then, his father has been working as a rickshaw puller and brought all his family members to Delhi about five years back.

Saroj started his work at the age of six in the Azadpur subzi mandi. He generally works from 8 a.m. to 11 a.m. His work place is one kilometer away from his home. Two years ago, when he was walking on the road to his workplace, he met an accident with an auto rickshaw and suffered a head injury. He purchases the tomatoes from the mandi and sales it in the chor bazaar. He gets six rupees profit from the sale of each pack of tomatoes. His eldest brother is working as auto rickshaw driver and is earning well, however his monthly rent of auto rickshaw is also very high as a result he is not able to save much. His other three elder brothers are also engaged as Kuli in tamato mandi. Saroj earns about Rs. 2000-3000/ per month from this job and gives all his earned money to his father. Sometimes he also keeps some pocket money with him and purchases eatables like samosa and pakoda in the market. His two younger brothers prepare *peti* in the mandi for packing of tomatoes. He works six days in a week except Sunday. When Saroj was asked why he was engaged in such job, he replied *'Sir kaam to karnaa padegaa, papa kaam nahi karte hain'*. His father doesn't go regularly for rickshaw pulling. Whatever money his father earns, he spends in drinking liquor at home. He even takes money from his elder sons and spends all money in drinking. His mother frequently comes to Delhi and stays here for couple of weeks. His father used to abuse her and when Saroj including his brothers objected for his behaviour, he also scolded and threatened them. Saroj said *"mujhe bahut buraa lagtaa hai jab mummy ki pitaai hoti hai. Main apni mummy se bahut pyaar kartaa hun"*. He is satisfied in this job and said *"mujhe ye kaam karnaa achchha lagtaa hai"*. He has planned to continue with this job for 4 to 5 years or more and then will look forward for a new kind of well paid job. He said *"main ye kaam aur kuchh dino tak karungaa par uske baad kyaa karungaa maine sochaa nahi hai"*.

They live in a one room rented pucca house with no toilet, bathroom and kitchen facilities. Their house is also not sufficient to accommodate all family members. Saroj along with his two brothers go to subzi mandi for sleeping in the night. Father and other family members take rest in the home. Except one cooking gas stove, they do not have any other electrical gadgets available in his house. Only one ceiling fan is there. Two tin boxes are kept in the house. Woolen clothes and some other valuables are kept in the box.

In the afternoon, usually he goes to watch T.V. in the nearby house or he goes to park to play cricket. He also visits cinema hall once in a month preferably to see Bhojpuri movie. He likes to see action movies with more fighting scenes. He also likes to play cricket along with his friends. Rakesh (name changed), his younger brother also often plays cricket with him in the park.

Saroj wears full sleeves clean clothes but his health condition is poor. His mother washes all the clothes (these days his mother was in Delhi). He takes roti, rice with dal and vegetables. His mother cooks food on the gas. He never takes milk in his diet. Saroj says, whenever he gets sick, he goes to private doctor who charges Rs. 40/ for consultation and extra charges is paid for medicines.

Saroj has no awareness about child labour legislations. He said, *"Mujhe iske baare mein koi jaankaari nahi hai."* When he was asked about his future plan, he replied that he wants to become a doctor but while discussions, he did not show any inclination of being ambitious in life.

The narrative analysis of the study reveals that poor economic condition of his family, unemployment of his father as well as father's addiction were the important reasons for his engagement in job.

Narratives 7

Name	:	Zakir (name changed)
Age	:	13 years
Permanent address	:	Lakheempur, Lucknow
Years of Working	:	one year
Place of Working	:	Nandnagari

Zakir stays along with his parents and two elder sisters in Sundernagari. His father migrated to Delhi in1990 along with one of his friend of his village. His father belongs to a village near Lucknow. The main reason of his migration was to get a suitable employment in Delhi. Since his father migrated to Delhi, he is working as a kabadibala.

Zakir started his work one year ego in an auto parts (garage) in E-block Nand Nagari, Gagan cinema road, Delhi. He works at stretch between 9 a.m. to 8p.m. with half an hour break during lunch generally in between 1p.m. to 2 pm. He has not changed his job in the last one year and is quite happy with the learning experiences from the garage. He helps the senior mechanic in various ways. He tightens and loosens the blots, removes the spare parts of the vehicle, and cleans the different spare parts of the vehicle etc. He said *"ghar mein sabse badaa betaa to main hi hun is liye kuchh kaam seekh kar kamaanaa to padegaa, aaj kaam seekhungaa to paanch saal baad jaakar khud ki kuch aamdani hogi"*. He gets one day off (on Tuesday) in every week and works even on Saturday and Sunday. He is paid

Rs. 20/ at the end of every working day. He said, his wage is very less because he is a trainee and acts as a helper in the garage. However, his employer pays him Rs. 100-200/ during festival times such as Eid, Holi, Diwali, etc. No other benefits are provided to him by his employer. The work place is at a walking distance of about 800 metres from his home. Zakir says *"ustaad mujhe kabhi-kabhaar gaali detaa maarta hai, par aise to school mein teacher bhi maartaa hai aisaa mere abbu kehte hain"*.

All his family members (7) stay in the jhuggi. It is a double storey pucca dwelling (20-22 sq.feet) comprising one room at each floor. Zakir said *"mere abbu ne hi yahaan aakar jhuggi daali thi tabse yaheen hamaaraa ghar hai."* The female members of his family use the public toilets located near M-Block Sundernagari School, whereas all the male members in the family visit the open ground located behind Gagan Cinema hall. For bathing purpose, they collect water from public tube well located in the community. They donot have refrigerator in the home. Zakir said *"jab koi mehmaan ghar par aataa hai to hum thande paani ke liye barf padosi se maang lete hain ya fir dukaan se khareed kar lete hain"*. They have one colour T.V along with cable connection used for entertainment purpose. His father has also a mobile phone. They have ceiling fan in each floor of the house. Food is cooked through gas stove. Plastic chairs and a wooden table are also in his home.

Zakir has attended school till 4th class and was then dropped out of school as he had to migrate to Delhi along with all his family members. He feels that being the elder son in the family, it is the natural obligation on his part to contribute for the family. He said, he was never interested in going to school as it pays nothing and on the other hand it makes you work a lot. That is why, he never felt bad on being dropped out of school. Now, he feels very happy that after some time he can contribute money to the family. He feels very much contented that now he can work independently on the puncture of the vehicles and also can help the adult mechanic in screwing the tyre of the vehicles.

During the working days, he does not get any time for any kind of recreational activities. He gets tired after working about eleven hours in the garage. After reaching home in the night, he has his dinner and goes to bed. During the major festivals like Eid, he used to go gagan cinema hall along with his friends. He likes to see salman khan movies. Once in a week, he gets holiday from his job and likes to play cricket with his community friends and also spends time in watching T.V. at home.

Zakir uses very dirty clothes and looks very thin. He says, even if he wears clean clothes it becomes dirty on the same day because of the nature of his job in the garage. Very often during the cold days, he suffers from cold and cough and purchases medicine from the near by medicine store. Some times he also visits the mobile health camp organized by St.Stephens hospital. On both the visits to the Zakir, his dresses were coloured with grease and other lubricants making his appearance quite untidy.

Zakir has no awareness about child labour legislations but he knows that child labour is a crime and the police and non-governmental organization staff catch him for this unlawful activity. He has no such specific future aspirations other than becoming a good mechanic and having his own motor garage.

The narrative revealed that due to the low income of his father, Zakir had to migrate to Delhi in search of employment. He feels that being the elder son in the family, it is his responsibility to contribute for the family.

Narratives 8

Name	:	Pankaj (Name changed)
Age	:	13 years
Permanent address	:	Gorakpur, Uttar Pradesh
Years of Working	:	3 years
Place of Working	:	Sunder Nagari market

Seven years ago, Pankaj's father came to Delhi from Gorakhpur along with his uncles. After two years of working in Delhi, his father brought Pankaj and his other three brothers and mother to Delhi. However, his elder brother (17 years old) left for village one year back to work in the village and to look after the family business. His elder brother stays in his village along with his grand parents and uncles. His elder brother looks after the small general store along with his uncles and also looks after the cultivation. Their family owns some cultivable land in Gorakhpur. Pankaj could not explain the reasons of migration however; he feels his father migrated to Delhi to earn more money.

Pankaj works in his father's Burgar shop located near Gagan cinema Bus stop at Sunder Nagari market (besides Hanuman mandir). He has no fixed time of working. His father and brother are involved in the shop throughout the day. He joins them in the shop whenever he desires. But in the evening from 5 p.m-11 p.m. he always remains in the shop because during the evening time, there is heavy rush in his shop. Pankaj said "*Dukaan ko sambhaalte wakt bheed bahut jyaadaa hoti hai, khaas kar shaam ko, aur unhein sambhaalne ke liye kam se kam do logon ki jarurat hai, agar teen log ho jaate hain to kaam kaa bhaar kam ho jaataa hai, isi liye main roz shaam ko paanch se gyaaraa dukaan par papa aur bhaai kaa haath bataane chalaa aataa hun.*". Pankaj is engaged in this job for the last three years. He said, the work demands to stand for long time and he gets tired. So, whenever, he feels tired he goes home which takes about fifteen minutes from the work place and takes rest over there. He said, sometimes his father gives him some pocket money. He is highly satisfied with this job.

He lives in Tahirpur Resettlement area in a rented pucca dwelling room along with six family members with a monthly rent of Rs. 1000/ per month. His parents, brothers (younger and older) and his younger uncle also stay with him. The water supply facility is available in his house. They have 'matka' in the house which is used for cooling water in the summer season. In his house, electricity connection is also there. They do not have .toilet in the house and have to rely on Saulabh Sauchalaya. They have a colour T.V. with cable connection.

Most of the time, Pankaj enjoys watching T.V. in his home. Though Gagan Cinema is located nearby to his house, he has never visited cinema hall for watching movies. However, he sees posters pasted on the cinema hall to have idea about the latest movie. He also enjoys playing cricket. He said *"Sunday ko kabhi-kabhaar doston ke saath cricket kheltaa hun, aur T.V. par Sehwag ko kheltaa huaa dekhtaa hun, Sehwag meraa best player hai. Isi lye mujhe Sehwag ki batting achchhi lagti hai."*

During the interactions, he was found wearing clean and colorful clothes. On the two occasions, the respondent appeared a happy person, always having smiling face, and extrovert in nature which was reflected during the interactions. Pankaj did not suffer from any major illness so far. On minor health problems like cold, cough and fever, he visits private clinics located in the community.

Due to his involvement in jobs, he feels less interested in study. However, he has attended schooling up to class II in his village school. After coming to Delhi, he is involved in his family business. He wants to become rich and wealthy after growing up.

The above narrative analysis reveals that due to his parent's pressure Pankaj had to migrate to Delhi and engage in the job.

Narratives 9

Name	:	Anisur (Name changed)
Age	:	12 years
Permanent Address	:	Madhepura (Bihar)
Years of working	:	3 years
Place of Working	:	Azadpur

Anisur and his father stay in Delhi. His two elder sisters and three younger brothers live along with his mother in the village. Anisur's father came to Delhi from Bihar about eleven years before in order to get a suitable employment. His father had about one bigha of agricultural land in the village which was the only source of livelihood. His father used to produce wheat, rice, maze etc. But the agricultural produce was not sufficient to maintain his family partly due to frequent loss in cultivation. So, his father left for Delhi for doing some job. After Coming to Delhi, he started work as a small vegetable vendor. With the passage of time, his father built rapport around the market area and now working as a vegetable whole seller in the Azadpur Subzi mandi. Anisur was forced by his father to come to Delhi to support him in his business.

Anisur does every household related work of his home. He wakes up at 4 am and start preparing the breakfast for him and his father. He cooks food (breakfast, lunch and dinner) and does various house related tasks including cleaning of clothes, cleaning the house and washing the utensils etc. He brings lunch for his father and works 5 to 6 hours along with his father in the subzi mandi. So, his father takes some rest in the subzi mandi itself. Some times he also sits in a nearby grocery shop and spends about 3 to 4 hours to earn some pocket money. He feels very proud of that he can cook all types of food which he has learned by himself. His father goes to work at 3 am in the morning and comes back home at 7 p.m. Anisur prepares dinner for his father before 7pm. He says his father saves three hundred rupees per day after all expenditures like food, travel and miscellaneous expenses.

Before his migration to Delhi, he was studying in Madrasa in his village. He was very much dissatisfied with the quality of education offered in the madrasa. After coming to Delhi, he feels satisfied with the facilities available in Delhi. In his village, they do not have electricity facility so they use kerosene oil for lighting the lamp. The entire village depended on one hand pump for drinking water. He feels satisfied to be at Delhi.

Anisur stays in a small single room accommodation at Bhadola village without any separate toilet and kitchen and pays a monthly rent of Rs. 1000/ per month and about Rs. 250/ electricity charges. About 20 people from his village stay near to his house. However, they have made a little space in the outside corner of the house which is used for bathroom. For toilet, they used to go open ground with a bottle of water. They have two folding beds along with blankets, bed sheets, pillows and other necessary things. They have also a very small size colour TV with cable connection, ceiling fan, and a cooler in his home. Anisur cooks food in cooking gas stove. His house and nearby surrounding is neat and clean. So Anisur feels very happy in Delhi because of all these facilities.

Anisur's physical appearance looks good. During the cold days, he usually suffers from cold and whenever he has any health problem, his father takes him to private clinics only. The consultation fee of the doctor is Rupees 40. Anisur says he doesn't find any time for recreation due to the overburden of work. During late evenings particularly after having dinner along with his father, he spends some time in watching Hindi movies. He has never taken any kinds of tobacco addiction and said *"Jo log nashaa karte hain main to unki taraf dekhtaa bhi nahi hun. Jo log mere pados mein Nashaa karte hain main unke paas bhi nahi jaataa"*. He goes home in every two months with his village people who live nearby and stays at least for a week

He wants to study in Delhi, but his father does not allow him to study. When he was asked about his future plan, then he replied *"Abba jo chaahenge main wo hi banungaa"*. He is interested to study and wants to become a teacher. He wants to educate all those children who could not able to educational facility like him. After becoming a teacher he can be able to educate all the poor children in his village.

The narrative analysis of the above revealed that poverty and lack of availability of educational facilities in his village were the primary reasons for his migration. Further, he was forced by his father to support him in his business.

Narratives 10

Name	:	Harish (Name Changed)
Age	:	13 years
Permanent native place	:	Faizabad, U.P.
Years of working	:	4 years
Present address	:	Sundernagari grocery shop

Harish was thirteen years old at the time of study. His parents have six children, 4 girls and 2 boys. Harish is the eldest son and is the third child among other siblings. His parents and other family members are staying in Faizabad in Uttar Pradesh.

Harish ran away from his house after a bitter fight with his father. He reported that he was going to school and was studying in class II. But his father pulled him out of school and put him in the work. So, at the age of seven he joined in work, not as choice but for his father's pressure to earn money. The low income of his parents compelled him to get engaged in remunerative job. He was working in a shop that sold purses, belts and toys and earned about Rs. 20 per day. His father always wanted him to earn more. But he tried a lot but could not earn more and was always being scolded and ill treated by his father. He said *"Maine bahut koshish kiyaa jyaadaa paisaa kamaane kaa kyonki baba aisaa kehte the"*. He was feeling miserable. So, he decided to leave his home and come to Delhi on being advised by a village friend who was working in Delhi. He reported that *"Mere dost ne kahaa Dilli mein bahut paisaa hai aur kaam bhi aasaani se mil jaataa hai."* He came to Delhi hoping to earn more money so that he could reduce the burden of his father's loan by sending him more money. Thus, it is revealed that poverty, low income of parents and large size of the family are the main causes of child labour.

Now Harish works in Sunderinagari in a grocery shop and gets about Rs. 1200 per month as wages with breakfast and lunch. His employer also gives him dresses and sweets and bonus money during Dipawali and other festive occasions. He starts working since 6 a.m. in the morning and works till 9.30 p.m. His place of work is quite at a distance from his jhuggis. After reaching the shop, he cleans the shop premises, arranges things in order. By 6.30 a.m. the shop is opened and ready for customers. He said *"Main roz subah jaldi uth jaataa hun chaahe garmi ho yaa sardi aur sab ke liye chay banaataa hun."* He also prepares tea for himself and the employer and also does some household work of the employer if required like purchasing of medicines, giving vegetables in his home etc. Thus, he spends generally 12 to 14 hours in work with about one hour break for breakfast and lunch. After working such long hours, he gets very tired. His main responsibilities are to weigh goods and give to customers.

Harish stays in the jhuggi along with his village friend and pays a monthly rent of Rs. 450 equally shared by both of them. The water supply facility is not available in the house. They collect water for drinking and cooking purposes from the nearby community water tab. They do not have toilet in the house and have to rely on sulabh sauchalya which charges a nominal payment. They have a 'matka' in the house used for cooling water in the summer. Temporary electricity connection is there which enables them to use a fan and an electric bulb. Harish and his friend cooks food in the night and both of them eat together.

Harish is not a very healthy child because of undernourishment and looks very weak. When he falls ill, he prefers to visit private doctors. When he was asked why he visits private doctors, he reported *"doctor sui nahi lagaataa hai."*

Harish has attended schooling up to class II. When he was asked whether he wants to continue his education, his eyes filled with tears and replied positively. He often watched many children going to school and often dreamt of going to school. However, he is very keen and eager to study if provided opportunity. He has no knowledge and awareness about the child labour legislations.

The narrative of the above revealed that bitter fight with his father for forcing him to earn more money was the immediate reason for his migration to Delhi. In his case, poverty, low income of parents and large size of the family were the main causes of his engagement in job.

Grounded Theory based on Narrative Analysis

One of the most commonly used approaches to coding is grounded theory. This approach has been used extensively across a variety of social science disciplines. Its central focus is on inductively generating novel theoretical ideas or hypotheses from the data as opposed to testing theories specified before hand. In so far as these new theories 'arise' out of the data and are supported by the data, they are said to be grounded. It is only at a later stage of the analysis that these new ideas need to relate to existing theory.

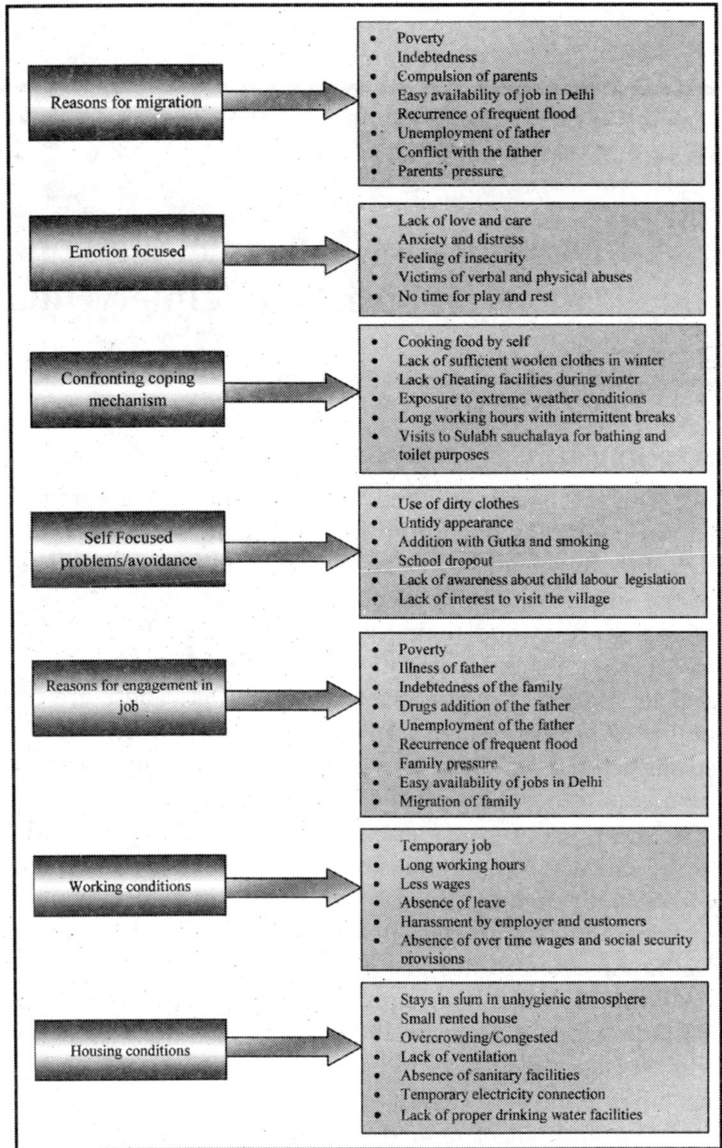

Fig. 8.1: Grounded Theory based on Narratives

9

Conclusions, Recommendations and Implications for Social Work Intervention

INTRODUCTION

This last chapter is aimed at concluding the research work by presenting the major findings of the study. This is followed by some suggestions extended for the abolition and mitigation of the practice of child labour and amelioration of situation of the children and their families. The same form the basis for drawing up the implications of the practice of social work and in suggesting appropriate intervention. These are based on the responses of the sample respondents, views of lawyers, social activists and social workers and also the researcher's own experiences during the research work.

The present study encompassed an in-depth study of child labour issues confronting the society. It aimed at providing a detailed description about the determinants and dimensions of child labour as it prevails in the context of Delhi. An attempt has also been made to critically examine the various child labour legislations in India as well as policy initiatives undertaken by the Government of India. Besides this, it has also presented the grounded theory based on narrative analysis of child labourers.

The study incorporated a quantitative analysis of the data gathered from the responses of child labourers, their parents and employers through interviews, coupled with a qualitative analysis sourced from the narratives from child labourers which uncovered some important aspects related to the problems of child labourers employed in small scale commercial establishments in Delhi.

The present chapter is divided into two sections. Section-I deals with major findings of the study and Section-II presents various recommendations as well as implications for social work practice.

SECTION - I

Section-I presents the major findings of the study under the following sub sections:

Demographic Profile of the Respondents
Child Labour Legislations in India: A Critical Analysis
Determinants of Child Labour
Dimensions of Child Labour

DEMOGRAPHIC PROFILE OF THE RESPONDENTS

Demographic Profile of Child Labourers

Nearly 43% of the children were 13 years or above, the remaining were less than 11 years of age at the time of data collection. It is significant to note that 7% of the respondents belonged to the age group of 7-9 years.

The sample comprised of a mix of children from Hindu and Muslim families, though a majority of them 73(60.8%) were Hindus. The findings of the study are in contrast with the study of Patil (1988). His study revealed that a large percentage of children were from Muslim and Christian families.

24.10% children belonged to the Upper Castes, 18.3% to Other Backward Castes and 17.5% to Scheduled Castes and Scheduled Tribes. So, it can be said that children, irrespective of religion and caste, were engaged in menial jobs in various small scale commercial establishments in Delhi.

The study revealed that 65.8% respondents belonged to nuclear families, while the remaining belonged to joint or extended families. So, it can be said that a large percentage of the child labourers come from nuclear families as against the common belief that larger families contribute more to quantum of child labour.

The study found that 37(30.8%) of the respondents had two siblings and 31(25.8%) respondents had more than three siblings. Only 18(15%) were the single child of their parents. Four children did not have any information regarding their families.

As far as the engagement of the siblings in petty jobs was concerned the study revealed that in the case of 75(62.5%) respondents, their siblings were also engaged in petty jobs and further out of this group 23(19%) respondents reported that their siblings were engaged in the same work as them.

The study found that 34(28%) respondents were the eldest among the siblings, 33(27.5%) were in the middle position and 31(25.8%) were the youngest in the family. It is significant to note that despite the fact that 18(15%) were the 'only child' in the family, yet they were engaged in petty employment probably due to poverty.

The study reported that, a majority of the respondents 103(85%) had both parents alive. The remaining 14(11.6%) respondents had only one parent. It was in three cases that both the parents were dead.

The demographic profile of child labourers showed that a majority of the children were from outside Delhi and belonged to the states of Uttar Pradesh and Bihar. Regarding migration of the respondents it was found that a majority of them had migrated before the year 2009.

The educational profile of child labourers as found by the study revealed that 58(48.3%) of the respondents were illiterate, 25(20.8%) had only literacy skills and 36(30%) of them had dropped out somewhere in the primary classes, or at the most completed primary schooling. Only one respondent had studied further i.e up to class seven. This reflects the extremely low educational attainment of these children and the low emphasis on education for them & their families.

As far as the occupational status of the parents of the child labourers was concerned, a majority of the children reported that their parents were wage labourers and were engaged in jobs which were by and large covered in unorganized sector. In few cases parents were found to be self employed. 17(14%) children reported that their parents were not doing any job and were mostly dependent on their earnings.

In keeping with the nature of occupation in which parents were involved it was noticed that the monthly earning of parents was also very low. Almost a negligible number of respondents (3) reported that their parents earned more than Rs. 5000/ per month. The low income of the parents could be a major reason for migration of families/children in search of jobs in metropolitan cities and their compulsion to work in small scale commercial establishments.

Profile of the Parents of Child Labourers

The age wise distribution of respondents (mostly fathers) revealed that a majority of the parents were less than 45 years of age. The family structure of the respondents revealed that a majority 36(90%) belonged to nuclear families. The mean size of the family was found to be 4 members. As far as the siblings' engagement in job was concerned, a majority of the respondents reported that their other children were also engaged in work. The parents of the respondents were either self employed in petty vocations like hawking, rickshaw pulling and fruits and vegetable selling or they were engaged in menial jobs like working as construction workers or employed in dhabas, tea stalls and garages. The study revealed that most of the children came from poor economic background with monthly earning of less than Rs. 5000/. The educational status of parents also presented a very dismal picture as 25(62.5%) of fathers had no education, 11(27.5%) had only basic education, 3(7.5%) had studied up to primary level and only one respondent was found to have studied up to middle level. In a manner of speaking, the poor educational attainment of parents may have reinforced the less than optimal desire within them to provide their childen with education.

Profile of the Employers of Child Labourers

The age wise distribution of employers revealed that a majority of employers were in the age group of 36-45 years.

The study reported that most of the respondents 29(72.5%) were Hindus with remaining being the Muslims. Majority of the employers who were Hindus either belonged to the Upper Castes or the Other Backward Castes. As far as the educational qualifications of the employers was concerned, a majority of the employers 24(60%) were found to have studied up to the primary level and very few of them 2(5%) had studied up to the middle class.

CHILD LABOUR LEGISLATIONS IN INDIA – A CRITICAL ANALYSIS

The review of literature revealed that child labour was prevalent in India even in ancient and medieval periods when children were engaged in agricultural and domestic activities. It was also found that during this period no significant initiatives were undertaken for the abolition of the problem of child labour. During the British rule (1757-1947 A.D.) under the patronage of the East India Company, certain specific industrial organizations grew in the 18th and 19th centuries which involved the employment of large number of artisans especially in weaving, carpentry, silk and other sectors. The prolonged scarcity of food, extreme poverty caused by famines, lack of education and absence of compulsion for education of children and large scale unemployment of adult workers resulted in the entry of children into the labour market. However, due to the pressure of social reformers, the British government enacted a few protective legislations for the child labour in India. The Indian Factories Act, 1881; Mines Act, 1901; Factories Act, 1911; Factories (Amendment) Act, 1922; Indian Factories Act, 1931; Children (Pledging of Labour) Act, 1935 and Employment of Children Act, 1938 were enacted with a view to prohibit the employment of children in factories carrying out hazardous work.

The major thrust of these laws was on regulating the conditions and hours of work of children. Moreover, these laws were mainly confined to factories and mines. Also, there was no effective process of verification and strict enforcement of rules. As per the Labour Investigating Committee Report (1946), the main cause of this was the inadequacy of the inspecting staff to enforce the provisions of those welfare legislations. It is also important to note that no unified attempt was made by the British government to prohibit child labour as such. Hence, child labour continued to exist as a means of providing cheap labour.

After independence, numerous provisions ensuring justice to children were envisaged in Part-III and Part-IV of the constitution. The Government of India enacted important legislations from time to time such as the Factories Act, 1948; the Minimum Wages Act, 1948; the Merchant Shipping Act, 1958; the Motor Transport Workers Act, 1966; the Plantations Labour Act, 1951; Beedi and Cigar Workers (Conditions of Employment) Act,1966 and Child Labour (Prohibition and Regulation) Act, 1986.

The basic aim of all these enactments was to prohibit the employment of children in certain employments and regulate the conduct of the employers of child labourers so that the latter were not exploited.

The major points of criticism of the child labour legislations enacted after India's independence are as follow:

- It is noteworthy that despite the fact that laws exist to regulate and prohibit employment of children in hazardous employments, there is neither a blanket prohibition on the use of child labour, nor is there any universal minimum age set for child labourers. This provides avenues for employment of child labourers. Therefore it would not be fallacious to say that inadequate legislation, as well as insufficient enforcement, is responsible for the continuation and perpetuation of the phenomenon of child labour.
- A major criticism of the legislations on child labour is the lack of uniformity. The various acts define the term 'child' differently. As already mentioned these legislations do not conform to a single agreed minimum age which differs from Act to Act, state to state and industry to industry. The same is also true with regard to the working hours, rest periods and night employment. Moreover, even where legislations apply, the employers do not conform

to them. There is also hardly any case when the government took the employers to courts for disregarding the various stipulations. Even if they were caught violating the provisions of the child labour laws, the judicial punishment given to them has been limited and is most often nominal. As a result, the legislation does not act as a deterrent and the tendency to employ children continues. Besides that, the administrative authorities have no powers to suspend or cancel the license of a factory violating these laws. This conveniently ensures that no effective steps are taken to alleviate the presence of child labour.

- Another major defect of child labour related laws is that they prohibit employment of children only in hazardous occupations. However, a large number of working children do not come under the term "hazardous labour" as they work in unorganized sectors like agriculture, cottage industries etc. All of these sectors provide inferior conditions and which are unsuited to their physical development (Weiner, 1996). The legislation also fails to include 'new' hazardous occupations and is unclear about the criteria that shall be used for defining what is 'hazardous' (Burra, 1986, Fernandes, 1986).
- The Child Labour (Prohibition and Regulation) Act of 1986 emphasizes regulation rather than prohibition of child labour. The legislation bans the employment of children in factories, but children are otherwise permitted to enter the labour force at any age. They can be legally employed in small workshops. They are free to work in numerous fields. For example, rag picking is not classified as hazardous, though thousands of children collecting scraps of iron, glass, paper and rags often pick up bits of food to eat and are prone to tetanus, skin diseases and other hazards. It is important to note that the legislation for child labour in the so called 'non-hazardous' occupations without regard for age is a violation of Articles 24, 39 and 45 of the Indian Constitution, which ban child labour and call for compulsory schooling.

Incidentally, in the Unnikrishnan and others Vs the State of Andhra Pradesh (1993) case, the Supreme Court had argued that free and compulsory education should be considered as a Fundamental Right.

- Again Section II of the 1986 legislation stipulates that a register must be maintained of all children employed in the establishment and the same should be scrutinized by inspectors. But the stipulation only applies to children employed on regular basis. Since a majority of child labourers are employed on a casual basis, these children do not show up in the official registers. Also, the provisions do not apply 'to any establishment wherein any process is carried on by the occupier with the aid of his family' and this somewhat subjective phrase provides a convenient loophole.
- Again a major chunk of the girl child labourers do not come under the definition of child labour because according to these laws there must be an identifiable employee and an identifiable employer. But most of the girl children are mainly confined to domestic sphere and are normally invisible. Moreover, children working as part of family labour do not come under the purview of Child Labour (Prohibition and Regulation) Act.
- Additionally, the governmental machinery to implement these laws is inadequate. Inspectorate system does not work at all and partly as a result of this, children are often not aware of their rights. For example, under Section 12 of the 1986 legislation, every establishment where children are employed is supposed to prominently display some of the provisions of 1986 legislation through notice, both in the local language and in English. Virtually no establishment complies with this provision. The employers are not punished as the inspectors never turn up. In fact, the jurisdiction of individual inspectors is also too extensive for them to keep a regular watch on activities within their purview. The labour inspector, whenever he gets a chance to book any violation, has difficulties in collecting evidence for proper prosecution.

- The government in the Act of 1986 claimed that it would abolish the serious problem of child labour within ten years. Despite the fact that it has enough powers to deal firmly with employers violating the provisions of the various child labour legislations, this abhorrent exploitation continues. The enforcement of the legislation of 1986 was again left in the hands of inspectors who have proved rather ineffective through all these years (Shandilya and Khan, 2003).
- The new Act of 1986 does not specify how the welfare, health and safety of child labourers are to be protected. The government has taken upon itself the task of providing all welfare measures, leaving the employers rather free of this responsibility.
- In addition to various legislations, the Government of India implemented the National Child Labour Projects Scheme in 1988 to rehabilitate the child labourers. An assessment of the projects revealed that no suitable mechanisms have been evolved for monitoring the implementation of the project either at the district level or at the state level. Also a number of defects were found in the implementation of the project.
- Besides formulating numerous legislations and welfare programmes for the children, the Government of India has also ratified various United Nations Conventions which put focus on three main issues (a) minimum age of employment; (b) medical examination of the working children; and (c) prohibition of night work by children. Most of the Conventions and Recommendations of the ILO show that only a few of them are relating to agricultural and non-industrial occupations; they are mainly concerned with industrial employment. In other words, they are more relevant to industrially developed countries. In a country like India where the bulk of the work force is in agriculture, their relevance is limited. It may not be wrong to say that these Conventions and Recommendations have been framed and adopted with reference to the conditions prevalent in the industrialized

countries and not much thought has been given to the needs of child labourers in non-industrialized countries. The Indian Government has not adopted and ratified all the Conventions of the ILO, which is also one of the important reasons for the unbridled growth of child labour in India.

DETERMINANTS OF CHILD LABOUR

Children's Responses

Determinants of Child Labour

The study revealed that the most important factor which led the children to work was to supplement their family income. About 62(52%) children started working only because their parents wanted them to work since the economic background was very poor for the entire family; they joined work so that they could provide extra income to the family. Some of the respondents also informed that since their father did not get any job throughout the year, they had to face financial crisis. So, in order to support the family, they joined in remunerative work Poverty of the household was an important factor and 48(40%) respondents started working due to the absolute poverty in which they and their families were placed. Again 59(49%) child labourers reported that they started working due to the family pressure only because their parents wanted them to work. This was due to the illiteracy and ignorance of the parents. Besides these, lack of interest in studies; dropping out of schools; migration of parents; desire for having a better living standard; to earn some pocket money and death of parents were also emerged as determinants of child labour.

Reasons of Leaving Schooling

The study revealed that about 54% of the drop outs were those whose parents could not afford to send them to schools due to financial constraints. These children reported that they had been pulled out of schools in order to supplement the family income. Thus, the poor income of the parents was an important factor for the children dropping out from schools. It was also found that around 46(38.33%) of the total drop outs were not interested in studies and considered work more beneficial than study. A majority of these child labourers 54 (45%) dropped out because of parental pressure to get engaged in either remunerative work or in family occupation. A significant number of respondents 38(31.66%) also dropped out due to the migration of their parents to Delhi. Thus, the underlying cause of dropping out of the school of the children was also rooted around the poverty of the parents.

However, the study reported that 16 (13.3%) respondents expressed unhappiness due to dropping out from school because they wanted to continue their study and wanted to stay in their village. One of the respondent said, *"Jab kaam karte-karte disturb ho jaata hun to kaam chhod kar padhaai karne ka mann karta hai, magar kya karu hamare is kaam ke alaawaa kamaai ka koi jariyaa bhi to nahi hai, isi liye main kaam karta hun. Jyada padhne ke liye jyada paisa chaahiye, mere poore pariwaar mein koi nahi padha hai"*. Another respondent said, *"jab mann mein padhaai ka khayaal aa jaataa hai to kaam mein mann nahi lagta hai."* In contrast, 25(20.80%) respondents opined that they felt very much relieved after dropping out. These respondents reported that they became economically independent and they preferred that.

Reasons of Migration

The study found that 59(49 %) children reported that financial problems of their families was the most important reason of migration. 47(39%) children reported that they had come to Delhi because of family problems. These children reported that their parents used to quarrel and they felt neglected and uncared for. 8% children said that they were allured by the city's charm and better job prospects, so they migrated from their home towns. One of the respondent replied, *"Har saal baadh ke kaaran kheton aur gharon mein paani bhar jaataa hai aur hamein bahut pareshaani hoti hai, kai baar to saari fasal barbaad ho jaati hai."* Thus, as the study reveals, the main reasons of migration included financial problems, family problems, natural disasters and pressure to search for livelihood opportunities. This is in tune with the findings of other studies like NIPPCD (1978), Gangrade (1978) and Khandekar (1972).

The study found that 64(53.3%) child labourers joined work force between the age group of 9-11 years followed by 27(22.5%) who joined between 7-9 years and 21 (17.5%) who started work at the age of 11-13 years. Only 8 (6.7%) started work at the age of even less than 7 years.

A majority of the respondents 58(48.3%) had never attended school before joining their work followed by 25(20.8%) who had done schooling up to 2nd standard and 36(30%) who had education up to 5th standard.

Aspirations of Child Labourers

The study reported that a majority of the respondents 94(78.3%) had never thought about their future. One of the respondent replied, *"ghar mein sabse badaa betaa to main hi hun, isi liye kuchch kaam seekh kar kamaanaa to padegaa, aaj kaam seekhungaa to paanch saal baad jaakar khud ki kuchch aamdani hogi."* Another respondent said, *"Abbaa jo chaahenge main wo hi banungaa."* Their immediate concern was only to fulfil their immediate basic needs. Besides that, a significant number of respondents had very low ambitions as they wanted to continue that work in the future also. The finding of the study is in contrast with the study conducted by Pant, 2006. His study revealed that the child labourers wanted to be doctors, police men, photographers, cricket players and actors.

Awareness about Compulsory Education and Legal Provisions

The study revealed that most of the child labourers were not aware of child labour legislations which ban employment of children below 14 years. These children also did not have any knowledge about free and compulsory education and the Right to Education Act. However, a significant number of children were aware of various non-governmental organizations working nearby for the education and empowerment of child labourers.

Parental Perspectives

Determinants of Child Labour

The study revealed that 22(55%) parents sent their children for work because of poverty. 6(15%) parents reported that they had sent their child to work as he was wasting his time. 8(20%) parents reported that their child was not interested in studies and 4(10%) viewed that children were sent to work to learn skilled work so that in future they would get employment easily. So, it was evident that poverty was the predominant factor which compelled the parents to send their children for remunerative work. The same was articulated both by the parents as well as the children.

Poverty and Inadequate Income of the Parents

In the present study, 40% of child labourers reported poverty as the main reason for their engagement in work and 55% of parents also reported that poverty was one of the important causes for sending their children for work. This finding is also supported by the studies conducted by Mishra and Mishra (1990), Patil (1988), Kulshrestha (1978), Rao (1996), Singh (1990) and Shah (1992).

Illiteracy of the Parents

The present study revealed that literacy level of the parents seemed to have a relation with the incidence of child labour as 25(62.5%) of the parents were found to be illiterate. Thus, parental illiteracy was also a contributory factor for existence of child labour. Majority of the child labourers came from illiterate families. Many other studies have also showed that the incidence of child labour has been found to be more in families where the father or the mother was illiterate. Sharma and Sharma (1997) also brought out with a similar result in their study on child labour in the glass industry of Firozabad. The study of George (1977) revealed that most of the children who came to the labour force belonged to families in the lower literacy group. His study reported that parents of 44% of child labourers were illiterate.

Occupation of the Parents

The study reported that a significant number of parents 21(48%) were either engaged in petty jobs or unemployed, which was of course an important contributing factor for the incidence of child labour. The study of Savitri (1985) also stated that unemployment of adult members in the family was also one of the reasons which contribute towards child labour.

Employers' Responses

Reasons for Hiring Child Labourers

As per the present study, 13(40%) employers reported that children were engaged in their establishment only because they wanted to learn the trade. 7(17.5%) said that the parents had requested them to give employment to their children. It may be that their parents were financially very weak and unable to fulfill the basic necessities of life. Again 7(17.5%) employers reported that children were very obedient and never complained on any issues. They work hard and were happy with their wages. However, 6(15%) employers reported that the children themselves had approached them directly for job due to family pressure to supplement family income. 4(10%) viewed that the work was basically child centric and the children could do these unskilled jobs efficiently.

So, it could be said that learning trade skills was an important reason cited by the employers for the employment of children in small scale commercial establishments. This finding is also supported by the study of Singh (1990) conducted in Varanasi.

DIMENSIONS OF CHILD LABOUR

Work History, Working Conditions and Terms of Employment

Age of Entry into the Workforce

So far as the age of entry into the workforce was concerned, the study found that a majority of the children 64(53.3%) entered between 9-11 years. The study also revealed that in Delhi, children of different age groups entered into some or other vocations either due to poverty, and/or large size of the families, or lack of parental care or some associated reasons.

First job of Child Labourers

The study revealed that before entering into the present work context, a majority of the children were in schools and once they entered into employment, they were continuing in that very work even when data was gathered by the researcher for the present study. So, it can be said that once the child was engaged in one type of work, he continued to be in that work for a long time frame.

Source of Getting Work

Regarding the source of getting Work, a majority of the respondents (53%) informed that, they got their work either though the help of relatives who were already employed or through friends (16%) who were working in Delhi. Some others had got employment by themselves. In some cases they were also found to be engaged in their family occupation.

Duration of Work

The study revealed that a majority of child labourers 59(49.2%) were in the present employment for last six months to one year. The children's length of engagement was found varying from six months to three years. Only 5% children were found working for more than 3 years in the same employment.

Distance from Home to Workplace

A majority of the respondents (57.5%) reported that their workplace was within walking distance (less than 1 km.) and that they used to come to their workplace by walking. The study revealed that the distance between homes to work place varied from less than 1 km. to 3 kms. In very few cases (5%) children used to travel more than 3 kms. to reach their place of work. Thus, the children preferred staying near the workplace by hiring cheap residential places nearby.

Employment Status of the Child

A majority of the respondents (55%) pointed out that they were having full time work whereas 33% of the respondents were occupied in part time work. 8% of the respondents reported that their work was permanent in nature. These respondents were mainly working in their family occupation or in the business of their relatives. Only 4% of the respondents reported that their work was casual in nature as they were not compelled by their parents to do the work. They were working to earn some pocket money for their personal expenditure.

Working Hours

Regarding working hours of children, the study revealed that their working hours varied from 4 hours to more than 12 hours a day. 25(20.8%) children reported that they worked for more than 12 hours per day. This confirmed the general observation that children are put to longer hours of work by the employers. This finding is also in tune with the study of Barooch (1977) and the Report of the National Commission of Labour (Government of India, 1969).

Weekly Holidays

Regarding weekly off days, it was very disheartening to note that most of the children (59.2%) did not get any weekly offs and if at all they got any, that was unpaid.

Overtime Work

The study revealed that a majority 73(60.8%) of the children were doing over time, as far as work hours were concerned. While doing overtime work, they were provided with free food and some pocket money. The children employed in tea shops/dhabas and subzi mandi were mostly working for more than 12 hours. So, it can be said that children even in that tender age were forced to do overtime work, much beyond their scheduled timings.

Children's Monthly Earning

The study revealed that the wages of child labourers depended entirely on the mercy of the employers. Further, nearly 51(42.5%) children received a monthly income between Rs. 500 to less than Rs. 1000. There were 38(31.66%) children who earned between Rs. 1000 to Rs. 1500. 18 (15%) children reported that their monthly earnings were even less than Rs. 500. Some of these children in this category were employed in family occupation and received only pocket money. Almost all the child labourers received their income in cash, either on daily, weekly or monthly basis depending on the type of work they were engaged in. Sinha (1994) in his study on child labour also found that the wages were low and they worked continuously without any interval.

Recipients of Children's Earnings

As per the present study, 42(35%) respondents received their wages by themselves and 59(49%) revealed that the wages were given to their parents/relatives. The rest of the respondents did not receive any wages as they were placed in family work. The practice of receiving wages on behalf of the children was prevalent in almost all sectors included in the present study. However, its occurrence was greater in tea stalls/dhabas. Singh (2006) also reported that in most of the cases wages were paid to the children and daily and weekly payment system was also prevalent in auto workshops and furniture industry.

Nature of Work Performed

A majority of the respondents 87(72.5%) reported that they were doing unskilled work. 25(20.8%) were employed in semi skilled work and a few children 8(6.7%) reported that they were engaged in skilled work. Thus, most of the children employed in the informal sector were doing unskilled work.

A majority of the employers reported that child labourers mostly assisted adult workers particularly those engaged in garages/tea shops/dhabas. A sizeable number of the employers also viewed that children were able to work independently.

Degree of Work Satisfaction

Regarding the level of Work satisfaction of child labourers, the study found that about 38% of them were satisfied in their present work as they felt satisfied that they had economically independent and were able to support their family financially to meet their basic needs. Those who were partially satisfied reported that they got less pay and worked for long hours. A significant number of child labourers reported that they were not satisfied with their present work because of the rude behavior of their employers, temporary nature of work, lower wages, longer hours of work, physical assaults by the employers and lack of facilities at the work place.

Attitude of Family towards Children's Engagement in Work

Majority of the children 90(108%) reported that their family had a positive attitude towards their engagement in work. The same was reported by the parents (95%) as well.

Attitude of the Employers/Co-Workers and Customers

As reported by the child labourers, the attitude of the employers/co-workers/customers was very cordial and kind. However, a few of them reported that they were sometimes harassed by the employers/co-workers and customers on small faults and sometimes without any reason. One of the respondents said, "*Ustaad mujhe kabhi-kabhar gaali detaa aur maartaa hai, par aisaa to school mein teacher bhi maartaa hai, aisaa mere abbu kehte hain*".

Impact of Work on Health of Child Labourers

Majority of the respondents reported that no health hazard was associated with their present occupation. However, a very small number of them also reported that they had no idea whether the work that they did was harmful to their health.

Disciplinary Actions Taken by Employers

Majority of the employers (84%) reported that they used to counsel the child to work properly if his performance and behaviour was not satisfactory. However a very few of them reported that they sometimes scolded and gave some kind of physical punishment to such children.

Recruitment System for Hiring Child Labourers

The study reveals that there was no formal recruitment system for hiring children below 14 years of age. Unlike the formal sector, no such proper recruitment procedure was followed. Children were hired on the basis of recommendations of internal employees, parent's requests for engaging the child and sometimes on the basis of children's request and needs.

Living Conditions

Type of Housing

The study revealed that about half of the child labourers were staying in *kuchcha* houses and a few of them were even staying on foot paths and in parks.

Ownership of the House and Monthly Rent

The study revealed that the respondents mostly stayed in the rented accommodation in the slum areas and the monthly rent varied from Rs. 500 to Rs. 2000 depending upon the size of the dwelling, proximity to the market area and the facilities available in the house.

Water and Sanitation Facility

The study also reported less availability of water and sanitation were a major problems faced by the child labourers living in Delhi. A majority of them had to get water from public tube wells/community water taps or Delhi Jal Board tankers. These respondents used *Sulabh Sauchalayas* (public lavatories) and open spaces for defecation purposes.

Recreational Activities

The study revealed that the child labourers could hardly get time for playing or to engage in any other recreational activities. They rarely spend their leisure time in watching T.V, cinema or sleeping at their homes. One of the respondents replied, *"Khelna achchaa lagtaa hai, par T.V. par programme zyaadaa achchaa lagtaa hai. Ek din main bhi kamaakar T.V. kharidungaa aur apne gaon le jaungaa."* Another respondent viewed that *"hamaaraa chhotaa kamaraa hai, par T.V. par programme hameshaa chaltaa rehtaa hai, dekh ke mann ko bahut khusi hoti hai"*.

Addiction

The study also found that a majority of the children were addicted to smoking and chewing *gutka* (tobacco) which was cheap and easily available. The researcher found that the family environment and the surroundings in which they lived and worked; the influence of peer group and sometimes curiosity to taste something new were some of the factors responsible for their addiction.

Social Interaction with Friends

The study revealed that the children hardly got any free time to spend with their friends. It was during the celebration of festivals that got relatively more opportunity to spend time with friends.

SECTION - II

RECOMMENDATIONS FOR ABOLITION/REGULATION OF THE INCIDENCE OF CHILD LABOUR AND IMPLICA-TIONS FOR SOCIAL WORK INTERVENTION

Child labour is a complex socio-economic demographic problem which can be reduced and eliminated by multiplicity of actions, both by the government and the civil society sector. On the basis of the research findings, views of lawyers, social activists and social workers and experience emanating from the research process, the following recommendations emerge for dealing with the multiple dimensions of the phenomenon.

Promoting Income Generation Activities

Indisputably, child labour is rooted in poverty. The progressive elimination of this problem will lead to a reduced need for the family to push their children into labour. The income deficiency can be made up by providing sustainable livelihood opportunities to the lower stratum of society through creation of more jobs/livelihood options, agrarian reforms, and enforcement of minimum wages and social security.

Self-employment schemes should be intensified. Poor families must be provided social security including medical and sickness benefits.

Various studies have observed that the parents are compelled to send their children for work only because they had to fulfill their basic needs and repay loans. These sections of the society must be provided with easy and cheap loans returnable in small installments. This type of facility can alleviate the problem to a large extent because the debt is a big compulsion for the parents to put children to work.

A large chunk of the rural population still depends on agriculture therefore it is imperative that this sector should be developed more adequately. Poor families with children should be provided free or subsidized inputs like fertilizers, insecticides and seeds. In rural areas, investment in better irrigation, credit and market facilities should be made available, so that rural people can get more out of their land.

The dairy and fisheries development programme must be given importance. Agro based industries should be promoted to all possible extent for income generation and enhancement among the rural people.

Rural Cooperatives/Self-help Groups should play a more vital role in giving loans, offering help in procuring raw materials and in marketing so that it could add to the rural incomes. Small-scale industries could be promoted on a large scale for reducing unemployment among adults.

Providing Social Safety Nets/Social Protection Schemes

Provision of unemployment allowance, and old age pension schemes should be properly and fairly implemented. Benefits should reach genuine and deserving people. Systems of social protection provided by the state or non-state agencies must be carefully designed and implemented. Microfinance schemes, organized by civil society groups at the local level can be linked into larger structures, such as banks. The state can help by providing start-up funds, and develop a supportive legislative and regulatory frame work.

Providing Educational Opportunities

The school represents the most important means of drawing children away from the labour market. School provides children with guidance and the opportunity to understand their role in the society. So, top priority should be given to universalization of elementary education for children between 6 to 14 years within a time frame not exceeding more than five years. Along with general education, vocational training should be imparted to the children to make them economically independent in their adulthood. Apart from that, to increase the interest towards schools, handsome incentives should be provided to children belonging to the socio-economically backward sections of society in the form of scholarships, free books, stationery, dress and nutritious meals for, at least, up to their fourteenth year of age. These incentives would not only raise the education level but also provide opportunities for skill acquisition and better employment in adulthood.

Flexible timetables and other forms of flexibility in education can also help to accommodate the needs of the child labourers and their families. Not only the child labour enrolled in schools should be given regular guidance but their parents also should be given continuous advice, guidance and financial support for continuing education of their children. This is because the poor economic conditions of parents very often make conflicting demands between work participation and schooling on the children. Thus, even the easy accessibility to schools does not necessarily increase the enrolment of children if economic status of parents does not permit it. Parents belonging to low socio economic groups should be motivated to send their children to school rather than to work place through education, publicity and propaganda.

Many parents involve their children in work because they do not understand and realize the significance of education. It is therefore necessary to develop education consciousness among them by making use of all possible means especially by effectively organizing adult education programmes and work through community based organizations. It is suggested that the government intensify the steps to achieve cent per cent literacy by undertaking adult education programmes, which in turn will enable parents to realize the need and importance of education.

Awareness Generation

Increasing public awareness is critical for the elimination of the problem of child labour. A large number of persons are unaware of the unsafe working conditions in which children work and the repercussions of early employment on children in particular and the society in general. There is need to arouse awareness among the child labourers, their parents and employers of the negative consequences of children's engagement in work. People, specially employers and the parents of the children should be made aware of the existing laws concerning child labour and the penalties imposed for flouting them.

The mass media has a critical role to play in communicating information about child labour. The information it conveys can have a significant influence on public policy and legislation both in terms of formulation and enforcement. Initiatives should be taken to ensure that child labourers get a fair and balanced portrayal and hearing in the media. Mass media should be used for imparting regular information on regular basis and running educational campaigns.

Public lectures can also be organized with more emphasis on the problem and its repercussions. People, specially employers and the parents of children should be made aware of the existing laws concerning child labour and the penalties imposed for non adherence.

There is a need to bring consciousness among children so that they may become aware of their constitutional rights, which is possible with the help of radio, television, spread of education and literacy campaigns.

Efforts should also be undertaken by the voluntary organizations to involve the local public and parents/ guardians of child labourers, so that they become aware of the efforts made by the government for the mitigation of the problem and enhancing the well being of the families.

Strict Implementation of the Legislations

The state governments should take concrete steps to strictly prohibit the employment of children in occupations, which have been banned under the Child Labour Act. The state government must activate and strengthen the law enforcement machinery to see that all the legislative measures are properly enforced. The enforcement machinery must be geared up to ensure effective enforcement of the Child Labour legislations and take effective steps to prosecute those who violate the act. There is a need to strongly view the violation of child labour laws as serious offences. The need of the hour is to apply the provisions of legislations strictly so that the employers of the child labourers must be severely punished in case of their violation of child labour legislations.

The legal system should be framed in such a way that the people violating this law may not be spared. The law can be formed in such a way that it may leave no loophole where the employer of the children may be left free.

Involving Local Governance Institutions

On account of the fact that, child labour is a localized phenomenon, the panchayats and municipalities can play a potential role in the eradication of child labour by providing local information, enhancing communication, and evolving local monitoring and mobilization.

Implementing and Supporting Fair Trade Labeling Initiatives

There is an urgent need to promote social labeling. Social labeling consists in putting a label on an item- or in the shop where it is sold- which guarantees to consumers that the product has been manufactured without using child labour.

Encouraging Trade Unions

The trade unions can play a very important role in the implementation of existing laws on the minimum age for admission to employment, minimum wages, working hours and rest intervals. Trade unions can work more effectively if they comprehend the physical and mental havoc the child labourers have to face, and the fact that child labour reduces adult wages as well as adult employment.

Role of Non-Governmental Organizations

Non-Governmental Organisations can also help vulnerable and marginalized groups, including child labourers, have their voices heard by government and other decision makers at local, national and even international levels.

NGOs often have a comparative advantage in piloting and evaluating alternative strategies and interventions at community level. They have also played a vital role in advocacy for the elimination of child labour by publishing materials in local languages.

Community based organizations are often best placed to ensure that programmes to combat child labour are realistic and adapted to the local context. There is a need for formation of 'Community Surveillance Groups' which can play an active role in preventing the migration of children by identifying, monitoring and supporting "at risk" families and children.

It is now a challenge for the Non-governmental organizations to address the issue not just on the periphery but aim at structural reforms. Attempts like organizing the unorganized sector, reforms in the primary education system, microfinance for the weaker sections and instilling process for community participation and ownership are some of the essential issues that NGOs would have to address at the outset because lack of such systems contributes heavily to the inflow of children into the workforce.

Provision of Proper Housing/Avenues for Recreation/ Purposeful Utilization of Leisure Time

Proper housing is important for healthy growth, which, in turn, is necessary for higher efficiency. Lack of proper housing not only impairs the healthy growth of children, but also brings them in contact with undesirable elements leading to anti social and delinquent behaviours. In our study, the child labourers were staying in slums, which were devoid of proper water supply, sanitation and lighting arrangement, leading to an unhealthy growth and development. Therefore, provisions should be made for housing with basic amenities. Besides, avenues for meaningful engagement of children in their free/leisure time also need to be provided to ensure that children (working and non-working) are provided stimulation for healthy growth and development of the body and the mind. Availability of recreation centres/clubs/Bal sabhas, etc. can go a long way to ensure that children are suitably engaged and also stay from delinquency and harmful activities.

In sum, there is an urgent need for attitudinal change, social awareness and an aggressive campaign against the scourge of child labour. It should be our national obligation to ensure physical and mental development of children with measures for regulating and humanizing child labour along with an attack on poverty. The eradication of child labour must be an explicit objective of development discourse and must be implemented with perseverance and as a matter of priority. In the absence of a proper development perspective, it is very difficult to keep the child labour away from the labour market. The elimination of the practice of child labour, requires people's participation and cooperation from all sectors i.e. from their families to society at large. The eradication of the problem is a long process, which requires intensive efforts on many fronts and also creation of general social awareness. There is also the urgent need for political mobilization to completely prevent the demand and supply of child labour. The basic strategy concerning child labour should be to gradually reduce and eliminate it through improving and enforcing legislation, promoting school enrolment and raising public awareness. The coordinated efforts of government, NGOs, employers and social workers through active public support are likely to help in ameliorating or controlling the problem.

ROLE OF SOCIAL WORKERS IN THE ABOLITION/ REGULATION OF THE INCIDENCES OF CHILD LABOUR

Social workers should provide guidance and counseling to the child labourers in confronting their problems and tackling them. Counseling is also needed for the families of the child labourers as well as those who are on the verge of sending their children to the labour market. Counseling and guidance are also needed for those children who are poor in studies and are truants so that they are prevented from dropping out of the school and entering into the labour market.

Social work intervention is necessary at the family level, especially where the fathers are alcoholics or drugs addicts or are unemployed. Voluntary agencies need to work closely with these families and provide counseling and referral services depending on their need.

Social workers should work with children to bring about a change from an essentially welfare-based, charitable approach to a more children-centered, rights based approach. Every child of the age of 6-14 years has a right to free and compulsory education in a neighborhood school till completion of elementary education. No child is liable to pay any kind of fee or charges or expenses which may prevent him/her from pursuing and completing the elementary education.

Social workers should take systematic efforts to ensure that work places and communities remain child labour free.

This can be facilitated by awareness raising activities by using participatory approach involving employers, parents, and adult workers in the work places, community leaders, service providers and enforcement agencies. The social workers should ensure that the children withdrawn from work remain and complete their schooling and that new children do not enter work force. This can be done in the schools or educational centers, in the work places and in the communities.

Social workers should focus on the establishment of local child welfare and vigilance committees to oversee the welfare of the children in the community. The social workers should have participatory approach and actively involve the children, their parents, community leaders and teachers.

The social workers should mobilize the media to focus on the rights of the children when dealing with exploitation of children, and should encourage them to give ample coverage to issues related to children, and child labourers.

Children-friendly schools can provide a safe learning environment, equitable access, and also recognition of children's rights and responsibilities. Social workers should use a multifaceted approach to prevent early dropout and involvement in job, by motivating parents, and bridging the gap between home and school.

Lets us all share the following feeling from sense of empathy:

"The child of the new age is arrived,
and a place must be made for him.
And so, we of the worn out world
Must leave bearing the debris
of the frustrated and the dead on our back.
To the new born
I give my firm word of honour.
I shall make this world
a fit place for him to live in".

(Quoted from "Credentials"- in English version of the Bengali poem 'ChharPatra' by Sukanta Bhattacharya, translated by Kshitis Roy, cited in Sen, A (2000) in Development as Freedom.

References

Aldridge, J. and Becker, S. (1995) 'The Rights and Wrongs of Children Who Care', in Franklin, B. (ed.), *The Handbook of Children's Rights: Comparative Policy and Practice*, Rutledge, London.

Ahmed, I. (1999). Getting Rid of Child Labour, Economic and Political Weekly, Vol. 34, No. 27, pp. 1815-22.

Arulmani, G., & Arulmani, S.N. (2010). Applying Psychology for Children in Poverty: The Experience of Non-Governmental Organization. Retrieved from http://www.thepromisefoundation.org/TPFRes01.pdf 16/1/10.

Becker, G.S. (1960). An Economic Analysis of Fertility. In Demographic and Economic Change in Developed Countries, Princeton University press , New Jersey.

Barooah, P. (1977). Working Children in Urban Delhi, A Research Report, Indian Council of Child Welfare, New Delhi.

Bequele, A., & Boyden, J., (1988). Combating Child Labour, ILO, Geneva.

Burra, N. (1995). Born to Work, Child Labour in India, Oxford University Press, New Delhi.

Burra, N. (1986) "Old Flaws in New Child Labour Bill", The Times of India, 7 November.

Berger, L.X., (1991). Medical Aspects of Child Labour in Developing Countries, American Journal of Industrial Medicine, Vol. 19, No. 6.

Basu, K., & Van, P.H., (1998). The Economics of Child Labour, American Economic Review, Vol. 88, pp. 412-427.

Bhat, B.A., & Rather, T.A. (2009). Child Labour in the Handicrafts Home Industry in Kashmir: A Sociological Study, International NGO Journal Vol. 4 (9), pp. 391-400.

Chaudhari, D.P. (1997). A Policy Perspectives on Child Labour in India with Pervasive Gender and Urban Bias in School Education, Indian Journal of Labour Economics, Vol. 40, No. 4 , pp. 789-808.

Castle, R., Chaudhri, D.P., Nyland, C. & Nguyen, T. (1997). Labour Clauses, the World Trade Organization and Child Labour in India, Indian Journal of Labour Economics, Vol. 40 No. 1 January-March, pp. 51-65.

Colombini, J. (2008). Combating Child Labour and Promoting Youth Empowerment. Refugee Survey Quarterly, 27(4), 74-82.

Cockburn, J., & Kabubomaria, J. (2010). Child Welfare in Developing Countries, Springer, London, pp. 162-164.

Dinesh, B.M. (1988). Economic Activities of Children, Daya Publishing House, Delhi.

Duraiswamy, M. (1997). Changes in Child Labour Over Space and Time in India, Indian Journal of Labour Economics, Vol. 40 No. 4, pp. 809-818.

Dessy, S.E. (2001). A Defense of Compulsive Measures Against Child Labour. Journal of Development Economics, Vol. 62, No. 1 (June), pp. 261-275.

Desai, K., Raj, N. (2001). A Study of Child Labour in the Diamond Industry of Surat, V.V. Giri National Labour Institute, NLI Research Studies, Series No 019/2001, Noida.

Dak, T.M. (2002). Child Labour in India, Serials Publication, New Delhi.

Das, D. (2011). Child Labour in India, Rights, Welfare and Protection, Deep and Deep Publications, New Delhi.

Dhar, R.L., & Joshi, R. (2008). Child Labour in the Restaurants and Eateries: A Case Study of Pune City, Paper Submitted in the International Conference on Child Labour & Child Exploitation, Cairns Convention Centre, Queensland, Australia.

Encyclopedia of Social Sciences, (1963), Vol. 11, Tata MacMillan Co., New York.

Elizabeth, B.H. (1972). Child Development, McGraw Hill, London.

Encyclopedia of Social Work in India, (1997), Vol. I, p. 94.

Ennew, J., Myers, W.E., Plateau, D.P. (2007) Defining Child Labour as if Human Rights Really Matter, in an Edited Book Child Labour and Human Rights (eds. Weston, B.H.) Viva Books Private Ltd, New Delhi.

Folks, H., (1946). US Child Labour Commission Report, United States Government, Washington, D.C.

Fernandes, W., Burra, N., Annad, T.S. (1986). Child Labour in India–A Critique of NCLP: Shivkashi, Paper Presented in the Seminar at Indian Social Institute, Delhi.

Fype, A. (1989). Child Labour, Cambridge Polity Press, p. 4.

Foster, J.E., & Sen, A. (1998). On Economic Inequality, Oxford University Press, Delhi.

Flick, (2006). An Introduction to Qualitative Research (3rd edition), Sage, London.

Government of India, (1936). Report of the Royal Commission on Labour.

Government of India, (1946), Labour Investigation Committee Report.

Gore, M.S., (1968). Urbanisation and Family Change, Popular Prakashan, Mumbai.

Gangrade, K.D. (1979). Child Labour in India, Department of Social Work, University of Delhi, Delhi.

George, K.N. (1977). Child Labour in the City of Madras, Paper Presented in the National Seminar on Employment of Children in India, National Institute of Public Cooperation and Child Development, August, 1977, New Delhi.

Gaur, G.L., (1999). Child Labour in College Canteens. A Case Study of Jaipur City, in an Edited Book, Child Labour (Ed. Y.S. Reddy), Anmol Publications Pvt. Ltd., New Delhi.

Government of India, (1969). Report of the National Commission on Labour, Ministry of Labour.

George, K.N. (1977). Child Labour in the City of Madras, Paper Presented in the National Seminar on Employment of Children in India, National Institute of Public Cooperation and Child Development, August, 1977.

Gangrade, K.D. (1979). Child Labour in India, Department of Social Work, University of Delhi, Delhi.

Government of India, (1979). Report of the Committee on Child Labour (Gurupadhasamy Committee), Ministry of Labour, New Delhi.

Gathia, J.A. (1983). Women and Child Workers in Unorganized Sector, Concept Publishing Co., New Delhi.

Gaur, A. (2005). Analytical Study of Girl Child – With Special Reference to the NCT of Delhi, Indian Council of Social Science Research, New Delhi.

Gibbs, G.R. (2007). Analyzing Qualitative Data, (Book6), Sage Qualitative Research Kit, Sage, London.

Hammond, J.L., & Hammond, B. (1919). The Skilled Labour, London.

Hutchins, B.L., & Harrison, A. (1926). A History of Factory Legislation (3rd edition), M.W.Thomas, London.

Hiraway, I., (1991). Towards Eradication of Child Labour: An International View, Gandhi Labour Institute, Ahmedabad.

Hensmen, R. (2001). The Impact of Globalization on Employment in India and Responses from the Formal and Informal Sectors. CLARA Working Paper No. 15, IIAS/IISG, Amsterdam.

Hazarika, G., & Bedi, A. (2003), "Schooling Costs and Child Work in Rural Pakistan, Journal of Development Studies, Vol. 39, pp. 29-64.

Hussain, S., Sarwar, M. (2005). Child Labour: A Poverty Shape, Pakistan Journal of Social Sciences, Vol. 3, Sl.No. 5, pp. 803-808.

ILO. (1973). Population and Child Labour, ILO, Geneva.

Indian Council of Child Welfare, (1977). Working Children in Urban Delhi, ICCW, New Delhi.

IAMR, (1998). Child Labour in Informal Sector, Institute of Applied Manpower Research, New Delhi.

ILO. (1983). Population and Child Labour, ILO, Geneva.

ILO (1997). Technical Paper: Practical Action to Eliminate Child Labour. International Conference on Child Labour, Oslo, Norway.

Impulse Net Work, (2004). Child Labour in Shillong, A Research Study, Retrieved from http://www.jansamachr.net/pof.php3?num=4238&lang=English, Shillong.

Juyal, B.N. (1988). Child Labour and Exploitation in Carpet Industry, Indian Social Institute, New Delhi.

Jain, M. (1996). Elimination of Child Labour in India-Government Initiatives, The Administrator, Vol. XLI, Lal Bahaduar Shastri National Academy of Adminstration, Mussorie.

Jeyaranjan, J. (2001). A Study of Child Labour in the Knitwear Industry of Thirupur, V.V.Giri National Labour Institute, NLI Research Studies, Series No. 024/2001, Noida.

John, J., & Ghosh, R. (2003). Study of Child Labour in the Zardari and Hathari Units of Varanasi, V.V. Giri National Labour Institute, Noida.

Khandekar, M. & Naik., R.D. (1972). Working Children in Greater Bombay, Indian Journal of Social Work, Vol. 32, No. 4, January, pp. 369-86.

Kulshreshtha, J.C. (1978). Child Labour in India, Ashish Publishing House, New Delhi.

Kothari, S., (1983).There is Blood on those Match Sticks, Economic and Political Weekly, July 2, p. 1 197.

Karunanidhi, G. (1990). Child Labour in Melapalayan, Social Welfare, January, pp. 6-7.

Kumar, S., (1993). Child Labour and Eradication. In Children at Work, Problems and Policy Options (Singh, B.D. & Mohanty, eds.), S.B., Publishing Company, Delhi.

Kulshreshtha, J.C. (1994). Indian Child Labour, Uppal Publishing House, New Delhi.

Lumpkin, K.D. & Douglas, D.W. (1938). Child Workers in America, R.M. Mc Bride, p. 7.

Lieten, G.K., Srivastava, R., & Thorat, S. (2004). Small Hands in South Asia: Child Labour in Perspective, New Delhi, IDPAD/Manohar Publisher, Delhi.

Marx, K. (1971). Capital, Vol. 1, Progress Publishers, Moscow.

Manheim, H.L. (1977). Sociological Research: Philosophy and Methods. Homewood, Ill. The Dorsey Press.

Murthy, G.K., & Rani, T.J. (1983). Wages of Child Labour, Yojana, Vol. 27, Sl. No.18, pp. 12-14.

Mishra, P.K., & Mishra, B.N. (1990), Child Labour – A Study in Cuttack City, Indian Journal of Labour Economics, Vol. 33, No. 4.

Mitra, S., (1994). Factors in the Socio-cultural Environment of Child Labourers: A Study in a Small Scale Leather Goods Industry in Calcutta, Occupational and Environmental Medicine, Vol. 51, pp. 822-825.

Mehta, P.L., & Jaswal, S.S. (1996). Child Labour and the Law: Myth and Reality of Welfare Measurers, Deep and Deep Publications, New Delhi.

Mathur, K., & Bhargava, P. (2000). Child Labour in the Home Based Industries in the Wake of Legislation, Institute of Development Studies, Jaipur.

Misra, G., & Mohanty, K.A. (2000). Consequences of Poverty and Disadvantage: A Review of Indian Studies: K.A.Mohanty and G.Misra (editors), Psychology of Poverty and Disadvantage, Concept Publishing Company, New Delhi, pp. 121-148.

Mishra, L. (2000). Child Labour in India, Oxford University Press, New Delhi.

Murthy, S. (2001). Child Labour in India: Causes, Consequences and Cures, RBSA Publishers, Jaipur.

Manimekalai, N. (2001). Child Labour Elimination through NCLP- Some Micro Level Evidences from TamilNadu, in the Book 'Economics of Child Labour '(eds. K.P. Kannan), Deep and Deep Publications, New Delhi. pp. 163-184.

Myers, W.E. (2001). The Right Rights? Child Labour in a Globalised World, Annals of American Academy of Political and Social Science, Vol. 575, pp. 38-55.

Mathur, K., Singh, R.G. (2001). Child Labour in the Home based Zem Polishing Industry of Jaipur, V.V.Giri National Labour Institute, NLI Research Studies, Series No. 025/ 2001, Noida.

Manimekalai, N., (2001). Child Labour Elimination Through NCLP – Some Micro Level Evidences from Tamilnadu, in, Economics of Child Labour (K.P.Kannan, eds.), Deep and Deep Publications, New Delhi, pp. 163-184.

Mishra, R.N., & Pradhan, S.K. (2003). Child Labour in Transport Sector – A Study, in an Edited Book, Child Labour in Hazardous Sectors, Discovery Publishing House, New Delhi, pp. 29-43.

Mishra, S.N. & Mishra, S. (2004). Tiny Hands in Unorganized Sector, Shipra Publications, Delhi.

Mustafa, M. & Sharma, O. (2008). Child Labour in India – A Bitter Truth, Deep & Deep Publications, New Delhi.

Mohapatra, S. & Dash, M. (2011). Child Labour – A Product of Socio-economic Problem in India, A Case of Bhubaneswar, Educational Research, Vol. 2, No. 6, pp. 1199-1209.

NIPPCD, (1978). Child Labour in Bombay, New Delhi

Nangia, P. (1987). Child Labour. Cause - Effect Syndrome, Janak Publishers, New Delhi.

Naidu, U., & Kapadia, A.K., (1985). Child Labour and Health Problems and Prospects, Tata Institute of Social Sciences, Bombay.

National Commission for Protection of Child Rights, (2007), Abolition of Child Labour for the 11th Five Year Plan.

Nanjunda, D.C., (2008). Child labour and Human Rights, A Prospective, Kalpaz Publications, Delhi.

NasirUddin, M., Hamiduzzaman, M., & Gunter, B.G., (2009). Physical and Psychological Implications of Risky Child labour: A study in Sylhet City, Bangladesh Development Research Centre, USA.

ORG, (1993). Child Labour Law – An Overview, V.V.Giri National Labour Institute, Noida.

Perloff, H.S., (1960). Regions, Resources and Economic Growth, John Hopkins University Press, Baltimore.

Pati, R.N., (1985). Rehabilitation of Child Labourers in India, Society for International Development, Bhubaneswar.

Panicker, N & Nongia, P. (1992). Working and Street Children in Delhi. V.V. Giri National Labour Institute, Noida.

Patil, B.R., (1988). Working Children in Urban India, D.B. Publishers (P) Ltd., Bangalore.

Pant, J.C. (2006). Child Labour, A Blot on Indian Belief System, in an Edited Book 'Child Labour from Different Perspectives' (Mahaveer Jain & Sangeeta Saraswat Eds.), Manak Publications, Delhi pp. 234- 243.

Rao, J.S., (1980). Agricultural Child Labour, Indian Journal of Labour Economics, Vol, XXIV, January.

Rodger, G., & Standing, G. (1981). Child Work, Poverty and Unemployment, ILO, Geneva.

Rao, B.V.R., & Mallik, B. (1992). Street Children of Hyderabad V.V. Giri National Labour Insititue, Noida.

Raman, V (1997) Globalization and Child Labour, Paper Presented in the Seminar on 'Globalization and Democracy in the Third World', Academy of Third World Studies, Jamia Millia Islamic University, New Delhi on 7-8 October.

Raj, M., & Chauhan, D. (2001). Nature and Issues of Child Labour in India, Yojana, May, pp. 11-16.

Reddy, B.S., and Ramesh, K. (2002). Girl Child Labour, Dominant Publishers and distributors, New Delhi.

Ramanathan, U. (2009). Evolution of the Law on Child Labour in India in an Edited Book ' The World of Child Labour – An Historical and Regional Survey' Edited by (Hugh D.Hindman), Armonk, New York, p. 783.

Srinivas, M.N. (1979). The Field Worker and the Field, Problems and Challenges in Sociological Investigation, Oxford University Press, Delhi.

Savitri, S., (1985). A Survey of Child Labour in Tamilnadu, in Edited Book "Child Labour and Health: Problems and Prospects" Tata Institute of Social Sciences, Bombay, Series No. 54.

Srivastava, S., & Bhanumathi, R. (1990). Child Workers in Farms, Domestic and Catering Sectors, Indian Journal of Educational Planning and Administration, Vol. 4, No. 1.

Shukla, B.N. & Shukla, B. (1993). Child Labour in the Informal Sector. In Children at Work, Problems and Policy Options (Singh, B.D. & Mohanty, eds.), S.B., Publishing Company, Delhi.

Singh A.N. (1990), Child Labour in India: Socio-Economic Perspectives, Shipra publications, Delhi.

Shah, N.A. (1992), Child Labour in India, Anmol Publications, New Delhi.

Saxena, R.C., & Saxena, S.R. (1992). Labour Problems and Social Welfare, Prakasan Kendra, Lucknow. pp. 535.

Singh, B.D., & Mohanty, S.B. (1993). Child Labour in the Informal Sector. Children at Work, Problems and Policy Options (eds.) S.B., Publishing Company, Delhi.

Sharma, I., Kumar, B., & Padmadeo, K.B. (1993). Child Labour in India: An Exploratory Child at Work: Problems and Policy Options, B.R. Publishing Corporation, Delhi.

Sinha, N. (1994). Child Labour in the Indian Silk Industry, Uppal Publishing House, New Delhi.

Sharma, R., & Sharma, R.K. (1997). The Case of Glass Bangle Industry of Firozabad, Indian Journal of Labour Economics, Vol. 40, No. 4, pp. 869-875.

Singh, S.P. (1997). Child Labour-The Malady and Remedy, Yojana, Vol. 41, No. 7, p. 21.

Sinha, A., (1998). Child Labour and Health, Social Change, Vol. 48, No. 1, January-March.

Singh, J.K. (1998). Labour Economics: Principles, Problems and Practices, Deep and Deep Publications, New Delhi.

Sen, A. (2000). Development as Freedom, Oxford University Press.

Srivastava, R.S., Raj, N. (2000). Children of Carpet Looms: A Study of Home Based Productions of Carpet in Uttar Pradesh, V.V.Giri National Labour Institute, NLI Research Studies, series no 011/2000, Noida.

Sekar, H.R., Mohammad, N. (2001). Child Labour in the Home Based Industries of Aligarh, V.V. Giri National Labour Institute Research Studies, Series 018/2001.

Shandilya, T.K., and Khan, S.A. (2003). Child labour: A Global Challenge, Deep and Deep Publications, New Delhi.

Subramanian, M.S. (2003). Gender Bias in Child Labour in India: Education as a Causative Factor' in R.K.Sen and A.D.Gupta (eds.) Problems of Child Labour in India, Deep and Deep Publications, New Delhi.

Sekar, H.R. (2004). Child Labour in Urban Informal Sector: A Study of Rag Pickers in Noida, V.V.Giri National Labour Institute, Noida.

Shacklock G, Thorp L (2005) Life History and Narrative Approaches. In: Somekh B, Lewin C (Eds) Research Methods in the Social Sciences. Sage Publications, London, 156-163.

Singh, A. (2006). Problems of Child Labour and Their Working Conditions: A Case Study of Agra City, in an Edited Book 'Child Labour from Different Perspectives' (Mahaveer Jain & Sangeeta Saraswat eds.), Manak Publications, Delhi pp. 12-25.

Shandilya, T.K., Kumar, N., & Kumar, N. (2006). Child Labour Eradication, Deep and Deep publications, New Delhi.

Singh, A. (2006). Problems of Child Labour and Their Working Conditions: A Case Study of Agra City in Child Labour from Different Perspectives (Eds. Mahaveer Jain and Sangeeta Saraswat), Manak Publications, New Delhi.

Sekar, H.R. (2007). Child Labour: Situation and Strategies for Elimination, V.V.Giri National Labour Institute, Noida.

Sarshar, M. (2010).Sociological Study of Children (Pledging of Labour) Act, 1933, Dissertation Submitted at National Law University, Delhi.

Suresh, L.B. (2011). An Empirical Study on Child Rag Pickers in Warangal City, Andhra Pradesh, India, Retrived from http://community.eldis.org/lalbsuresh/. 59e05148/ .59e68905.

Singh,A.P.(2012). Political Economy of Child Labour in India: A Study of Brassware Industry of Moradabad, Unpublished Dissertation, Delhi Univeristy, Delhi.

Tripathy, R.S (1985). History of Ancient India, Motilal Banarasi Das Publishers, Delhi, p. 49.

Tripathy, S.N. (1996). Child Labour in India: Issues and Policy Options. Discovery Publishing House, New Delhi.

Tripathy, S.N. (1997). Migrant Child Labour in India, Mohit Publication, New Delhi.

Tiwari, A. (1997). Child Labour: Ways and Means to Tackle the Malady, Social Change, Vol. 27, No. 34, September-December.

Tiwana, S.S. (1999). Child Labour in India, An Appraisal. Published in Child Labour, Reddy, Y.S. (eds.), Anmol Publications, New Delhi.

Tiwari, R.T. (2005). Child Labour in Foot Wear Industry, Possible Occupational Health Hazards, Indian Journal of Occupational and Environmental Medicine, Vol. 9 No. 1 pp. 7-9.

UNICEF, (2001). Beyond Child Labour, Affirming Rights, March.

United Nations, (1998). United Nations Report on Development in India (1998) 'Position Paper on Child Labour', Development Organization in India http://www.un.org.in/iawg-cl.pdf.

Vagale, L.R. (1968). "Rent Control in Nigeria: A Policy Framework", in Onibokun, P. (ed.) (1985), *Housing in Nigeria* (Ibadan, National Institute for Social and Economic Research), pp. 133-138.

Vaid, K.N. (1970). Labour Welfare in India, Shriram Centre for Industrial Relations, New Delhi.

Vidyasagar, R., & Kumarababu, G. (2002). Child Labour in the Home Based Match Industries of Sivakasi, V.V. Giri National Labour Institute, NLI Research Studies Series, No. 028/2001, Noida.

Weiner, M. (1991). The Child and the State in India, Delhi: Oxford University, Press, p. 79.

Weiner, M. (1996). Child Labour in India: Putting Compulsory Primary Education on the Political Agenda, Economic and Political Weekly, Nov. 9-16, p. 3007.

Index

R

❖ ❖ ❖ ❖ ❖